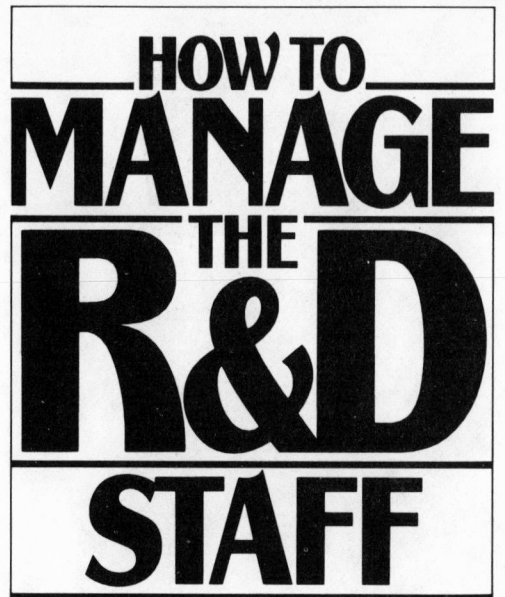

HOW TO
MANAGE
THE
R&D
STAFF

HOW TO MANAGE THE R&D STAFF

A LOOKING-GLASS WORLD

JAMES E. TINGSTAD

amacom

American Management Association

This publication is designed to provide accurate and authoritative
information in regard to the subject matter covered. It is sold with the
understanding that the publisher is not engaged in rendering legal,
accounting, or other professional service. If legal advice or other expert
assistance is required, the services of a competent professional person
should be sought.

Library of Congress Cataloging-in-Publication Data

Tingstad, James E.
       How to manage the R&D staff : a looking glass world / James
E. Tingstad.
         p.   cm.
Includes bibliographical references and index.
ISBN 0-8144-5048-2
1. Research, Industrial—Management. I. Title.
T175.5T55   1991
658.5'7—dc20   90-56194
                                                                      CIP

Printing number

10 9 8 7 6 5 4 3 2 1

To
Phyl, Mike, Judy, and Janet

Grateful acknowledgment is made to the following for permission to reprint excerpts from previously published material.

United Media for *Peanuts* comic strips.

Pharmaceutical Technology for material from "Technical Manager" columns by James E. Tingstad.

Bil Gilbert for material from "Competition," from *Sports Illustrated* (May 16, 1988).

The Tom Peters Group, © 1989 TPG Communications, all rights reserved, for material from the syndicated columns "Some Management and Economic Myths That Need to Be Debunked," "Involvement Unlimited: Untried But True Performance Elixir," "Firms May Be Dancing Last Macho Tango," and "Control Paradox: Less Yields More."

Anne C. Bernstein for material from "Feeling Great (About Myself)," *Parents' Magazine* (September 1982).

Harvard Business Review for material from "Barriers and Gateways to Communication" by Carl R. Rogers and F. J. Roethlisberger (July/August 1952).

Richard D. Irwin, Inc., for material from *Eupsychian Management* by Abraham Maslow.

Harper & Row, Publishers, Inc., for material from *Motivation and Personality* by Abraham Maslow. Copyright 1954, © 1987 by Harper & Row, © 1970 by Abraham Maslow.

McGraw-Hill Publishing Company for material from *The Human Side of Enterprise* by Douglas McGregor (1960) and *Managing the Managers* by Robert C. Sampson (1965).

Houghton Mifflin Company for material from *On Becoming a Person* by Carl Rogers, © 1961.

Contents

Acknowledgments *ix*

Preface *xi*

Introduction: Two Looking-Glass Worlds 1

Part I The R&D Setting 9

1 Characteristics of Technical People 15
2 Characteristics of a Fertile Work Environment 22
3 Characteristics of an Effective R&D Manager 29
4 Characteristics of an Effective R&D Vice-President 33

Part II Basic R&D Managerial Tasks 39

5 Five Cornerstone R&D Managerial Tasks 41
6 Planning for Productive Research 48
7 Organizing R&D Work Groups 55
8 Supervising and Controlling 63
9 Delegating and Monitoring 68
10 Advocating and Sheltering 74

Part III Developing a Productive R&D Team 81

11 The Cohesive Research Group 87
12 Effective Communication 94
13 Recruiting Technical People 104
14 Motivating Your Employees 116
15 Fostering Employee Growth 122
16 Building Subordinates' Self-Confidence 132
17 Evaluating Professional Performance and Potential 147
18 Formal Performance Reviews 156
19 Transferring and Terminating Unproductive Researchers 169
20 Promoting Laboratory Workers Into R&D Management 179

Part IV The R&D Function   **193**

21 Interacting With R&D Peers and Superiors   199
22 Working With Committees and Project Teams   205
23 R&D Budgets   215
24 Computers and R&D   220
25 Outlicensing and Inlicensing Concerns/Government
      Contracts and Regulations   228
26 Industry and Academia   236

Part V R&D and the Corporation   **245**

27 Interactions With Other Divisions   247
28 Managing International R&D   262
29 R&D Management and Corporate Management   268

      Index   *279*

Acknowledgments

First things first. I am grateful to my wife, Phyllis, for her encouragement, understanding, patience, and stamina and especially for her expert editing. I am also grateful to all my friends, advisers, and colleagues who have taught me so much; it would be unfair to hundreds of people to mention anyone in particular. Finally, I wish to thank the editors at AMACOM, Myles Thompson and Kate Pferdner, and particularly copy editor Carole Berglie, who worked so hard and so well.

Preface

Technical people are different. The world of R&D is different. In your experience with R&D you've undoubtedly suspected this but have not known how to adjust the standard management dogma to fit the R&D situation.

Here is a book that meets that need. Yes, technical people are different: They are highly self-motivated and appreciate a manager who respects them as adults. Most important, they need a lighter management hand. This is the management philosophy that pervades this book. The manager seeking to increase productivity—in quality and quantity—of his or her team, department, or division will find here both the theory and the practice of proven, effective management tailored to R&D.

The book is in five parts. Part I describes the R&D setting—the people it attracts, the environment most fertile for innovation, the manager who gets results, and the vice-president who oversees it all.

Part II presents the basis of good management—in any setting. These are the fundamentals—the guiding stars by which enlightened leaders serve both their employees and the corporation. Applied to R&D, these qualities of person and method ensure planned productive research through team effort.

Part III sharpens the focus on R&D, with chapters that concentrate on management's guidance of R&D teams or groups. Recruiting the right people and then encouraging them to grow are the route to a cohesive, productive team. Also here are chapters on evaluating employee work, ways to deal with unproductive workers, and promotions or other rewards for work well done.

Part IV widens the book's view of R&D management by considering other aspects of the manager's job: interactions with peers and supervisors, budgeting, computer applications, out- or inlicensing, patents, government regulations, and industry's relations with academic institutions.

Part V sees R&D against a corporate background and speaks of interrelationships with divisions such as marketing, sales, engineering, and the like. We also look here at an interesting development of recent years: international R&D and multinational corporations or global markets for technology. And the book concludes with an overview of R&D's interaction with corporate management—how to get on with those at the top.

Throughout the book are both general theories and specific case studies to show the relationship of theory to practice. Whether you're a first-line manager or an R&D vice-president, you'll find here the basic tenets of good management in the 1990s—adjusted for and focused on the R&D situation.

HOW TO
MANAGE
THE
R&D
STAFF

Introduction

Two Looking-Glass Worlds

"I don't understand. It's dreadfully confusing!"

Alice, from Lewis Carroll, *Through the Looking-Glass
and What Alice Found There*

People in the physical sciences...tend to despise the uncertainty
and disorder of managing and want to impose both certainty and
exactitude where none exists.

Robert C. Sampson, *Managing the Managers*

Alice was comfortable in her normal world. She disciplined her cats, wondered
whether "the snow *loves* the trees and fields, that it kisses them so gently," and
played a fair game of chess. But her curiosity about the Looking-Glass House
(one room of which she could see in the mirror over the fireplace) caused her
to climb up and enter the Looking-Glass World, a world that proved to be "as
different as possible." For example, flowers talked, bees were as big as
elephants, memory went both ways in time, and you had to run very fast just
to stay in one place.

A Scientist Enters the World of Management

Carroll's classic is a useful analogy to emphasize the many differences between
the realm of laboratory science and the world of R&D management. For the
person trained and educated in technology, the laboratory is quiet, familiar,
and relatively orderly and predictable; it is a realm of test tubes and electronic
circuits, of reasoned hypotheses and careful experimentation. But the world of
management is dominated by crowds of people, and that world can be strange,
capricious, confusing, and, at times, clamorous. Recognizing these differences
and learning to deal with them is the surest path to R&D managerial competence.

Technical/Managers or Technical/Managers : A World of Difference

Scientists are usually promoted into management because of their scientific expertise and performance, with little or no regard given to their interpersonal skills. Once promoted, they often behave, not as managers, but as superscientists.

To succeed as R&D managers, scientists must first take seriously their supervisory responsibilities. As management consultant Robert C. Sampson *(Managing the Managers)* emphasizes, "Management of people is a matter treated much too superficially and casually. It is highly dangerous to exercise power over others, to direct and control them, and to determine their futures." Jay Hall, another management consultant *(Ponderables: Essays on Managerial Choice—Past and Future)*, agrees: "Management of people is a major profession, affecting the productive and social well-being of hundreds of thousands of people."

Not all R&D managers realize that their promotion into supervision is, in fact, a major change in profession. This can best be described by examining the differences between a **technical**/manager and a technical/**manager. Technical**/managers regard themselves primarily as technical people with some added supervisory responsibilities. Technical/**managers** view themselves principally as supervisors of people who have technical training. The difference is not trivial; it leads to major differences in managerial behavior.

Technical/managers tend to treat their supervisory responsibilities as a distraction, a minor component of their jobs. As part-time supervisors, they shortchange both the organization and their subordinates. Underestimating the seriousness of their new managerial responsibilities, they seldom develop the additional talents needed to succeed in their new profession. In contrast, technical/**managers,** recognizing the complexities of management, work hard to develop the necessary interpersonal and organizational skills, and they do this while retaining an appropriate level of scientific sophistication.

Let's examine the problem more closely. Typically, a scientist spends four to ten years at a university mastering the fundamentals of the profession, followed by several years at the bench in an R&D organization. Then, most often as a reward for technical proficiency, the individual is promoted to first-line supervision—usually with little or no training in management or interpersonal relations. Although a few gifted individuals can excel at both science and management, most have to make a choice: Either retain and polish their technical expertise, or concentrate on mastering their new profession. Just as all of us tend to resist change, many fledgling supervisors choose to stay in the familiar, comfortable world of science and thus become **technical**/managers. But to excel as leaders in R&D, they must become technical/**managers** and focus primarily on management.

Minimally, we need to emphasize the importance of management far more than we presently do. On the other hand, I do not advocate that R&D managers allow their technical skills to atrophy completely; they need a certain amount of scientific sophistication to do their jobs well. For example, they need to have an appreciation for the complexity, capabilities, and limitations of

Figure 1. Continuum of leader behavior. *Source*: Adapted with permission from Robert Tannenbaum and Warren H. Schmidt, *Harvard Business Review*, vol. 51 (May-June 1973), p. 164.

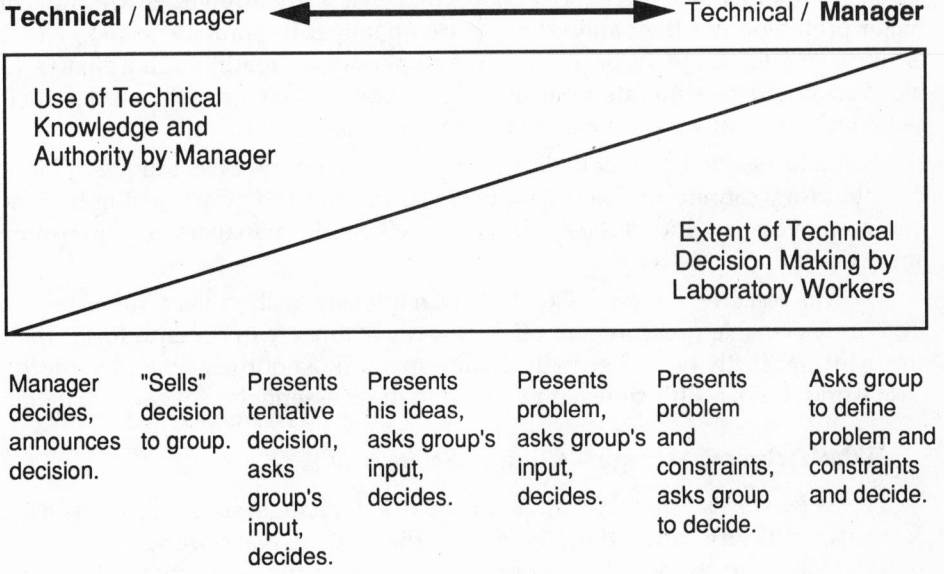

Technical / Manager ◄──────────────► Technical / **Manager**

Use of Technical
Knowledge and
Authority by Manager

Extent of Technical
Decision Making by
Laboratory Workers

| Manager decides, announces decision. | "Sells" decision to group. | Presents tentative decision, asks group's input, decides. | Presents his ideas, asks group's input, decides. | Presents problem, asks group's input, decides. | Presents problem and constraints, asks group to decide. | Asks group to define problem and constraints and decide. |

science. Also, they should not feel threatened by the scientific competence of subordinates.

As a rule of thumb, a 50:50 ratio of managerial-to-technical skill is appropriate for first-line supervisors; certainly a 90:10 ratio, with heavy emphasis on either managerial or technical skill, is excessive. Clearly, the technical **manager** should retain major involvement in selecting projects and assigning resources, since usually he or she has the broadest vision. As the individual ascends the organizational ladder, however, the managerial-technical balance should shift increasingly toward the managerial side.

Danger Areas of Being a Technical/Manager

1. *Competition.* If R&D managers regard themselves primarily as scientists, they will be seen by their subordinates as competitors for technical resources, scientific recognition, and attendance at technical meetings. But a supervisor is a competitor with an unfair advantage; he or she holds the power of management.

2. *Decision Making.* **Technical**/managers are inclined to make most of important scientific decisions themselves; this soon drives out independent, competent subordinates, leaving behind passive "assistant scientists" (see Figure 1).

3. *Mediocrity.* As word of their style spreads throughout the scientific community, **technical**/managers have difficulty recruiting high-quality people, moving their groups toward mediocrity.

4. *Redundancy.* If too many levels of supervision review technical/reports and judgments, bench scientists will sense that management does not trust them, to say nothing of the inefficiency from redundancy.

5. *Major Professor.* R&D supervisors may view themselves in the role of major professor, but their subordinates are no longer in graduate school, and it is necessary for them to be relatively independent. Treating subordinates as glorified graduate students demeans them, stunts their growth, erodes their self-confidence, hurts their pride, and fosters resentment.

6. *Individuality.* R&D managers need to treat employees as unique individuals, but they cannot do this unless they spend time and effort getting to *know* the employees as individuals. This is unlikely if managers are part-time supervisors.

7. *Unreasonable Pressure.* Good R&D managers will protect subordinates from unreasonable pressure and other sources of anxiety in order to foster their creativity, productivity, and growth. If they spend most of their time in the technical world, there is little time left to attend to these essential managerial matters.

Why Technical/Managers Cling to Science

1. *Lack of Flexibility.* We all tend to resist change, but scientists have particular difficulty when they move into the looking-glass world of supervision, which is, in the words of Lewis Carroll, "as different as possible." Most **technical**/managers welcome their promotions into supervision, but they don't realize the attitudinal and behavioral changes that must accompany their switch in profession.

2. *Value System Linked to Science.* **Technical**/managers spend many years developing a value system based on science, treasuring technical expertise and scientific publications. When they enter supervision, that value system must be modified to accommodate interpersonal relations, schedules, budgets, and bottom lines, which taxes one's flexibility.

3. *A Gray vs. Black-and-White Orientation.* A major goal of science is movement toward certainty: to view the world in black and white. But the world of management is the realm of interpersonal relations, with its infinite shades of gray. The properties of chemical compounds, electronic circuits, and oil shale are relatively predictable, but laboratory workers, accountants, secretaries— even R&D supervisors—are chock-full of surprises.

4. *Fear of Looking Foolish.* **Technical**/managers retain their scientific expertise because they don't want to feel foolish or appear uninformed during detailed discussions of technical matters.

5. *Anxiety.* When they were at the bench, these individuals produced results themselves. As R&D managers they are one step or more removed from hands-on productivity; this creates anxiety, especially when problems arise. When we are anxious, we tend to migrate toward familiar ground. For technical people, "home country" is the land of experiments, data, equations, and statistics.

6. *A Tendency to Meddle.* Many organizations have too much management, so technical supervisors start looking for things to do. Meddling in scientific matters is usually the action of **technical**/managers, but soup is not the only commodity spoiled by too many cooks.

7. *Need for Praise and Respect.* Although it is true that management is where the money and power are, it is equally true that praise and respect from scientific colleagues comes—understandably—from the realm of science. Most **technical**/managers are loath to relinquish this source of gratification. Unfortunately for their subordinates and the organization, these individuals want to have their cake and eat it, too, leaving little sustenance for their employees.

8. *Fear of Losing Their Identity.* As with their value systems and need for praise and respect, new supervisors become "faces in the management crowd." This threatens their sense of identity and worth, and they are reluctant to give up their starring role in the world of science.

The Successful R&D Manager

To succeed in the looking-glass world of R&D supervision, **technical**/managers must learn to become technical/**managers**. This requires that they (1) learn how to supervise people well; (2) learn how to evaluate people accurately; (3) become familiar with the basics of their company's business; (4) acquire a broad, comprehensive understanding of the entire R&D operation; and (5) develop style as well as substance.

Learning How to Supervise People Well

R&D managers must find ways to optimize productivity and employee growth. This requires—

- ▲ a working knowledge of basic social science principles (cognitive skills learned from seminars and the social science literature); and
- ▲ development of new attitudes and behaviors (experientially learned skills).

Learning How to Evaluate People Accurately

Since technical/**managers** cannot (and should not) be as technically current and competent as laboratory scientists, and since they do not (and should not) want to make technical decisions themselves, they must learn to evaluate their subordinates accurately, especially regarding their subordinates' technical judgment. This requires—

- ▲ perceptiveness concerning people;
- ▲ experience;
- ▲ hard work;

▲ perseverance; and

▲ minimizing personal bias based on friendships or familiarity with veterans (while still appreciating the value of their experience).

Becoming Familiar With the Basics of the Company's Business

The wise technical/**manager** becomes familiar with the basic financial and business aspects of the company. This does not mean expending a significant amount of energy on financial or business matters but, rather, spending time early in one's management career getting a broad perspective of the company. That means knowing its—

▲ history;

▲ current short- and long-range plans;

▲ structure (e.g., its divisions, including international);

▲ organizational culture;

▲ basic way of operating (e.g., in addition to R&D, Marketing and Sales, especially its view of "who is the customer"; Production Planning, Manufacturing, and Distribution; Engineering; Patents; Accounting; and Inlicensing/Outlicensing, especially the company's basic philosophy on licensing products); and

▲ "the system" (e.g., how to minimize bureaucratic delays and move things along efficiently in cooperation with Personnel, Purchasing, and Accounting).

Acquiring a Broad, Comprehensive Understanding of the Entire R&D Operation

The wise technical/**manager** becomes an expert on how the overall R&D process works in the company, including—

▲ project or product flow from idea all the way to manufacturing;

▲ responsibilities of each department;

▲ how each group fits into the overall picture; and

▲ interactions among various R&D departments.

Developing Style as Well as Substance

As R&D managers ascend the organizational ladder, they need to pay more attention to "style," to be aware of and sensitive to corporate politics. Successful R&D managers do this without sacrificing principles or substance.

▲ ▲ ▲ ▲ ▲

The realities of the looking-glass managerial world demand that R&D managers focus on becoming successful technical/**managers.** It is hoped that the material in this book will help managers with the practical aspects of supervising technical people, while acquainting them with the business and organizational concerns of R&D management.

References

"Chicago's B-School Goes Touchy-feely: The University of Chicago Adds Practical, People-oriented Courses." *Business Week*, November 27, 1989.

Hall, Jay. *Ponderables: Essays on Managerial Choice—Past and Future*. Woodlands, Tex.: Teleometrics International, 1982.

Sampson, Robert C. *Managing the Managers*. New York: McGraw-Hill, 1965.

PART I

The R&D Setting

My definition of success is peace of mind. That can be obtained only in self-satisfaction, in knowing you made the effort to do the best you are capable of doing.

John Wooden, Former UCLA Basketball Coach

Some schools of management imply that you must become a different person to be a good manager; others give the impression that it doesn't matter what kind of person you are—one management style is as good as another. Actually, the practical truth lies somewhere in between.

Part I of this book examines the setting in which R&D managers find themselves. Chapter 1 takes a look at what makes technical people tick—what motivates them and how best to structure their work. Chapter 2 examines the R&D environment, with ideas for promoting greater achievement of goals. Chapter 3 offers a view of R&D management, pairing human characteristics with favorable managerial qualities. Chapter 4 discusses the characteristics of an effective R&D vice-president, the leading advocate of R&D in the corporation.

Whether you are a first-line R&D supervisor or chief assistant to the R&D vice-president, your management efforts will be successful only if you manage within the context of the person you are. Before considering the factors that contribute to management in the R&D context, take a little time to consider the kind of person you are, and then make your management style as people-centered as possible.

You Have to Be You

Psychologists say that our basic personality is in place by age 6 or 7; from then on, life consists of attempts to cope, grow, mature, and succeed while maintaining a reasonable equilibrium and of satisfying our needs while getting along in a sometimes hostile, sometimes friendly world.

But we are not rigid, one-dimensional creatures. We have upper and lower

limits of behavior, within which we operate. For example, if you've just successfully completed a complicated task, you feel good about yourself and can deal with
an unexpected problem with patience and good humor. However, if you have
been in a frustrating work situation for two years and have just been chewed out
by your boss, a subordinate in need of your help is likely to find you impatient and
grumpy. The key to being an effective R&D manager is to move steadily toward
your upper limit. This is how you grow and mature as a professional and as a
person.

How Do You Move Toward Your Upper Limit?

Most learning takes place experientially (on the job), but relying solely on
personal experience is both naïve and dangerous. Why? Because no one views
reality as it truly is; perceptions are always clouded by personal bias. It has been
said that "we see things not as *they* are, but as *we* are." Social scientists
emphasize that human beings are self-deceiving, self-justifying creatures. Therefore, we need to check the validity of personal experiences with the general
observations about people and management that experts have provided us.
The way we do this is by attending seminars and reading the social science
literature.

What Are the Best Paths for Growth?

Certainly R&D managers can begin by improving their interpersonal skills and
becoming more people-oriented. Experiments by social scientists have shown
consistently and conclusively that managers who develop their "people" skills are
the most effective leaders. For example, Management Professor and Consultant
Rensis Likert studied supervision in some 5,000 assorted organizations. He
found "people-oriented" managers to be high producers while "results-oriented"
managers (those who regarded workers only as tools to get the job done) were
low producers. Specifically, high producers—

- ▲ were good delegators;
- ▲ allowed workers to participate in decisions;
- ▲ were nonpunitive; and
- ▲ encouraged open, two-way communication.

Low producers, on the other hand, were—

- ▲ poor delegators;
- ▲ autocratic;
- ▲ punitive; and
- ▲ relatively inaccessible to their subordinates.

Likert adds that "genuine interest and unselfish concern on the part of a supervisor in the success and well-being of his subordinates have a marked effect on performance" *(New Patterns of Management)*.

Jay Hall *(Ponderables)* came to the same conclusions in a five-year study involving over 16,000 managers in more than fifty different types of organizations.

Psychologist Carl Rogers *(Carl Rogers on Personal Power)* cites a case of an executive who was allowed to set up experimental plants where person-centered management was practiced. The results:

> In the experimental plants the average cost of a particular unit is about 22¢. In the control plants the average cost of the same item is 70¢!

Part of the increased efficiency was a reduction in managerial overhead:

> In the experimental plants there are now three to five managers. In the control units of comparable size there are seventeen to twenty-three managers!

Rogers concludes:

> All of this seems to point to the somewhat surprising conclusion that the person who is able to develop close personal relationships, who is primarily person-centered, who does not place a high value on power, who is a growing person with understanding of himself, is, all in all, likely to be the most effective and productive manager of an enterprise.

The preeminence of people-centered management is confirmed by the vast majority of the social science and management experts listed in the Suggested Reading at the end of this section.

Crossing Into the Looking-Glass World

People-centered management, then, asks the R&D manager to step into the uncertain world on the other side of the looking glass. While that journey can be difficult, wisdom, sensitivity, and stamina can help ensure success—for the individual, the group, and the corporation.

References

Hall, Jay. *Ponderables: Essays on Managerial Choice—Past and Future.* Woodlands, Tex.: Teleometrics International, 1982.

Likert, Rensis. *New Patterns of Management.* New York: McGraw-Hill, 1961.

Rogers, Carl R. *Carl Rogers on Personal Power: Inner Strength and Its Revolutionary Impact.* New York: Delacorte Press, 1977.

Suggested Reading

Argyris, Chris. *Integrating the Individual and the Organization.* New York: John Wiley and Sons, 1964.

———. *Interpersonal Competence and Organizational Effectiveness.* Homewood, Ill.: Irwin-Dorsey, 1962.

———. *Personality and Organization: The Conflict between System and the Individual.* New York: Harper & Brothers, 1957.

———. *Reasoning, Learning, and Action: Individual and Organizational.* San Francisco: Jossey-Bass, 1982.

Bennis, Warren. "How to Be the Leader They'll Follow." *Working Woman,* March 1990.

Blake, Robert R., and Jane S. Mouton. *The Managerial Grid.* Houston: Gulf, 1964.

De Pree, Max. *Leadership Is an Art.* East Lansing: Mich. State University Press, 1987.

Drucker, Peter F. *Innovation and Entrepreneurship: Practice and Principles.* New York: Harper & Row, 1985.

———. *Management: Tasks, Responsibilities, Practices.* New York: Harper & Row, 1974.

———. *The Practice of Management.* New York: Harper & Row, 1954.

Greenleaf, Robert K. *Servant Leadership: A Journey into the Nature of Legitimate Power and Greatness.* Mahwah, N.J.: Paulist Press, 1977.

Guest, Robert H., Paul Hersey, and Kenneth H. Blanchard. *Organizational Change through Effective Leadership.* Englewood Cliffs, N.J.: Prentice-Hall, 1977.

Hall, Jay. *The Competence Process: Managing for Commitment and Creativity.* Woodlands, Tex.: Teleometrics International, 1980.

Hersey, Paul, and Kenneth H. Blanchard. *Management of Organizational Behavior: Utilizing Human Resources,* 3rd ed. Englewood Cliffs, N.J.: Prentice-Hall, 1977.

Herzberg, Frederick. *The Managerial Choice: To Be Efficient and to Be Human,* 2nd ed. Salt Lake City: Olympus, 1982.

———. *Work and the Nature of Man.* Cleveland: World, 1966.

Herzberg, Frederick, Bernard Mausner, and Barbara Block Snyderman. *The Motivation to Work.* New York: John Wiley and Sons, 1959.

Ingalls, John D. *Human Energy: The Critical Factor for Individuals and Organizations.* Austin, Tex.: Learning Concepts, 1979.

Kanter, Rosabeth Moss. *The Change Masters: Innovation for Productivity in the American Corporation.* New York: Simon and Schuster, 1983.

Kolb, David A., Irwin M. Rubin, and James M. McIntyre. *Organizational Psychology: An Experiential Approach,* 3rd ed. Englewood Cliffs, N.J.: Prentice-Hall, 1979.

Leavitt, Harold J. *Managerial Psychology: An Introduction to Individuals, Pairs, and Groups in Organizations,* 4th ed. Chicago: University of Chicago Press, 1978.

Likert, Rensis. *The Human Organization: Its Management and Value.* New York: McGraw-Hill, 1967.

McGregor, Douglas. *The Human Side of Enterprise.* New York: McGraw-Hill, 1960.

————. *The Professional Manager,* ed. Caroline McGregor and Warren G. Bennis. New York: McGraw-Hill, 1967.

Maslow, Abraham H. *Eupsychian Management: A Journal.* Homewood, Ill.: Irwin-Dorsey, 1965.

————. *Motivation and Personality,* 2nd Ed., ed. Wayne G. Holtzman and Gardner Murphy. New York: Harper & Row, 1970.

Peters, Tom. "Ask Dumb Questions and Fail with a Flair." *The Arizona Daily Star,* February 13, 1990.

————. "Control Paradox: Less Yields More." *The Arizona Daily Star,* April 11, 1989.

————. "Firms May Be Dancing Last Macho Tango." *The Arizona Daily Star,* April 4, 1989.

————. "It's Management Author's Greatest Hits." *Chicago Tribune,* July 18, 1988.

————. "Nine Traits for Victory, in War or Business." *The Arizona Daily Star,* May 16, 1989.

————. "Some Management and Economic Myths That Need to Be Debunked." *Chicago Tribune,* September 19, 1988.

Peters, Thomas J., and Nancy Austin. *A Passion for Excellence: The Leadership Difference.* New York: Random House, 1985.

Peters, Thomas J., and Robert H. Waterman. *In Search of Excellence: Lessons from America's Best-run Companies.* New York: Harper & Row, 1982.

Rogers, Carl R. *On Becoming a Person: A Therapist's View of Psychotherapy.* Boston: Houghton Mifflin, 1961.

Sampson, Robert C. *Managing the Managers.* New York: McGraw-Hill, 1965.

Sargent, Alice G. *The Androgynous Manager.* New York: AMACOM, 1981.

Sargent, Alice G., and Ronald J. Stupak. "Managing in the '90s: The Androgynous Manager." *Training and Development Journal,* vol. 43 (December 1989), 30.

Schein, Edgar H. *Organizational Psychology,* 3rd ed. Englewood Cliffs, N.J.: Prentice-Hall, 1980.

Shtogren, John A., ed. *Models for Management: The Structure of Competence.* Woodlands, Tex.: Teleometrics International, 1980.

Chapter 1

Characteristics of Technical People

Consideration of people and their behavior seems a prerequisite to any conscious attempt to learn how better to "manage" people.

Harold Leavitt, *Managerial Psychology*

Managers should indeed know more about human beings.

Peter Drucker, *Management: Tasks, Responsibilities, Practices*

To manage successfully, managers need to learn as much as possible about people in general and about themselves and their subordinates in particular. Only then can they identify management practices that are—

- ▲ realistic;
- ▲ appropriate;
- ▲ effective; and
- ▲ productive.

This chapter takes a look at technical people—how they are different from other employees as well as how they are similar—in an attempt to define the successful R&D manager.

People and Their Behavior

What can we learn about people and their attitudes, motivations, and behavior? Suggestions from experts such as Sampson, Rogers, and McGregor follow.

▲ Consultant Robert C. Sampson believes that the fundamental motive in human behavior is the preservation of self-image. This can manifest itself in

many ways, including self-interest and self-protection—both normal, healthy human emotions. The keys to good management are to—
- minimize the need for self-protection and
- harmonize self-interest with the interests of the organization.

▲ According to Psychologist Carl Rogers, people want to learn and grow throughout their lives, but they want to determine for themselves the direction and pace of growth. This relates to Sampson's point because, as people mature, their self-image constantly changes. When employees are treated in ways that reinforce their self-image, the manager who does so will be viewed as their partner and the group will be productive. If, however, they are treated in a manner contradictory to their self-image, they will resist the manager at every turn. They will consider him or her an adversary—even an enemy—and things will go poorly.

Each individual has a unique self-image, but useful generalizations can be made:

- A healthy person's self-image is positive, so any managerial action that implies otherwise will be strongly resisted and greatly resented. For example, if managers control their subordinates restrictively— if they run a tight ship—employees will view that as a sign of mistrust. Since being trustworthy is an essential component of a positive self-image, the employees can't help but regard their manager's actions as hostile.
- Employees consider themselves—and indeed are—adults. Therefore, when managers give subordinates the freedom to make decisions and to do their jobs without excessive interference, they are treating them with respect and reinforcing the employees' self-image. If, however, they always give subordinates detailed orders and make most of the decisions, they are treating them disrespectfully, and that means big trouble.
- Individuals believe they are well-intentioned, responsible, reasonably intelligent people. Thus, when an employee makes a mistake, the manager who does not get angry, but rather expresses sympathy and support, is saying the following:

> "I know your intentions were good."
> "I'm sure you're not reckless."
> "I don't consider you stupid."
> "I'm confident you can do better."

- Everyone feels he or she has value as both a unique human being and a productive worker, and is therefore important to the organization. When managers give subordinates recognition for a job well done, they emphasize those people's worth. When they treat people as individuals and not as interchangeable parts of the corporate machinery, employees feel important. However, if managers fail to share important information with employees, the employees feel demeaned.
- Management professor and consultant Douglas McGregor supports the

concept of employees' positive self-image. He says that people enjoy working and, given the chance, prefer to exercise self-direction and self-control. They seek responsibility and can be a major positive force in company operations if management allows them.

Skeptical readers should reflect on their own self-image. Most certainly it will be similar to the above; why should managers assume they are emotionally different from and superior to nonmanagement workers?

Let's allow employees to speak for themselves. As Kenneth Kovach ("What Motivates Employees?") explains, in 1987 tens of thousands of workers (both technical and nontechnical) were asked: "What is important to you in your job?" Their composite reply, in descending order of importance was (1) interesting work; (2) full appreciation of work done; (3) feeling of being in on things; (4) job security; (5) high wages; (6) promotion; (7) good working conditions; (8) personal loyalty of supervisor; (9) tactful discipline; and (10) help with personal problems.

Let's look at each of these:

1. *Interesting Work.* Relates to Carl Rogers's point that we all want to learn and grow throughout our lives.
2. *Full Appreciation of Work Done.* We want to feel important, appreciated, and respected.
3. *Feeling of Being in on Things.* Being treated as an outsider makes us feel isolated and unimportant.
4. *Job Security.* Loss of livelihood threatens our sense of well-being—the emotional equilibrium that stabilizes our self-image.
5. *High Wages.* Has to do with feeling important, appreciated, and secure; also allows us to learn and grow off the job—additional education, challenging hobbies, and so on.
6. *Promotion.* Sense of importance, new challenges, and growth opportunities.
7. *Good Working Conditions.* Security, well-being, and lack of distractions. Allows us to expend our energy on useful work.
8. *Personal Loyalty of Supervisor.* Feelings of importance (I deserve his loyalty), individuality, stability, and togetherness.
9. *Tactful Discipline.* Respect (relates to importance).
10. *Help With Personal Problems.* Respect, importance, support, and individuality.

Technical People and Their Behavior

Business people have often viewed technical people as different, with somewhat different motivational needs and management approaches. For example, the well-known management consultant Peter Drucker has commented that "the knowledge worker will not produce if managed [restrictively]. Knowledge has to be self-directed and has to take responsibility."

Scientists tend to be independent, creative, ambitious, self-motivated, and self-disciplined. Good management greatly increases their productivity, while bad management causes for scientists more problems than it does for the average employee.

As Harold Leavitt points out, in one sense people are the same but in many ways they are different. Technical people often have advanced education, generally higher motivation, and potentially high productivity. For example, while ditchdigging is honorable work, a ditchdigger's potential for growth on the job is considerably less than that of a scientist. This means that good R&D management enjoys a significantly higher payoff.

To further elaborate, let's look at the most common job categories in R&D organizations, together with typical characteristics of people in those positions. Finally, I'll discuss the best work-group arrangements for typical R&D projects.

Technicians (Assistant Scientists). In general, technicians tend to be—

- ▲ highly motivated, especially if they are viewed as "partners in experimentation" by their laboratory supervisors and given as much responsibility and independence as possible and appropriate;
- ▲ eager to learn; and
- ▲ willing to work hard, especially on challenging projects.

In addition, they—

- ▲ want to know the "why" of experiments and can grasp many scientific concepts when explained by their laboratory supervisors;
- ▲ can learn to conduct experiments carefully and precisely if properly taught;
- ▲ resent being treated disrespectfully, as a "pair of hands";
- ▲ want additional schooling or training, especially if partially financed by the organization; and

---

Case Study: The Sky's the Limit

George was an excellent R&D technician with three years of college but no degree. When Molly, a B.S. scientist who supervised the R&D prototype assembling operation, retired, George approached Florence, the department manager, and said, "I was so excited about this idea I didn't sleep at all last night. How about considering me for Molly's job? I'm sure I can do it."

Florence had been looking at B.S. people within the organization, but George's fervor touched her and his previous high-quality performance reassured her. After short but due consideration, she promoted George, and he went on to perform admirably.

▲ function best if they are associated with a small laboratory project team rather than in a random pool of technicians.

Assistant scientists usually have high school, associate, or bachelor's degrees with post-high school training in science. The principal advantage of people with associate or bachelor's degrees over technicians with only a high school education is that their additional education usually makes them more flexible concerning complicated technology. But some technicians are capable of advancing to the level of associate scientist or scientist (see case study that follows), and as manager, you should encourage those moves.

Associate Scientists. Associate scientists usually have bachelor's or master's degrees in science. They generally tend to—

▲ have most of the characteristics described for technicians;
▲ do best if they work in small groups where the scientists are partners or advisers rather than laboratory supervisors;
▲ understand most scientific theory and application, especially when explained by their laboratory advisers;
▲ quickly learn sound laboratory experimental procedures;
▲ do well when given additional responsibilities—e.g., administrative management of projects;
▲ become envious of scientists, especially if the associate scientist is experienced and if the manager has not created a climate of mutual respect and recognition of the contributions of group members at all levels; and
▲ have the potential to advance to the scientist level.

Scientists. These senior laboratory workers usually have master's or doctoral degrees (depending upon the scientific discipline) and tend to—

▲ understand basic scientific theory in their field and employ sound laboratory experimental procedures;
▲ operate at the highest level of self-motivation;
▲ prefer self-direction even more than the average worker;
▲ become frustrated and demotivated if tightly controlled by their supervisor;
▲ suffer from ennui after four to six years in the same position and technical area;
▲ be independent and proud;
▲ be interested in management, especially if the organization does not have a meaningful scientific ladder; and
▲ have the ability and the desire to be the technical authority on projects and to run the department (as a group) from a scientific standpoint.

In organizations with a meaningful dual-ladder system (that is, a management path and a scientist career path), scientists can rise above a standard laboratory position—for example, to senior scientist—and enjoy greater challenge, more freedom, higher salary, additional resources, and more frequent interaction with upper management.

Arrangement of Laboratory Work Groups

The nature of technical work and the behavior of technical people call for special work groups. Any specific arrangement of laboratory work groups depends upon the—

- ▲ company's business (high-tech or low-tech);
- ▲ nature and scientific complexity of the project;
- ▲ categories of technical employees (e.g., all scientists; scientists and technicians; or scientists, associate scientists, and technicians); and
- ▲ specific talents and interests of the laboratory workers.

In general, it's best to have small work groups so that each member can feel important, involved, and committed. Laboratory workers at all levels should be given as much freedom and responsibility as possible.

The major function of scientists is to ensure the scientific excellence of the project. It's best to leave the administrative details of the project to associate scientists, unless the scientist wants the experience. This gives the associate scientists more responsibility while allowing the scientists to concentrate on theoretical technical matters, which they do better than anyone else. As mentioned, technicians should be given as much information, freedom, and responsibility as possible.

In three-tiered laboratories, in general it's necessary for scientists to be intimately involved in the first 10 to 15 percent of the project to ensure a technically sound beginning. Associate scientists should be in charge for the next 65 to 70 percent, and technicians in charge for the remainder. Everyone should stay involved throughout the project as needed. Obviously, these percentages will vary depending on the project, the technology, and the individuals.

Most important, if all group members feel challenged and respected, and if each person is allowed to fully apply his or her particular talents to the project, productivity will be maximized and the prejudices that usually separate people with different levels of education will largely disappear.

References

Drucker, Peter F. *Management: Tasks, Responsibilities, Practices.* New York: Harper & Row, 1974.

Kovach, Kenneth A. "What Motivates Employees? Workers and Supervisors Give Different Answers," *Business Horizons*, September-October 1987.

Leavitt, Harold J. *Managerial Psychology: An Introduction to Individuals, Pairs, and Groups in Organizations.* Chicago: University of Chicago Press, 1978.

McGregor, Douglas. *The Human Side of Enterprise.* New York: McGraw-Hill, 1960.

Rogers, Carl R. *On Becoming a Person: A Therapist's View of Psychotherapy.* Boston: Houghton Mifflin, 1961.

Sampson, Robert C. *Managing the Managers.* New York: McGraw-Hill, 1965.

Chapter 2

Characteristics of a Fertile Work Environment

The three basic components of an R&D group are (1) laboratory employees, (2) the work environment, and (3) the manager. In *The Professional Manager,* Douglas McGregor eloquently links these three elements as follows:

> Management must seek to create conditions [an organizational environment] such that members of the organization at all levels can best achieve their own goals by directing their efforts toward the goals of the organization.

Carl Rogers, in *On Becoming a Person,* goes a step further:

> We know how to provide conditions in a work group . . . which will be followed by increased productivity, originality, and morale. . . . When workers in industry participate in planning and in decisions, when supervisors are sensitive to worker attitudes, and when supervision is not suspicious or authoritarian, production and morale increase.

Throughout this book, there is a continual melding of these three fundamental components of R&D groups. Only when employees, environment, and management are a harmonious whole will there be fertile ground for the successful development of new ideas. Chapter 1 discussed employees. This chapter turns to the work environment, and management is discussed in Chapters 3 and 4.

Characteristics of a Fertile Work Environment

Understanding the basics about people, especially technical people, allows us to formulate the characteristics of a fertile R&D work environment. But how do you recognize a fertile environment? There is a combination of brisk efficiency and relaxed congeniality, of creative independence and reasoned orderliness. It exists where group members accomplish their personal goals by focusing on organizational goals.

Managers need to recognize that R&D groups are a special challenge because they are often so diverse. Employee educational levels will vary from high school to Ph.D., for example. Also, many departments or groups are multidisciplined—with engineers, chemists, biologists, mathematicians, and so on—each with a potential for scientific chauvinism that can lead to competition or misunderstanding.

R&D managers, through their attitudes and behavior, largely determine the climate in their group or department. A fertile R&D work environment is characterized by the following elements.

▲ *Respect.* Respect—for each person as a unique human being, not just as a member of the group—is essential. It is a fact of life that the president receives more respect than does a janitor, but it is equally true that each deserves and needs respect as a human being. If a manager has little respect for a subordinate or, for that matter, vice versa, they are both in an untenable, unworkable situation.

▲ *Trust.* Trust flows from respect and is an essential component of everything good in human relationships. Certainly trust is crucial to effective supervision. Without it, a "we-they," adversarial mood is sure to develop.

▲ *Sense of Purpose.* Why are we here? The manager and all group members know how their department fits into the R&D function or division.

PEANUTS ® by Charles M. Schultz

Reprinted by permission of UFS, Inc.

▲ *Commitment.* The leader and all group members have a strong commitment to the long-term health of the division and to harmonized company, R&D, group, and personal goals.

▲ *High Competence and Dedication.* The manager and all group members are highly competent and have confidence in each other's ability and dedication.

▲ *Urgent but Reasoned Goal-Focused Activity.* There is goal-focused activity, with a work pace that is a healthy blend of urgency and contemplative, well-reasoned, and deliberate progress.

▲ *Involvement.* Productivity, personal growth, and morale will be high if employees feel involved in the planning, decision making, and movement of the department toward its goals.

Case Study: Individuality

In one nonunion R&D department of an automotive manufacturer, Bill, the manager, required all technicians to work exactly the same schedule, allowing no exceptions. To him, sameness equaled fairness. However, many technicians considered the policy unfair. Some preferred to work the standard hours, but others had problems doing so.

For example, working parents with young children needed flexibility to accommodate babysitters. Technicians taking college courses to improve themselves had trouble meeting strict course schedules. Medical or dental appointments were also a problem. As a result, some technicians called in sick for the entire day when actually they needed only an hour or two off. Laboratory scientists needed Bill's permission to have technicians work modified schedules to accommodate special experiments, and if Bill was not available to make a decision, progress on some projects suffered.

Although Bill could not prove malfeasance, he instructed the secretary to keep a strict log of all technicians' absenteeism. Then when an individual's record was poor, Bill berated him, regardless of whether his absences were legitimate. Over time, relationships, especially between Bill and departmental technicians, deteriorated.

When Bill retired, Mabel took over the department and, after becoming aware of the situation, changed the policy. Technicians were allowed to work any reasonable schedule as long as they obtained their laboratory supervisor's approval. At the next department meeting, Mabel emphasized that she trusted every group member—until and unless she learned differently. She then instructed the secretary to throw away the "lost-time" log, since Payroll kept track of sick time and vacation from time cards. The technicians began to feel trusted, important, and fairly treated, and the laboratory scientists appreciated the increased flexibility. Soon work schedules and absenteeism became nonissues and employee morale and productivity rose dramatically.

▲ *Individuality.* Harold Leavitt, in *Managerial Psychology,* emphasizes that the units of management are "people, one at a time." A leader does not supervise people in general, but as separate, unique individuals. When managers regard employees as interchangeable parts (all janitors have the same job, therefore all janitors are the same), they disregard the strong human need to be treated as an individual. When leaders cite fairness as the justification for treating everyone alike, they are being neither fair nor realistic. To be sure, most official company policies must be administered uniformly, but in many interpersonal situations, regarding everyone the same can be the most unfair treatment of all.

▲ *Concern (Caring).* Some years ago, "Have a good day!" became part of people's conversation. When employees feel that their boss—or anyone else in the work group—really cares whether they have a good day, they feel part of the group. They perceive that their identity as individuals has been established. Nothing does more for a feeling of warmth and safety than the realization, in the midst of personal difficulty, that coworkers care deeply and are offering sympathy and encouragement. The idea that a work environment should be cold and impersonal to improve efficiency is contradicted by the reality concerning people and their feelings.

▲ *Acceptance.* The leader and group members accept one another—that is, they value one another and tolerate idiosyncracies because everyone is an individual and no one is perfect. Carl Rogers *(On Becoming a Person)* says it best:

> By acceptance I mean a warm regard for him as a person of unconditional self-worth—of value no matter what his condition, his behavior, or his feelings. It means a respect and liking for him as a separate person.... [Acceptance creates] a relationship of warmth and safety, and the safety of being prized as a person seems a highly important element in a helping relationship.

Rogers, a clinical psychologist, was primarily addressing the therapeutic situation, but as Abraham Maslow, another clinical psychologist, has pointed out in his book *Motivation and Personality,* psychological principles that make sick people well will surely make well people even better.

▲ *Civility.* "Good management starts with good manners, society's means of ensuring consideration of others as people," suggests Consultant Robert Sampson *(Managing the Managers).* When coworkers are polite to one another and avoid treading on others' dignity, they create an underlying tranquillity, even in the most hectic work environment. Civility can compensate for unintentional slights, and a person left with dignity intact recovers much more quickly from criticism. Of all the mistakes managers make, none is more grievous or damaging to morale than being rude and disrespectful to subordinates. Few managers intentionally "put down" employees, but since most organizational cultures consider managers to be superior to nonmanagement workers, such behavior comes all too easily.

▲ *Honesty, Candor, Openness.* Just as trust is basic to all things good in human relationships, honesty, candor, and openness are basic to sustaining and strengthening those relationships. When one person can depend on another to tell the truth, even when it might hurt a little, all sorts of good things start to happen between them.

One of the very worst dislocations between management and employees is management's assumptions about how things are done in the organization versus what *really* takes place in the employees' world of work. The more employees trust a manager and the more honesty, candor, and openness there is between them, the more they will share their world of work. Then managers can do a better job of managing because they will have a more accurate picture of reality.

▲ *Stability, Security, Predictability.* Managers need to be ethical, fair, and consistent without being inflexible. This minimizes uncertainty and anxiety and makes employees feel safe and secure; more energy can then be focused on productive work.

▲ *Cooperation.* When coworkers respect and care for one another, and when all people feel safe and secure about their "place in the sun," the stage is set for cooperation rather than competition, for mutual esteem and pride rather than envy.

▲ *Effective Communication.* Defined as "the creation of understanding," effective communication is indispensable in any good work environment. For example:
  —The level of trust among a group of people is directly proportional
     to the quality of their communication.
  —Good communication minimizes gossip and shuts down the rumor
     mill, optimizing feelings of safety and security.
Managers who listen carefully and inform abundantly will soon be surrounded by good communicators.

▲ *Recognition.* When people are recognized for their accomplishments and their value to the organization, they feel good about themselves, their coworkers, and their boss.

▲ *Thoughtfulness (Consideration for Others).* It has been said, probably correctly, that nothing is more contagious than nervous tension, but surely thoughtfulness must run a close second. This can take many forms, but it generally involves getting outside oneself, being significantly oriented toward others rather than solely toward oneself. It means *giving* rather than *taking*.

▲ *Agreeableness, Amiability, Friendliness.* These characteristics are potent antidotes for nervous tension and anxiety and create as much tranquillity in a work environment as civility. Good-natured bosses, especially those with a sense of humor, are one step ahead in creating an atmosphere of warmth and safety. The concept of an aloof, formal manager stems largely from the military, where life-and-death decisions in wartime are commonplace—hardly a realistic model for other organizations.

▲ *Genuineness (Realness).* A quality work environment helps people feel safe and secure, thus encouraging them to be themselves, warts and all. This reduces façades, protectiveness, and defensiveness and allows people to focus their energy on productive work.

▲ *Independence and Interdependence.* When people are valued for their basic worth and are respected for their individuality, they develop a strong sense of independence. But it is precisely because employees feel prized and respected that they find little need to throw their weight around, to assert their individuality at the expense of others. Thus when people feel good about themselves and receive emotional support from other members of their work group, they develop a strong sense of both *inde*pendence and *inter*dependence.

▲ *Cohesive Group Spirit.* Under good management a group of people will develop a close, family-type working relationship in which individual members care for, trust, respect, and have confidence in each other. For example, concerning an R&D manager, a subordinate wrote, "I have personally witnessed in two different companies where his approach to management created high-quality working groups whose atmosphere would rival that of a close-knit family."

▲ *Deference.* If the aforementioned characteristics are operative, if group members feel good about themselves and about each other, and if managers seek advice from and defer to their subordinates, group members will defer to one another's expertise and judgment when appropriate. When the authority of knowledge, talent, and experience is freely recognized and supported, problems are given to the persons best equipped to solve them and opportunities are presented to those best able to take advantage of them. Then turf considerations are minimized.

▲ *Pride (But Not Arrogance).* Realistic pride in oneself and in one's work group strengthens group cohesiveness and individual self-confidence and fosters a can-do attitude toward innovation and technical challenge.

▲ *Loyalty and Enthusiasm.* People can work at being civil and respectful, but loyalty and enthusiasm must arise spontaneously. As Napoleon said, "An army's effectiveness depends on its size, training, experience, and morale . . . and morale is worth more than all the other factors combined."

A full supply of these qualities in a group requires considerable emotional capital, and it is the manager who has to make the first deposit—a generous investment of one's self. The interest that accrues in the group will depend partly on the maturity of its members, but primarily on the manager's interpersonal skills, which in turn depend significantly upon the extent of his or her knowledge of human motivation and behavior. Understanding people is crucial to success for an R&D manager because, as the saying goes,

In the world, people must be dealt with according to what they are, and not according to what they ought to be; and the great art of life is to find out what they are and act with them accordingly.

References

Leavitt, Harold J. *Managerial Psychology: An Introduction to Individuals, Pairs, and Groups in Organizations.* Chicago: University of Chicago Press, 1978.

McGregor, Douglas. *The Professional Manager,* ed. Caroline McGregor and Warren G. Bennis. New York: McGraw-Hill, 1967.

Maslow, Abraham H. *Motivation and Personality,* 2nd ed., ed. Wayne G. Holtzman and Gardner Murphy. New York: Harper & Row, 1970.

Rogers, Carl R. *On Becoming a Person: A Therapist's View of Psychotherapy.* Boston: Houghton Mifflin, 1961.

Sampson, Robert C. *Managing the Managers.* New York: McGraw-Hill, 1965.

Chapter 3

Characteristics of an Effective R&D Manager

I believe that effective leadership . . . is largely a function of the chief's vitality, willingness to empower others, and skill at exciting individuals about the purpose of themselves and their group.

Tom Peters

Managing research is a contradiction in terms. *Managing* implies control and order, while *research* involves creativity and freedom. Yet research *must* be managed—managed in such a way that good results are achieved, not choked by overmanaging. Now that we have studied what constitutes a good R&D work environment, we need to ask: What type of leader is most likely to provide such an atmosphere?

Many different kinds of people can and do become good R&D managers, and numerous supervisory styles have proved to be successful. Let's identify the characteristics most common among good leaders.

Good Managers Are Good Employees

As a start, good managers have an overabundance of the same qualities that characterize good employees. Therefore, good R&D managers are:

▲ Technically competent, defined for managers as follows:
  • Having a broad understanding of the scientific disciplines relevant to the company's business
  • Recognizing which technical literature is the best source of current information
  • Having a sense of what constitutes good science, good scientists, and appropriate methods of investigation
  • Being able to detect spurious science, scientists, and data, no matter what the discipline

▲ Highly productive, focused, and goal oriented
▲ Genuine (psychologically honest with themselves and with others)
▲ Open-minded and flexible, with a high capacity for growth
▲ Cooperative, yet independent
▲ Respectful toward and tolerant of others
▲ Deferential to others when appropriate
▲ Good communicators
▲ Not overly self-centered
▲ Self-confident and secure (have strong but realistic self-esteem)
▲ Not arrogant (don't take themselves too seriously)
▲ Not afraid to admit when they are wrong
▲ Self-starters
▲ At the self-actualization level of motivation
▲ Considerate of others
▲ Committed to their organization, their boss, their subordinates, and their peers
▲ Ethical, with a strong set of basic values

Nine Traits for Management Victory

1. An inspiring vision
2. Leadership by emotion
3. Managing by wandering around
4. Improvisation, autonomy, and creativity
5. Small-group dynamics
6. Partnership
7. Execution and the "little things"
8. People, not technology
9. Removing boot-lickers and bureaucrats

Source: Tom Peters, "Involvement Unlimited: Untried But True Performance Elixir," *Chicago Tribune* (February 11, 1989). TPG Communications.

Leadership Ability

On the other hand, Abraham Zaleznik, in an article in the *Harvard Business Review,* describes some *differences* between "caretaker" managers and leaders. Leaders, he says—

▲ tend to take risks and help their organizations break free from inertia, bureaucracy, and conservatism;
▲ adopt an active, personal attitude toward goals;

▲ relate to people empathetically; and
▲ value individualism.

Professor and consultant Warren Bennis, in an article in *Training and Development Journal*, adds that leaders—

▲ draw people to their vision;
▲ communicate that vision to their subordinates;
▲ establish an atmosphere of trust; and
▲ know their skills and how to use them effectively.

Psychological Health

Psychologist Abraham Maslow relates managerial excellence with psychological health, as does Rensis Likert, who, in his book *New Patterns of Management*, says: "The best managers . . . seem to be psychologically healthier people than the poorer managers [and they] increase the health of the workers whom they manage." Maslow studied the personal characteristics of many public and historical figures who were, to the extent feasible, prejudged to be psychologically healthy. Tentative composite impressions yielded some of the following characteristics. In each case, I've linked the characteristic (Maslow's finding) with a desirable managerial quality.

Characteristic	Managerial Quality
More efficient perception of reality and more comfortable relations with it:	Is fair in evaluating and treating subordinates.
Acceptance [of self, others, and nature]:	Is comfortable with one's self and others; values others and treats them with respect.
Spontaneity, simplicity, naturalness:	Is genuine, direct, candid, and straightforward.
Problem centering:	Is oriented toward others and toward solving problems; not self-centered.
The quality of detachment:	Handles adversity well; reflective about life, career, and the meaning of things.
Autonomy; independence from culture and environment:	Is an independent thinker; needs to be satisfied that one has done one's best.
Continued freshness of appreciation:	Is optimistic about life and about potential of employees.
Altruistic desire to help the human race:	Likes other people; rejoices when

	employees succeed; sympathizes with and encourages employees when they are struggling; a strong advocate for subordinates.
Meaningful interpersonal relations:	Develops trusting, caring relationships with subordinates; kind and patient most of the time.
Democratic character structure:	Respects and trusts subordinates; delegates well; not self-important.
Discrimination between good and evil:	Is highly ethical; has broad horizons.
Philosophical, unhostile sense of humor:	Is friendly, does not take him- or herself or life too seriously; doesn't laugh at others' expense.
Creativeness:	Is an original thinker, flexible, creative; does not have to go by the book.
Firm foundation for a value system:	Knows what he or she likes and doesn't like; feels strongly about things but is flexible.
Resolution of dichotomies:	Tends to do the right thing in any situation.

Simply put, the best way to ensure good management in an organization is to promote into supervision the individuals who are most likely to practice good management.

References

Bennis, Warren S. "Why Leaders Can't Lead." *Training and Development Journal,* vol. 43 (April 1989).

Likert, Rensis. *New Patterns of Management.* New York: McGraw-Hill, 1961.

Maslow, Abraham H. *Eupsychian Management: A Journal.* Homewood, Illinois: Irwin-Dorsey, 1965.

Maslow, Abraham H. *Motivation and Personality,* 2nd ed., ed. Wayne G. Holtzman and Gardner Murphy. New York: Harper & Row, 1970.

Peters, Tom. "Nine Traits for Victory, in War or Business." *The Arizona Daily Star,* May 16, 1989.

———. "Some Management and Economic Myths That Need to Be Debunked." *Chicago Tribune,* September 19, 1988.

Zaleznik, Abraham. "Managers and Leaders: Are They Different?" *Harvard Business Review,* vol. 55 (May–June, 1977).

Chapter 4

Characteristics of an Effective R&D Vice-President

The person most responsible for the success or failure of an R&D organization is its leader. For brevity's sake here, the leader of R&D is assumed to be a vice-president.

In many ways, this individual has the most difficult job in the corporation. Because of the inherent disorder in science's "world of order [*the technical term is* entropy, *but Murphy said it better:* IF ANYTHING CAN GO WRONG, IT WILL GO WRONG]," there are many more experimental failures than successes. Indeed, success in R&D is difficult to measure. The winning R&D division and its leader learn from negative results without becoming overly discouraged, and they take quick advantage of positive results.

In many industries, the payoff from R&D is far distant—ten years or more—thus the effect of a particular decision or policy—and of the R&D vice-president's strengths and weaknesses—may be far removed from the action itself.

The successful R&D vice-president needs good fortune, but certain personal characteristics lend a hand to Lady Luck. To begin, the vice-president needs all the characteristics of an effective R&D manager (see previous chapter). In addition:

1. The individual should be able to inspire both managers and bench scientists.

2. Because of the high position, the R&D vice-president must spend considerable time focusing on the larger picture, such as finance and policy issues; thus "people management" time is diminished. Strong interpersonal skills can help the individual, such as the ability to do the following:

> ▲ Develop and maintain a good working relationship with corporate management.
> ▲ Make the best use of limited subordinate-managing time.
> ▲ Be a strong role model for all R&D managers in the organization.

3. The vice-president needs strong diplomatic and political skills, and they must be founded on integrity and genuineness, not deviousness, duplicity, and deceit. For example, the R&D vice-president must generate strong financial support from corporate management, but in doing so, must paint an accurate picture of R&D for corporate management (rather than telling them what is expedient or what they want to hear) and take the responsibility when things go wrong (rather than blaming others, especially governmental regulatory agencies).

4. The individual should be a problem solver rather than a problem creator.

5. He or she must have the ability to sort out the important from the unimportant.

6. A vice-president must enjoy working with line R&D managers and not develop a large personal staff. If the individual does the latter, staff personnel will have a broad view of the R&D operation while most line managers will be compartmentalized.

7. The R&D vice-president must be a good scientist. This does *not* mean he or she stays "current"—he or she must rely on laboratory employees for that—but the person should have a general appreciation of and "feel" for science, both its potentialities and its limitations. For high-tech industries, this often requires a Ph.D. in a basic scientific field.

8. He or she needs to have the rare and subtle qualities of broad vision and good judgment. In particular, the vice-president must be able to judge accurately which subordinates are high-quality R&D managers and which are not, no matter how well the latter "manage upwards." Then he or she needs the courage and will to get rid of substandard managers.

9. The R&D vice-president must be able to judge when to discontinue projects with little or no chance of success, while continuing to support those

---

Case Study: The Problem Is Perry (and Also Rebecca)

Perry, a subordinate of Rebecca, the R&D vice-president, was grossly incompetent, devious in his dealings with everyone, imperious to all except his boss, and detested by all who really knew him. Because Rebecca was imperceptive, struggling in *her* job, and busy pleasing *her* boss, Perry survived in his position for many years. When something went awry in an important, complicated R&D function under Perry's supervision, outside consultants were brought in to assess the problem and suggest a solution. Their report drew only one conclusion: "The problem is Perry." The remedy was obvious, but Rebecca did nothing, which made her part of the problem.

with reasonable promise. Most important, the vice-president must choose and act long before the decision becomes obvious to everyone in R&D. Sometimes this is done on the basis of accumulated experimental evidence, but usually it depends on the judgment of subordinates, both laboratory scientists and middle R&D managers. (See case study on Listening to Others' Opinions.)

10. A good R&D vice-president is able to determine which subordinates' judgment he or she can trust.

Case Study: Listen to Others' Opinions

Most subordinates agreed that Theo, an R&D vice-president, was not up to the job. For example, he continued to support two pet projects even though his subordinates were unanimous in recommending they be cancelled. On the other hand, he procrastinated on a multimillion-dollar inlicensing decision for two years, until it became obvious to every R&D employee that the project was a sure winner. In the end, Theo made the correct decision, but the organization lost two precious years in a very competitive market.

Case Study: Who Is Right More Often?

Leo, an R&D vice-president, became enthusiastic about a project championed by Leona, one of the R&D managers. When Ingrid, another R&D manager, told Leo that Leona's project was technically correct but irrelevant because it was a solution looking for a problem, he replied, "Technically I'm in over my head. But I don't know who to believe; Leona tells me one thing and you tell me another. In fact, Leona says you're dead wrong." "Leo," Ingrid pointed out, "eventually you're going to have to decide whether you're best off trusting my judgment or Leona's. The best way to do that is to keep score over time and see who is correct more often."

Leo thanked Ingrid for her candor and counsel, kept score, and within eighteen months realized that Leona, while an innovative scientist, had a relatively closed mind and tended to come to inadequate conclusions because she refused to learn from her colleagues.

Evaluating the R&D Vice-President's Performance

Accurately evaluating the performance of an R&D vice-president is as difficult as the vice-president's job because so many factors enter into the equation.

Ultimately, an R&D vice-president's performance is measured by three interrelated factors: (1) the degree of success in the organization, (2) the quality of the R&D work environment, and (3) the quality of the R&D employees—both laboratory and management.

Measuring the R&D division's degree of success is discussed in the introduction to Part IV. The quality of the R&D work environment can best be measured by asking employees to anonymously evaluate the boss's performance. Perhaps the four most telling signs of a fertile R&D work environment (and an effective R&D leader) are: pervasive enthusiasm, a general sense of purpose and direction, a work pace characterized by brisk efficiency and relaxed congeniality, and low employee turnover, except when improving the quality of the work force.

In contrast, a poor work environment shows up in widespread malaise, constant employee griping and grousing, a general state of confusion, and high employee turnover coupled with a proliferation of dead wood.

The R&D vice-president is doing the job well when the overall quality of the R&D staff—management and laboratory workers—is high and constantly improving. This is a result of good leadership, including effective recruiting, fostering growth, promoting the right people, and ensuring a low turnover.

High-quality technical people can be spotted by the following:

▲ Internal accomplishments, including the quality and number of new products developed
▲ Patents and external publications involving peer review
▲ Recognition by scientific societies, including awards and election as officers
▲ Recognition by academicians and industrial competitors, especially if they actively recruit from the organization
▲ Ability to recruit top candidates from universities

Perhaps one of the best uses of consultants is to ask them how the quality of your R&D staff compares with that of your competitors.

Ethics in R&D Management

In John Steinbeck's novel *Cannery Row,* the character Doc remarks:

> It has always seemed strange to me, the things we admire in men; kindness and generosity, openness, honesty, understanding and feeling are the concomitants of failure in our system. And those traits we detest, sharpness, greed, acquisitiveness, meanness, egotism and self-interest, are the traits of success. And while men admire the quality of the first they love the produce of the second.

In spite of Doc's cynicism, one of the most critical qualities for an effective R&D vice-president (but true for all R&D managers) is high ethics. In fact, good management is impossible without consistent ethical behavior. As Tom Peters (*Arizona Daily Star,* September 26, 1989) emphasizes: "Ethical concerns surround us all the time, on parade whenever we deal with people in the course of an average day... treating people decently."

Ethical management is also a prerequisite for high productivity. Rensis Likert's social science experiments convinced him that, "Genuine interest and unselfish concern on the part of a supervisor in the success and well-being of his subordinates have a marked effect on performance."

Many R&D experimental results must be taken on faith, and this likewise calls ethics into play. For example, most projects involve extensive experimentation, frequently equivocal results, and complex interpretation. Much of the work must be taken on faith, assuming that laboratory workers are competent in conducting experiments, that they are honest in reporting results, and that managers have made honest use of the group's work.

It has been said that honor is the quality of personal integrity. It is won slowly by a lifetime of small decisions, where one places the virtues of compassion and justice ahead of one's own advancement.

The R&D vice-president is ultimately responsible for the ethical attitude, behavior, and performance of the division. Here are three ways to ensure success:

1. *Set a good example.* The leader sets the tone for any group; he or she is the role model. When subordinates see the vice-president consistently doing business in a highly ethical manner, they will set similar high standards for themselves and for one another (see case study below).

2. *Minimize unethical conformity and "group-think."* Peer pressure naturally dominates most teenagers ("all my friends do it"), but adults must resist

---

Case Study: Ethics and Regulatory Agencies

Drugstor, a pharmaceutical company, marketed a combination product that had some annoying, though not serious, side effects. An R&D project team found that if one of the active ingredients was micronized to a fine powder, twice as much was available for absorption, eliminating the side effects. Jody, a high-level manager in R&D, suggested submitting the new procedure to the Food and Drug Administration as a simple "manufacturing change," without revealing the medical ramifications, an action that would speed up FDA approval. Fortunately, Victoria, the R&D vice-president, was a sensible, ethical individual, and the company valued its pristine reputation. Jody's inappropriate recommendation was rejected without discussion and the FDA supplement was filed with the required biological data.

conforming to "slightly" unethical behavior norms. (Journalist-novelist Alistair Cooke diagnosed the problem of a particularly troubled U.S. president's administration as "too many shabby men.") A leader emphasizes healthy independence and interdependence, a strongly principled value system, and free, open communication.

3. *Create a safe environment.* Unless they are pathological, people suffer ethical lapses out of fear and insecurity, not evil. Consequently, vice-presidents can elevate the ethical behavior in their division by creating an atmosphere in which people feel psychologically safe and secure. For example,

▲ When laboratory workers are afraid of punishment or of losing their jobs if they don't stay on schedule, work tends to become sloppy.

▲ When an R&D vice-president fears his or her job is in jeopardy, the individual tends to "manage" the information that goes to corporate management so that the division is viewed in the best possible light.

▲ A subordinate who lacks self-confidence may become a yes-man, telling the boss what he or she thinks the boss wants to hear.

PEANUTS ® by Charles M. Schultz

Reprinted by permission of UFS, Inc.

References

Likert, Rensis. *New Patterns of Management.* New York: McGraw-Hill, 1961.
Peters, Tom. "Ethics Is Everyday, Lifetime Endeavor." *Arizona Daily Star,* September 26, 1989.

PART II

Basic R&D Managerial Tasks

The key to becoming a highly successful manager is to learn to behave like one.

Jay Hall, *Ponderables: Essays on Management Choice*

Most R&D managers no longer perform hands-on laboratory work; yet they are still responsible for experiment results. This means they must get the work done through the efforts of others.

To accomplish this, R&D managers must learn a new set of skills: interpersonal managerial skills involving human motivation and behavior. These "people responsibility" skills can be seen as separate tasks, discussed in Part II and in portions of Part III. While considering each task, however, keep three important points in mind.

A. *There are seven cornerstones of effective R&D people management.* As a good manager, you must do the following:

1. Inspire employees.
2. Respect each and every employee.
3. Trust your subordinates.
4. Involve as many employees as possible in the operation.
5. Manage empathically—that is, look at every aspect of your managerial behavior and ask yourself, "How would I want *my* boss to treat *me* in this situation?
6. Be a servant to subordinates.
7. Manage with a light touch—that is, interfere with workers as little as possible and give them as much responsibility and freedom as possible.

Of these seven cornerstones, two—Be a servant to subordinates and Manage with a light touch—are general. The other five (dealing with inspiring, respecting, trusting, involving, and empathizing) are discussed in Chapter 5.

B. *In general—*

▲ the more you can inspire people and instill in them a sense of purpose and commitment to group goals,
▲ the more you can supervise with a light touch,
▲ the more you can prize people for what they are instead of pressuring them to change,
▲ the more you can respect and trust your subordinates and treat them as individuals,
▲ the more you can share your power with them and involve them in running the organization, and
▲ the more giving, caring, candid, communicative, and genuine you are toward others,

the more fertile will be the work environment. This will lead to significant personal growth, improved group spirit, and steadily rising productivity.

C. *Most major supervisory functions are not performed—at least not well—as discrete tasks or even as combinations of easily identified segments.* Rather, they are multidimensional activities involving complex attitudes and behavioral patterns. A supervisor cannot improve his or her performance simply by practicing these skills as one practices, say, a musical instrument. Improvements in performing managerial tasks come with changes in attitudes and behavior. Such progress is not easy; it usually takes place on the job and occurs in small increments; it requires time, effort, stamina, and patience. In the end, you decide for yourself whether excellence—or at least significant improvement—is worth that effort.

Superficial, "quick-fix" pathways to managerial excellence are unworkable. They trivialize the difficult practice of management, implying that its complex functions can be distilled down to a brief flurry of simple activities. As Albert Einstein said, "Everything should be made as simple as possible—but not simpler."

This said, the chapters in Part II move us on to a discussion of the most fundamental functions associated with R&D management.

References

Hall, Jay. *Ponderables: Essays on Managerial Choice—Past and Future.* Woodlands, Tex.: Teleometrics International, 1982.
Labovitz, George. *Motivational Dynamics-I: Mainsprings of Motivation.* Minneapolis: Control Data Corporation, 1980.

Chapter 5

Five Cornerstone R&D Managerial Tasks

The introduction to Part II lists seven cornerstones of effective people management. Five of those important tasks are described in this chapter.

Inspiring Laboratory Workers

Most managers don't include "inspiring subordinates" in their job descriptions, but it should be first on the agenda. Consultant Tom Peters considers a manager's role to be that of cheerleader. Ford Motor Company Manager J. S. Ninomya and management educator and consultant Warren S. Bennis (see References at end of this chapter) both believe that managers should be visionary and draw employees to their vision.

Each person's work life has some bad, some good, and many routine—or neutral—moments. The manager's job is to reduce the subordinates' bad moments and increase their good ones. But excellence in management goes well beyond that. To stretch or grow, people need something extraordinary, something inspiring in their work lives; they need to feel exultant and triumphant. The manager does not so much provide those moments as refrain from snuffing them out when their subordinates come upon them. Only then does an R&D manager receive a thank-you similar to this handwritten note from a laboratory technician:

"You are truly an inspiring person and manager."

Why is inspiring one's subordinates so important? Hodding Carter, aide to former President Jimmy Carter and now a journalist, hinted at it: "There are only two lasting bequests we can give our children. One is roots, the other wings." Employees are not children, but the analogy fits.

Compared to some areas of a technical company, R&D is a complex world filled with both uncertainty and promise. For optimum employee well-being and productivity, a leader must infuse the work environment with a measure of stability and security—*roots*. With firm support beneath them, laboratory workers are more likely to rise to greater heights.

Inspiring your subordinates involves more than offering stability. As W. Shedd wrote, "A ship in the harbor is safe, but that is not what ships are for." When an R&D manager inspires subordinates, they take wing; and H. Mabry reminds us, "The higher we soar the farther we see." When laboratory workers have faith in themselves and in their leaders, they confidently focus their energies on creativity and innovation.

Remember:

I	Infusion of spirit and confidence
N	Nary a discouraging word
S	Security and safety emancipate creativity
P	Pride and progress
I	Independence for a sail; interdependence for an anchor
R	Roots and wings
E	Enthusiasm, élan, excellence, and everything else

Respecting Others

In his book *Management: Tasks, Responsibilities, Practices*, Peter Drucker says, "The work relationship has to be based on respect." Respecting your employees is just as important as inspiring them. Your success as an R&D manager depends on your ability to have and show esteem for other people. A manager *must* respect each subordinate as a unique individual and as a valuable, contributing member of the work group; only then will there be a trusting, caring, productive work relationship. Well-educated technical people are espe-

---

Case Study: Respect and the Action Team

Perry was asked to take over as head of an R&D department; he noticed that morale and productivity were low. Always a respectful person, Perry first concentrated on showing respect for all group members, including laboratory technicians. He emphasized to the group that creating a high-quality organization was primarily *their* responsibility. The technicians responded most dramatically, forming an Action Team. They examined the department's operations and physical facilities, and they took the responsibility for improving one situation after another. Within two months, their demeanor changed from that of being passive lackeys to being enthusiastic, confident, decisive, take-charge members of the organization.

cially capable and have high potential. They need and respond to respect more than the average person. Without mutual esteem, little goes right in an R&D organization, no matter how talented the manager or the subordinates. Mutual respect contributes to all other managerial tasks.

Deferring to Others

When we ask others for advice, we enhance their feelings of worth. We are also very likely to learn something. Deferring to others is an aspect of respect. It is submitting to another's opinion, wishes, or governance, out of respect. It is good R&D management, since it harmonizes with and combines so many other managerial tasks.

For example, nothing shows more respect for your subordinates than your deferring to their scientific, organizational, or operational judgment when appropriate. Likewise, deferring to your employees is one of the most eloquent demonstrations of trust you can make to them.

The deferential manager provides an excellent role model for subordinates; they will tend to defer to colleagues when it is best for the group. Simultaneously, it ensures good relationships with subordinates, peers, and superiors, and it reduces errors by deferring decisions to more knowledgeable people.

Considering the unavoidable politics within an organization, the deferential manager is both ethical and pragmatic. Deferring to others makes friends, not enemies, and mends fences instead of building barriers.

Trusting Your Subordinates

Psychologist Carl Rogers *(Carl Rogers on Personal Power)* has pointed out that, "The human organism is, at its deepest level, trustworthy." Trust, although not a task but an attitude, is basic to effective management.

Social scientists contend that people are able to trust others in direct proportion to their own self-esteem. When a first-line supervisor has trouble trusting subordinates, the problem is often a lack of self-confidence. The solution is not—as is often done—to pressure him or her to loosen the reins; that may threaten the individual's self-esteem even more by suggesting that the boss doesn't trust him or her to do the job. Instead, the manager needs to show in genuine ways that he or she trusts the supervisor, thus increasing the latter's self-confidence and ability to trust others.

An indirect approach is the best way to solve most personnel problems. Figure 2 shows both good and bad ways to approach the problem. As shown in the figure, the first small measure of improvement increases the subordinate's feelings of worth and self-confidence, which fosters growth and a snowball effect takes over. And since an indirect approach is most compatible with human nature, it produces longer lasting effects. (Note: The struggling supervisor who doesn't respond favorably may not be suitable for management.)

Managers should review their activities to determine the substantial posi-

Figure 2. Two ways to solve personnel problems.

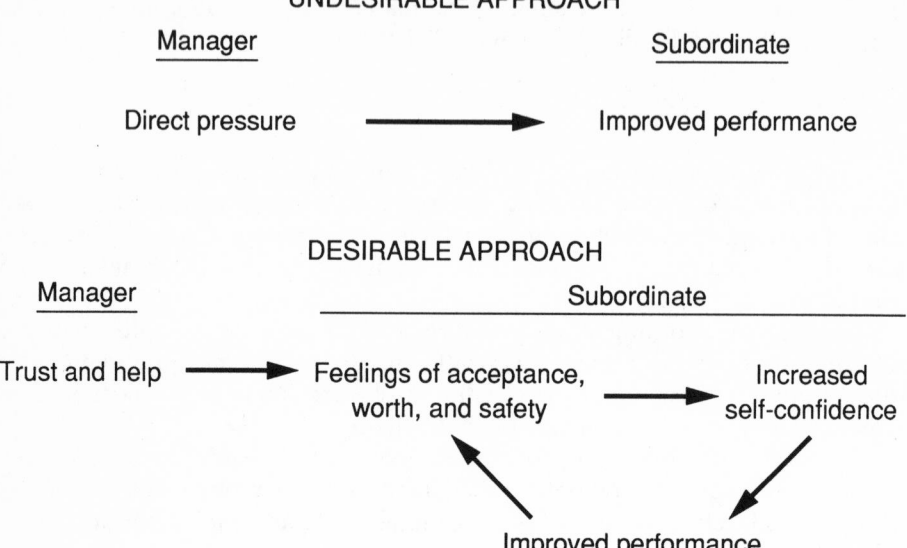

tive contribution that trust can make. Consider delegating as much as possible, monitoring as little as necessary, and relying primarily on employees' self-evaluation.

The obvious question is: Should you withhold trust until someone proves worthy, or do you assume trustworthiness until the individual's actions warn you otherwise? The second approach is preferable, not just because most people *are* trustworthy, but also because—

▲ assuming trustworthiness in subordinates (obviously) makes a manager more trusting as a person, and therefore a better manager;
▲ people tend to be more trustworthy if they sense an assumption of trust from another person—a classic self-fulfilling prophecy; and,
▲ most important, assuming trustworthiness in others is the right thing to do.

Involving Employees in the Operation

The wise R&D manager will involve group members in as much of the running of the operation as possible (including planning for reorganization). Tom Peters ("Some Management and Economic Myths") points out that "continuous improvement and spirited performance are a result of full-time, not sometimes, involvement." When employees don't feel involved, disinterest and lethargy reign. Involving others is linked to all other managerial tasks; you'll see it as an

---

Case Study: They Really Trust Me Again!

Jake, a scientist who, for various reasons, fell out of favor with manage-ment, was monitored constantly and given only menial, routine laboratory tasks to perform. After a change in management, Jake's new supervisor, Maryann, determined that the problem was primarily one of inappropriate *managerial* actions by his former supervisor, although Jake was not blameless.

In a heart-to-heart talk with Jake, Maryann said she would like to make a fresh start. From then on, Jake was treated with respect and afforded the same amount of freedom, trust, and responsibility as his colleagues. Soon his performance matched that of his counterparts, and his demeanor changed from that of a whipped dog to that of an enthusiastic, liberated laboratory worker. Jake confided to friends that "they really trust me again!"

---

element discussed throughout Parts II and III of this book. The experts agree. In an article in *Business Week*, business columnist Alan Blinder cites references from a conference sponsored by the Brookings Institution. He concludes: "Employee participation, if done right, can and does raise productivity."

Tom Peters, in a *Chicago Tribune* column entitled "U.S. Firms Overlook Worker Involvement," provides several case studies and concludes: "At [major] companies . . . the power of involvement . . . among hourly workers and work teams has amazed management in terms of what stunning results can be achieved."

Subtle differences in how to involve subordinates can have a substantial impact on the group's work environment. For example, suppose another manager writes a memo to you requesting that your department's personnel do things in a certain way in regard to her operation.

Case A: Because you do not consider the matter important, you do not think much about it and you circulate the memo to your group with a cover note saying, "Please comply."

Case B: You doubt that the matter is important, but out of habit you circulate the memo with a cover note asking, "Any reason why we shouldn't comply?"

In Case A, some subordinates will perceive that you didn't bother to ask their opinion. In Case B, you have—in a subtle but critically important way—shown them respect and courtesy; you have *involved* them in a situation that affects them. While the weight of this particular incident may be negligible, the accumulated impact of similar incidents is precisely what generates a good or bad organizational environment.

Managing Empathically

In Harper Lee's *To Kill a Mockingbird*, the attorney Atticus Finch explains, "You never really understand someone until you consider things from their point of view." In business too, *everything* managers do will be done better if they first consider how they would feel if *their* boss managed that way. Put simply, if one of your parents dies and mine are still living, I can only offer you sympathy. But if I, too, have lost a parent, I can empathize with you—I know how you feel.

Since managers begin their careers in a nonsupervisory position, and since all managers save one (the CEO, ignoring for the moment the board of directors and stockholders) are also subordinates, they should be able to empathize with their employees. Unfortunately, managers often seem oblivious to the impact of their decisions and behavior. They are equally unmindful of the profound effect empathizing with others can have on *every* managerial task.

Case Study: Managers as Subordinates

A seminar leader suggested that managers should manipulate their subordinates to improve productivity. Over lunch, one enthusiastic participant was asked by a table companion how she would feel if *her* boss had attended this same seminar the previous year and had been manipulating *her* (without her knowledge) for the past twelve months. She admitted she hadn't thought of that and agreed she would not like it one bit. Thereafter during the seminar, she was a vocal opponent to any suggestion of manipulation of employees.

Some managers may reject the suggestion that they look at their management practices through a subordinate's eyes, contending that management people are different from nonmanagement. This is akin to the ancient belief that kings and queens are not ordinary mortals. Certainly social scientists would have difficulty understanding the basis for such a claim.

Concerning the managerial task of delegating, ask yourself: How do I feel when my boss gives me interesting, challenging, important jobs to do? The obvious answer is: *It makes me feel good.*

The next question is: How do I feel when he makes it clear that I should do those assignments in whatever way I think best? The equally obvious answer is: *Even better; I feel prized and trusted.*

The last question is: How much effort am I going to put into those delegated tasks, and am I going to make sure they're done right? Answer: *I am going to do my damnedest to justify his faith and confidence in me.*

Going through this intellectual exercise will demonstrate the proper way for *you* to delegate; your actual behavior depends on your management style.

A final point: Many times we are insensitive to the feelings and blind to the views of others, not because we don't care, but because we unconsciously assume their reactions are identical to ours. This is an unrealistic assumption. Each person is a unique individual, and, in our pluralistic society, people come from varied cultures and are of different generations. It is best to ask the other person how he or she feels, then listen!

▲ ▲ ▲ ▲ ▲

Historian Henri Fayol, a French engineer, was first to define the functions of management as (1) planning, (2) organizing, (3) directing, (4) coordinating, and (5) controlling. These will be discussed in the next three chapters.

References

Bennis, Warren S. "Why Leaders Can't Lead." *Training and Development Journal*, vol. 43 (April 1989).

Blinder, Alan S. "Want to Boost Productivity? Try Giving Workers a Say." *Business Week*, April 17, 1989.

Drucker, Peter F. *Management: Tasks, Responsibilities, Practices*. New York: Harper & Row, 1974.

Fayol, Henri. *General and Industrial Management*. New York: Pitman, 1949.

———. *Industrial and General Administration*. London: Sir Isaac Pitman and Sons, 1930.

Ninomiya, J. A. "Wagon Masters and Lesser Managers." *Harvard Business Review*, vol. 66 (March-April 1988).

Peters, Tom. "Some Management and Economic Myths that Need to Be Debunked." *Chicago Tribune*, September 19, 1988.

———. "U.S. Firms Overlook Worker Involvement." *Chicago Tribune*.

Rogers, Carl R. *Carl Rogers on Personal Power*. New York: Delacorte Press, 1977.

Chapter 6

Planning for Productive Research

"Would you tell me, please, which way I ought to go from here?" "That depends a good deal on where you want to get to," said the Cat. "I don't much care where...." said Alice. "Then it doesn't matter which way you go," said the Cat.

Lewis Carroll, *Alice's Adventures in Wonderland*

R&D managers don't want to follow in Alice's footsteps. They don't want to be like the rider who "mounted his steed and rode off in all directions." And they certainly need to do better than the traveler who sent a letter back home saying, "I'm lost but I'm making wonderful time!"

Successful R&D managers plan first, then act. Nevertheless, it is important to recognize that planning involves more than answering the question: What should I do next? True managerial planning involves conscious decisions concerning your total approach to supervising a group. This is best illustrated with the case study on the next page. The subject's thoughts and actions provide a practical example of highly successful planning and execution.

Set Your Management Style

Before you can even consider strategies for meeting the R&D division's goals, you must establish an environment of trust within the work group. At this juncture, review the following:

Guidelines for Establishing Trust

1. Because one of the primary barriers to trust is unfamiliarity, get to know each person as an individual. Meet with your employees on a one-on-one basis as soon as possible, and ask them about themselves and their aspirations. Schedule the technicians first and work your way up the department; this

---

Case Study: Setting the Management Tone

Alan, an R&D manager, was asked to supervise a different R&D department within the same company. Here are his thoughts during the first few days of his new assignment:

"I change jobs tomorrow. Right now I have mixed feelings: sadness about leaving good friends and colleagues behind; enthusiasm because of the new challenge, and yet apprehension about exploring new territory."

"What are my goals? Where do I want to go? Better yet, because the essence of management is *we*, not *I*, where will my new colleagues and I want to go?"

"The emphasis needs to be on *we*, but as the leader I must have a clear, long-range vision, a consistent philosophy of management, and the flexibility to modify my personal views to accommodate, as much as possible, those of my new colleagues. Simply put, I want to create an organizational environment—a kind of fertile ground—in which all employees learn and grow while contributing optimally to organizational goals. I want to build in the workplace a family of competent, caring, and cooperative achievers who are strongly independent yet healthfully interdependent. The way to start is by building trust."

One year later, the positive changes in the group's attitude and performance were widely applauded by other managers (including the vice-president of R&D) as "amazing" and "a miracle."

---

sends the clear message that technicians are not second-class citizens. You'll want to stay in touch with every department member during the months and years to come.

2. At the same time, help employees get to know you. Be straightforward. Whenever possible, tell them what you're thinking and feeling. Because you have a great deal of power over your employees, no news is *bad* news to them, so communicate as much as possible. Fill a huge bulletin board with all the nonconfidential memos that come across your desk. People won't want to read everything, and different individuals will have different interests, but a bulletin board allows the employees to decide what information they receive. To reduce confusion and to focus attention, divide the board into three parts: urgent, new, and old information. Spend fifteen minutes or so each week to reorganize and update the information; if the board gets too messy and out of date, people will stop reading it.

3. Be trustworthy; deliver what you promise and promise only what you can deliver. Don't take advantage of subordinates—be a giver, not a taker. Don't poison the environment with deviousness or secrecy; rather, clear the air with directness and candor. Assume that everyone can be trusted until you have evidence to the contrary. Show employees that no one ever gets into trouble by telling you the truth, no matter how bad the news.

Case Study: Department Meeting, First Thing, First Day

Alan held a get-acquainted department meeting first thing in the morning on his first day in the department. His introductory remarks were limited to the following:

> "I'm glad to be here. I'm looking forward to working with you; I'll try to make a contribution to the group.
> "The previous manager and I are different people, so things will be different. You'll have to judge for yourselves whether they are better or worse, but they will be different.
> "I have a tendency to talk too much, so let's start by having all of you talk first. What do you want to know about me? What's on your minds?"

After a time, the discussion lagged, so Alan spent about twenty minutes explaining his general managerial philosophy:

> "In a very real sense, you don't work for me; I work for you. You produce the results; I'm simply overhead, as the accountants will tell you. I'm here as a facilitator to remove obstacles that impede your progress. I'm here to help and to provide leadership without smothering you.
> "Think of our departmental structure as a circle, not a triangle with me at the top. Like you, I have a contribution to make based on my responsibilities and particular talents, but your contributions are just as important as mine.
> "Since we are a circle, I need your help in planning the future of the department. If you help me with this process, the end result will not only be a better plan, but all of us will be more committed to its success.
> "A good plan answers the following questions, among others:
> ▲ "What should our goals be?
> ▲ "How should the department be organized?
> ▲ "How does this department fit into the overall R&D operation?
> ▲ "How can we do things better and more efficiently?

▲ "Should we be making more of an impact on the R&D organization and on the company as a whole? I encourage you to take risks and innovate.
▲ "In general, what do we want to be, as a department and as individuals?"

"You will be treated as well-intentioned, responsible adults.

"The two most frequent words you'll hear from me are, 'You decide.' All departmental supervisors will be encouraged to become very familiar with that vocabulary.

"I'll do my best to delegate as much as possible, but it's your responsibility to keep me informed on important matters.

"You are strongly encouraged to place group welfare first; this reduces internal strife and unhealthy competition. One of my major responsibilities is to create a situation in which your individual well-being, growth, and progress are compatible with—and even enhanced by—focusing significant attention on the group's accomplishments and reputation.

"As soon as possible, I would like each of you to ask yourselves the following questions and submit the answers to our secretary; she will compile all responses to preserve confidentiality:
▲ "What do you like about your job?
▲ "What don't you like about your job?
▲ "What can management do to make your job better?"

"I realize this is an extremely busy department, but it is important that each of you take time to think about what you are doing and to reflect upon the meaning and the significance of the data you are gathering. It is especially important that scientists explain to technicians the reasoning behind each particular experiment; otherwise technicians' work becomes meaningless drudgery.

"High performance is expected, and as long as you and I do our best, it will usually be attained. When we fall short, I'll look at myself and see what *I* need to do to improve. I'm sure all of you will do the same. When things go wrong and we are criticized, I'll take the blame. When things go right, you'll receive the credit. I'm no saint; that's what I get paid for.

"Speaking of high performance, perhaps we should borrow Newport News Shipbuilding's creed and make it our own: 'We shall build good ships here; at a profit if we can, at a loss if we must, but always good ships.' "

It was, at the start, a group of high-quality people. With Alan's leadership, they became even better.

Planning That Meets R&D Divisional Goals

Individual and departmental goals must be harmonized with the overall goals of the R&D division. The goals should be challenging so that people stretch and grow. Likewise, they need to be realistic enough to ensure some success lest people get discouraged.

The more a manager involves employees in the general planning process, the more successful the group will be. Since, in R&D, circumstances often change because of unexpected laboratory results, the manager and the group must be flexible. While the manager needs to be involved with significant changes in major plans, it is important that laboratory scientists have the authority to change the direction and approach on medium-range issues without checking everything with the boss.

In short, to plan well, the R&D manager needs to do the following:

1. Always involve subordinates in the process, especially when planning research.
2. Set challenging but realistic goals.
3. Be flexible when circumstances dictate that goals be revised.

Ethical Considerations

Many companies have formal goal systems, and how well a particular employee or department meets those goals is an important consideration for year-end performance evaluations. These systems are generally reasonable, but management needs to guard against a very common danger: conflict of interest.

When unforeseen circumstances cause a manager's formal personal goals to become adverse to the well-being of employees or of the R&D group, the manager experiences conflict. Under a rigid goal-performance review system and in a punitive work atmosphere, if managers don't meet their formal personal goals, they run the risk of getting a lower performance review, which may lead to criticism, a blot on their record, less financial compensation, and a dimmer future for their managerial career. On the other hand, if they focus on achieving their personal goals, they may cause problems for other employees or for the organization.

> Minimal ethics require that managers do what's best for the organization and that they do not benefit themselves at the expense of their subordinates. However, the organizational climate and goal system must be such that ethical behavior is encouraged.

These are not casual concerns; consider the following case studies. As both these case studies show, conflicts of interest can cause serious problems.

Case Study: Individual Employees Count

Tom, a laboratory technician, was busy running an experiment and inadvertently broke a flask, severely lacerating his thumb. When George, the manager, and Geraldine, the company safety director, heard of the accident, the first—and only—question they both asked was, "Was there any lost time?"

George and Geraldine both had as part of their formal individual goals for the year: No Lost-Time Accidents in Your Sphere of Responsibility. Obviously, something was wrong—with the system as well as with George and Geraldine—when the physical well-being of an employee took a distant, even unconsidered, second priority to management's goals.

Case Study: The Good of the Organization

The formal goals for Walter Wadsworth, a recently appointed vice-president of R&D for Doberman, Inc., a pharmaceutical company, included the following item: Five New Drug Applications to Be Submitted in the Coming Year.

Unfortunately, for various reasons the clinical proof of efficacy for two of the drug candidates fell nine months behind schedule. Nevertheless, Walter ordered his subordinates to submit all five new drug applications in December "to see what additional information the Food and Drug Administration wants before we go any further."

That reasoning could very well have been genuine, although its appropriateness is arguable. Still, the question remains: To what extent did Walter's concern about missing a crucial goal enter into his decision to submit the applications early?

Clearly, there has been potential damage to Doberman's reputation with the Food and Drug Administration, and incomplete submissions may lead the agency's reviewers to be skeptical about future submissions.

Involvement at All Levels

In most multitiered technical departments only the top level of laboratory workers get promoted into management. In many organizations, only management and a few key high-level scientists are involved in long-range planning. Therefore, some top-level and *all* lower-level laboratory employees are often disenfranchised from the long-range planning process, causing them to feel unimportant, isolated, and unrepresented. The situation may also threaten their career aspirations.

It is important for employees *at all levels* to be involved in long-range planning for the group. This can be accomplished with an *ad hoc* committee composed of representatives from all levels.

Chapter 7

Organizing R&D
Work Groups

Different industries require that R&D organize differently, but certain principles apply to most situations, no matter what products are involved. In an article in the *Arizona Daily Star*, Tom Peters lists management's 1990s survival requirements, two of which relate to organizing:

1. Hierarchy replaced with boundaryless, ambiguous networks of organizations
2. Team-centered organizations, without cop-supervisors or functional specialists

In this chapter we examine the organization of an R&D department in light of Peters' survival requirements.

Management

The flatter the organization, the better. Management at every level of an R&D organization needs to examine its operation and consider eliminating one or more levels of supervision.* Such change takes time and involves hard work, imagination, and tough decisions, but the payoff in productivity, efficiency, and employee morale is huge.

The Department or Group

Most R&D departments have two or three levels of laboratory employees. For organizational purposes, the technical characteristics of these workers can be described as follows, paralleling the groupings introduced in Chapter 1.

*Some laboratory workers may at first view this as decreasing their career opportunities, but the manager should emphasize that their responsibilities will be broadened at every opportunity—and then manage that way. In fact, this continual growth is preferable because it does not depend on scarce supervisory positions becoming vacant.

First Level: Scientist. Persons at this level have a Ph.D. or M.S. degree (depending on the scientific discipline) and—

▲ have mastered the theory of relevant technology;
▲ can often choose the most likely experimental path to technical success (e.g., know when to abandon unpromising approaches);
▲ can design experiments and interpret results, using statistics appropriately;
▲ have good laboratory skills;
▲ are familiar with laboratory instruments (their theory and capability) and keep abreast of advances in instrumentation and computers;
▲ know how their work fits in with the total R&D effort;
▲ can interact well with peers in other scientific disciplines and represent the department at project meetings involving their area of technical responsibility;
▲ give most of the technical presentations at project meetings;
▲ read and publish in the national and international scientific literature;
▲ make presentations at outside scientific meetings;
▲ are often responsible for major advances in technology;
▲ can serve as administrative project leaders when appropriate;
▲ interact with Manufacturing, Engineering, and Marketing when appropriate; and
▲ facilitate the personal and technical growth of people at the second and third level—and of colleagues at the first level. [*Note:* A veteran at any level can help train a neophyte at any level, and laboratory employees can facilitate the growth of their supervisors.]

Second Level: Associate Scientist (Omitted in some R&D organizations). The individuals have a B.S. or M.S. degree (depending on the scientific discipline) and—

▲ have good laboratory skills and understand the basics of their scientific field;
▲ are the "right arm" of the first-level person;
▲ grow in technical competence and interact well with scientific peers, with the occasional help of the first-level scientist;
▲ know how and where their work fits in with the total R&D effort and occasionally represents the department at project meetings, especially when they are the most knowledgeable about experimental details (but should be allowed to attend any project meeting they choose);
▲ can give technical presentations to project teams when appropriate;
▲ can serve as administrative project leaders but stay in close contact with first-level scientists on the project's technical issues to ensure scientific soundness;
▲ often are the "point person" when interactions with Manufacturing, Engineering, and Marketing are required;
▲ publish in cooperation with first-level scientists and occasionally alone;

- ▲ occasionally make presentations at outside scientific meetings;
- ▲ at least coauthor on all internal reports generated from their work; and
- ▲ facilitate personal and technical growth of people at the first, second, and third levels.

Third Level: Technician or Assistant Scientist. At this level good laboratory skills are paramount. Technicians have B.S., Associate, or high school degrees and—

- ▲ learn, with the help of others, reasons for experiments and various experimental approaches;
- ▲ do much of the hands-on laboratory work of the department;
- ▲ become expert on instrument use and capabilities;
- ▲ learn to detect anomalies in data while performing experiments and call them to the scientists' and associate scientists' attention; this is especially important so that valuable laboratory time and resources are not wasted on useless experimentation. The more respect technicians feel from their coworkers, the more alert they will be to experimental anomalies;
- ▲ keep the laboratory stocked with necessary supplies and equipment;
- ▲ know the ins and outs of the company's internal and external procurement system so that first- and second-level scientists need not be bothered by such matters;
- ▲ occasionally give presentations and often attend project meetings when they are of special interest;
- ▲ often interact with Manufacturing and Engineering personnel;
- ▲ should be coauthors of or are given special mention in external publications arising from their laboratory efforts;
- ▲ should always be coauthors on internal reports resulting from their laboratory work;
- ▲ facilitate the personal and technical growth of coworkers in the first, second, and third levels; and
- ▲ react positively to work assignments requiring travel if their involvement makes sense; such travel emphasizes strongly the value placed on technicians.

R&D managers must take care not to be myopic or rigid concerning degrees and credentials. For example, a few individuals with no college degree (Thomas Edison had only *three months* of formal education in his entire life!) or with a B.S. (Charles Kettering, the famous GM automotive inventor, and at least one of my former colleagues) are capable of performing, even excelling, at the first level. It should be the ability to perform, not a piece of paper, that determines an employee's position in an R&D department. (Peter Drucker once made the point that the only certainty about a person with a Ph.D. is that he or she has sat on a school bench for a *very* long time.) If managers do a proper job of hiring, however, Ph.D.s will end up in the first level. No matter what the employee's degree, *everyone* is better off if people are allowed to perform to their maximum potential.

What level a person works at depends upon the person, the company, the R&D group's philosophy, and the scientific field. Let's look at each of these factors in detail:

1. *The Person.* Numerous nondegreed laboratory workers at the 3M Company have risen fairly high in R&D because of their personal and technical qualities, and because of 3M's regard for individual accomplishment. However, managers need to recognize a subtle but important point: All else being equal, more education usually results in more flexibility and adaptability to change, both essential qualities when working in science.

2. *The Company.* High-technology companies, out of necessity, require more advanced degrees than do low-tech businesses, although work in either place can be challenging and rewarding. Also, a company's personnel policies regarding job descriptions and qualifications may differ.

3. *The R&D Organization's Philosophy.* In some R&D groups, B.S. people are technicians; in others, they are associate scientists. It often depends upon the past experience and the bias of management.

4. *The Scientific Field.* As an example of differing degrees of education required, B.S. degrees in pharmacy are primarily professional degrees—that is, they prepare individuals to practice in pharmacies and hospitals as registered pharmacists. In some pharmaceutical companies, B.S. pharmacists are technicians while in others, they are associate scientists.

With some exceptions, an M.S. research degree in pharmaceutical science does not qualify a person for the first level of laboratory work. In contrast, chemical, electronic, or mechanical engineers with a master's degree, because of the focus and curriculum at many engineering schools, often are hired at the highest laboratory level.

Case Study: Job Responsibilities

A product development department in a pharmaceutical company utilized three levels of laboratory employees: Ph.D.'s, B.S. pharmacists, and technicians (nonpharmacy B.S. or Laboratory Associate degrees). Part of the department's responsibility was to supply informal administrative leaders for project teams composed of people from various R&D departments as well as from Marketing, Quality Control, and Manufacturing. Work groups within Product Development were organized with the Ph.D. in charge of every project and the B.S. pharmacists and technicians as assistants. The pharmacists had more responsibility and freedom than did the technicians, but they never served as project team leaders. Consequently, they felt unimportant and underutilized because their five- or six-year professional degree prepared them for more than just glorified technician work.

At the same time, the Ph.D.s felt overburdened with routine administrative duties and paperwork. As a result, many of the B.S. pharmacists eventually transferred to other areas of the company (e.g., Production Supervision, Regulatory Affairs, and Clinical Research); and the administrative workload of the Ph.D.s was too high, resulting in little basic research and external publishing.

To solve the problem, Harriet, the manager, told her employees that they could arrange the responsibilities within their particular work group in any way they chose. Most work groups came up with the same solution:

1. The Ph.D.s preferred to be consultants on several projects and to conduct research that focused on the "why" and "how" of each venture. They were intimately involved during the early stages of a project, but as soon as a firm scientific foundation was established they withdrew, consulting only when asked by the B.S. pharmacists or the technicians. Occasionally they chose to be project leaders to gain administrative experience.

2. The B.S. pharmacists took over most of the project leadership for new products. They were the primary contacts with Marketing, Manufacturing, Quality Control, and other areas. The B.S. pharmacists felt that it was primarily their responsibility to shepherd new products from inception to the marketplace. In addition, they were actively engaged in the technology or science of the project until it became pro forma; then they turned most of that responsibility over to the technicians.

3. Technicians did much of the hands-on laboratory work and took charge of the technical aspects of the project after it became pro forma, consulting with the B.S. pharmacists and Ph.D.s when necessary. They assisted the Ph.D.s and B.S. pharmacists in the laboratory and were allowed as much freedom and responsibility as each situation allowed.

The arrangements in each work group varied depending upon the talents and preferences of the individuals involved, but how each group functioned depended entirely upon group-member preferences. Harriet was interested in only—

- ▲ optimum productivity;
- ▲ high-quality work;
- ▲ schedules being met;
- ▲ high morale and optimum cooperation;
- ▲ all employees being fully respected, utilized, and challenged; and
- ▲ optimum personal and professional development for all.

How that was accomplished was up to members of each group.

The results of this employee-determined reorganization were as follows:

1. Employees *at each level* felt challenged.
2. Administrative burdens for Ph.D.s decreased, allowing more time for their unique technical contributions.
3. Turnover of B.S. pharmacists decreased significantly.
4. Schedules were consistently met.
5. Morale, productivity, and employee growth all increased dramatically.

A few individuals complained that first choice of assignments was given to those with more education, and Harriet responded that the only equitable remedy was for them to either continue their schooling to obtain the necessary credentials or to climb the technical ladder via on-the-job growth and performance.

The R&D Division

The *raison d'être* for R&D is to supply new products for the corporation. Thus its span of operation includes developing new product ideas and conducting basic research leading to new products and new technology, reducing product ideas to practice, transferring developed products to Manufacturing, and servicing Manufacturing when problems arise after products are marketed.

Within its span of operation, R&D interacts with almost every other sector of the company, for example, top management, Manufacturing, Engineering, Marketing, Sales, Quality Control, Planning, Patents, and Legal. An R&D division, therefore, needs to be structured to facilitate these relationships.

Each company has its own structure and system, but there is usually a department that functions as a bridge between the generation of new product ideas and basic research on the one hand and the practical side of the business (Manufacturing, Engineering, Marketing, and Sales) on the other. Quite often the product development department serves that function.

A Centralized vs. a Decentralized R&D

There is no "best way" to organize R&D. What you do depends on factors specific to each corporation. For example:

▲ *Size.* A small company needs only one R&D group, whereas a large corporation, especially if divisionalized, often requires several units.
▲ *Physical Proximity.* The more the geographical separation between domestic divisions, the greater the demand for multiple R&D units.
▲ *Domestic vs. Multinational.* If a company operates within one country, a single R&D group may suffice. However, the more international the corporation, the more demand there is for multiple R&D units to serve local, area-specific needs.
▲ *Technology and Markets.* Large or small technical corporations may have one general market based on a single technology (e.g., oil refining or

specialty chemicals), while others may depend on multiple markets and technology (e.g., oil and general chemicals and pharmaceuticals, medical devices, diagnostics, and agricultural chemicals).

▲ *History.* Company tradition may dictate a centralized or decentralized R&D structure, although management should be flexible, willing to reassess the situation as circumstances change.

▲ *Focus.* Large, multimarket corporations (e.g., 3M) may have decentralized R&D groups to focus on specialized, shorter-range, more practical research, reserving their central research unit for longer range, more basic investigations.

The primary advantages of a centralized R&D group are greater efficiency, less redundancy, better communication, reduced competition; better, more supportive interaction among small groups of different scientific disciplines; and more control (in the good sense) over the R&D effort, especially its general focus and direction.

The primary advantages of multiple R&D units include a greater sense of ownership and relevance within each group, better communication with and responsiveness to local marketing, engineering, and manufacturing departments, a wider spectrum of new product ideas, more diversity in technology, and reduced risk that the company's R&D effort will become calcified.

Generally speaking, the most prudent course for a new company is to start with a centralized R&D group and then expand as the need arises. With multiple units, management and laboratory personnel must work hard to maximize communication and minimize competition. In addition, management and laboratory workers need to evaluate the situation every few years and make changes as appropriate.

Matrix vs. Product Line Structure

There are two primary ways to structure an R&D operation: matrix and product line. Let's look at each:

Matrix. Departments are primarily discipline oriented (e.g., organic chemistry, pharmacology, chemical engineering, biochemistry) or function oriented (e.g., process engineering, computer design, medical, analytical services). Interactions take place through various project teams, with team leadership provided either by an involved department or by members of a formal project management group. Project team leaders provide coordination but have no line authority.

The primary advantage of a matrix approach to R&D is that scientists have a professional support group and a sense of technical identity; this makes it easier to maintain high-quality science and accomplish technical breakthroughs. The principal disadvantages are scientific chauvinism; "ivory tower" syndrome; and a decreased sense of purpose, direction, and urgency.

Product Line. The R&D organization is arranged not by scientific discipline or function but by product line. For example, a computer company might have a personal computer R&D department or division, a mainframe industrial computer R&D group, and a pocket calculator–computer R&D effort. A pharmaceutical company may have numerous formal venture groups (e.g., cardiovascular, anti-infective, mental health), each composed of synthetic chemists, pharmacologists, physicians, and other disciplines. The venture manager is responsible for getting his or her line of products on the market, and has line authority over the group of scientists in various disciplines.

The advantages and disadvantages of this approach are mirror images of the matrix option. The group's sense of purpose, direction, and urgency is usually very high, but laboratory scientists may feel somewhat isolated from colleagues having a similar educational background. An additional disadvantage occurs if the group has, for example, only one electrical engineer. To the group she then becomes the smartest E.E. around—there is no one against whom to measure her technical competence. Likewise, if the situation forces group members to become generalists—for example, if a biochemist must perform too many engineering tasks—then the group may end up with a mediocre biochemist and a quasi-engineer.

For example, numerous pharmaceutical companies have reorganized from a matrix to a product-line arrangement. Most have been pleased with the experience. Top management, R&D management, R&D project leaders, and laboratory workers all have seen more goal-focused activity and more rapid progress. However, in those organizations with less than stellar R&D management, progress has been slower, and scientific chauvinism and turf protection have merely been replaced by fierce, disruptive competition among the various project or product teams.

Some R&D organizational options may work better than others, depending on the nature of the company's business and the talents and capabilities of the R&D staff. The two most important factors are:

1. All levels of R&D management should be flexible, changing their organization when circumstances so dictate. However, when an R&D organization is foundering because of poor management, reorganization often postpones the ultimate solution: replacing ineffective managers.
2. Staff positions should be kept to a minimum; otherwise staff people will have a broad view of the operation while line managers will tend to be compartmentalized.

Reference

Peters, Tom. "Firms May Be Dancing Last Macho Tango." *Arizona Daily Star,* April 4, 1989.

Chapter 8

Supervising and Controlling

The most appropriate roles of the manager vis-à-vis his subordinates are those of teacher, professional helper, colleague, and consultant. Only to a limited degree will he assume the role of authoritative boss.

Douglas McGregor, in *The Professional Manager*

Chapters 6 and 7 discussed the first two of Henri Fayol's functions of management. In this chapter, we explore supervising, which encompasses Fayol's concepts of directing and coordinating. We also take a look at controlling—the fifth and last of his traditional functions of management.

Supervising Laboratory Employees

Supervising is the appropriate title for the managerial task encompassing Fayol's directing and coordinating. One dictionary definition of *supervising* is: "overseeing workers during performance." However, the wise R&D manager looks beyond the obvious and realizes that employees do not work for the manager. The manager works for—provides a service to—the employees. As Tom Peters has said, "Leaders . . . are servants."

To some, this observation falls somewhere between blasphemy and heresy, but consider the logic of the matter:

1. The productivity of any organization is ultimately in the hands of those doing the actual work.
2. Most experts, e.g., Douglas McGregor and Peter Drucker (see References at the end of this chapter), agree that the biggest waste in any organization is underutilization of the talents and potential of employees.

It follows that the most likely cause of lower productivity is not lazy, irresponsible, antagonistic workers, but rather the situational and organizational obstacles (including inappropriate management practices) that lie in the paths of employees trying to do their best. It also follows that organizational goals are best served if management spends less time "overseeing workers during performance" and instead concentrates on removing as many obstacles as possible.

One of the best ways to break down the barriers to higher productivity is for managers to concentrate on improving *their* performance instead of worrying so much about their workers'. Better management practices invariably lead to improved employee performance and morale.

Since the R&D manager should be a helper and a facilitator, the best approach to supervising is:

1. Ask each employee: What do you think are the major impediments to your doing the best possible job for the organization? Please include what I am doing wrong in the way I supervise you.
2. Sit back and listen. Concentrate on being both nondefensive—so your subordinate is assured that candor is appreciated, not resented—and empathic. This is the quickest way to gain understanding of what the other person is trying to say.
3. *Together,* you and the employee decide how best to remove these obstacles, including what the subordinate can do on his or her own and what support he or she needs from you. When there is disagreement, defer to the employee unless a serious error is about to be made.
4. Go to work on *your* job, providing assistance so that the subordinate can do *his or her* job. You may discover that the best way to help is simply to get out of the way.

This approach reflects a subtle but important shift in management emphasis: from your making sure the job gets done to your helping the subordinate make sure the job gets done.

Some R&D managers may be uneasy with this scenario, thinking the employee will be intimidated and guarded, especially about criticizing a manager to his or her face. This may be a problem initially, but experience shows that as trust develops, candor is relatively easy to elicit.

Other R&D managers may feel this approach reduces their organizational power (using "power" in the good sense). The exact opposite is true:

▲ The manager "sees over" more clearly because the discussion with the employee has sharpened the view of the situation for both individuals.
▲ Control is increased because the employee is more likely to come back to the manager if the boss is viewed as a source of help, rather than as a giver of orders.
▲ Treating the employee as a competent, responsible worker greatly increases a supervisor's influence over him or her.

The mathematics of management are:

More oversight + better control + increased influence
= more organizational power

For the process to work, subordinates need to feel that it is their responsibility, not the manager's, to ensure the work is performed—and done in the best possible way. The workers also need to feel sufficiently safe and comfortable to speak candidly, even to criticize their supervisor and the organization.

The manager, on the other hand, needs to be nondefensive and a good listener. He or she also must be convinced that the employees are competent, responsible individuals with something valuable to contribute.

Controlling the R&D Operation

Fayol's fifth managerial function—controlling—originally meant "keeping a tight ship." The boss watched over everyone and everything, told employees what to do and when to do it, and made all the important decisions himself. Subordinates were expected to carry out orders to the letter and to inform the boss of any deviation. Today, as Tom Peters (*Arizona Daily Star*, September 27, 1988) has pointed out, "When we begin to understand that real control comes from *within* [workers] . . . then we will edge closer to unlocking the virtually unlimited potential that lies dormant in most of our work places."

Authoritarian control, a crucial element of the "boss" culture in management (see Chapter 20), originated with two ancient organizational models—the Roman Catholic Church and the military—neither of which applies to the workplace. In modern industrial corporations, control must take on a different character. Certainly, attempting to use managerial authority to establish absolute control over employees' behavior has proved to be ineffective.

Authoritarian control assumes that employees are totally dependent on their leadership. In fact, there are complex *inter*dependencies between management and nonmanagement workers. The most eloquent example is given by Douglas McGregor (*The Human Side of Enterprise*), with a story about the new manager of a textile mill who walked up to a union agent in the weave room and said,

> "I'm the new manager here. When I manage a mill, I run it. Do you understand?" The agent nodded, and then waved his hand. The workers, intently watching this encounter, shut down every loom in the room immediately. The agent turned to the manager and said, "All right, go ahead and run it."

Appropriate—that is, nonauthoritarian—control is especially important in R&D organizations where the emphasis is on high technology, creativity, and innovation. Since most people are trustworthy, the most effective managerial control is to emphasize employee self-control. Peter Drucker (*Management: Tasks, Responsibilities, Practices*) says: "To be productive, the individual has to have control, to a considerable extent, over [his work], . . . Control is a tool of the worker and must never be his master." Tom Peters (*Arizona Daily Star*, April 11, 1989) agrees: "I call such phenomena the control paradox: Less is more.

More precisely, less paper-driven central control and more genuinely ceded self-control for those closest to the action translate into tighter control overall."

In truth, the best form of control depends on many variables, and, as McGregor suggests, "effective control consists in 'effective adaptation' to these variables." Successful supervision is largely dependent upon the manager's ability to predict and control human behavior, and the essence of control is selective adaptation. We control the physical world around us, not by expecting nature to do our bidding, but by adjusting our actions to natural laws. For example, we do not control surface water by commanding it to flow uphill; rather, we dig channels, adjusting to the fact that water obeys the law of gravity.

Similarly, effective management control consists of channeling workers' energies, interests, and capabilities into activities that meet organizational objectives. Management controls the work force by adjusting its decisions and actions to the realities of human nature, not by telling people what to do and expecting blind obedience.

Case Study: Human Nature in Control

A product development department of a large corporation produced experimental devices used by researchers outside the company. This necessitated a well-defined paperwork system, which was made excessively complex by Wesley, an authoritative manager. The forms filled out by one laboratory scientist were checked by another. Then the completed forms were approved by three levels of management: Fay, the group leader; Bjorn, the section manager; and Wesley.

The department had an excessive number of errors, and punitive threats by Wesley had minimal effect. Why did Wesley's threats have little or no impact and why didn't the situation improve?

▲ The laboratory workers grew careless; they didn't feel ultimately responsible for the paperwork's accuracy, since three more people were going to review their efforts.
▲ Fay and Bjorn felt only partially responsible for accuracy because (1) the two laboratory workers were supposed to do careful work; (2) Wesley, the originator of the system when he was a lower-level supervisor, checked the completed forms in great detail; and (3) they were not as familiar with the system as were the laboratory workers or Wesley.
▲ Wesley felt ultimately responsible for the system's accuracy, but he grew tired of spending so much time correcting the mistakes of "careless, irresponsible, unresponsive" subordinates.

> Wesley retired, and Myra, his replacement, made it clear that the two laboratory workers were solely responsible for the accuracy of the completed forms and that only one manager (she) would sign off on them, and only to satisfy company regulations. She also emphasized that her signature would be merely a rubber stamp, and that she was depending on the laboratory workers to keep her out of trouble. Mistakes dropped immediately by a factor of five and, while a few errors cropped up occasionally, the accuracy issue disappeared.

The managerial tasks of supervising and controlling are important to an orderly, productive work group. Generally, successful R&D managers supervise best by acting as helpers to subordinates and control best by encouraging employee self-control.

References

Drucker, Peter F. *Management: Tasks, Responsibilities, Practices*. New York: Harper & Row, 1974.

McGregor, Douglas. *The Human Side of Enterprise*. New York: McGraw-Hill, 1960.

———. *The Professional Manager,* ed. Caroline McGregor and Warren G. Bennis. New York: McGraw-Hill, 1967.

Peters, Tom. "Book Explores Art of Good Leadership." *Arizona Daily Star,* September 27, 1988.

———. "Control Paradox: Less Yields More." *Arizona Daily Star,* April 11, 1989.

Chapter 9

Delegating and Monitoring

An effort should be made to allow the employee the right to choose *in any situation* in which he seems capable of bearing the consequences of his choice.

Carl Rogers, *Carl Rogers on Personal Power*

Delegating work and monitoring progress are closely interrelated R&D managerial tasks. These two management functions are discussed in this chapter.

Assigning Work in R&D

The primary reason R&D managers should delegate is that employees like, want, and need to do things in their own way. Nevertheless, assigning work to subordinates is not a task to be viewed casually. It requires thought and perceptiveness.

The wise R&D manager assigns research projects only after consulting with laboratory workers, preferably at a department meeting. This is because bench scientists tend to have a much better feel than a manager for who has the time, who is most qualified, and how best to divide up a responsibility. Also, the group feels respected and involved when they are part of the work-assignment process. Lastly, often someone will volunteer, especially for special or short-term projects, and this interest will guarantee commitment and hard work.

If most projects are assigned this way, the group will be more apt to accept and support the manager's decision.

Delegation, Not Relegation

The biggest waste in any organization is underutilization of talented employees. At the same time, the typical manager is depicted—usually accurately—

as a harried, overworked individual who never seems to find enough hours in the day. R&D managers are especially busy because the complex technical nature of the business adds to the normal burdens of management. If subordinates are underutilized while the leader is overwhelmed, the remedy is obvious: appropriate, effective delegation.

Experience tells us that, at most levels of an organization, at least one-third of each person's job could be permanently assigned to someone on the next lower level. This is especially true in R&D, where many employees have college degrees, are intellectually sophisticated, and have a strong motivation to succeed, grow, and perform well.

Although the solution is easy to identify, its proper application is often difficult. Too many managers confuse delegation with relegation. To *delegate* is to assign responsibility *and authority* to a representative. *Relegation*, on the other hand, connotes consignment to an inferior position. When managers give subordinates narrow, menial tasks or expect them to do all "delegated" work exactly as they would, then their action is relegation, not delegation. This is not to say that relegation is always undesirable, just that both parties should recognize the difference.

Likewise, not enough managers have confidence in their subordinates or are willing to share their power. This brings to mind an observation by historian and statesman Thomas Macaulay:

> Many politicians . . . are in the habit of laying it down as a self-evident proposition, that no people ought to be free till they are fit to use their freedom. The maxim is worthy of the fool . . . who resolved not to go into the water till he had learned to swim.

Such hesitancy to delegate quite often is a reflection of the manager's lack of experience, maturity, and confidence (in one's self as well as in the subordinates). But the problem can usually be overcome with a planned program—planned by the manager in concert with the employees—to gradually broaden the subordinates' spectrum of responsibility and authority.

Three Primary Goals of True Delegation

1. To relieve managers of some of their workload so that they have more time to think, meditate, plan, and grow.
2. To move work and responsibility as far down the organizational ladder as possible; this increases efficiency.
3. To offer all employees maximum challenge and opportunities for growth, even when formal promotions are not immediately available; this increases productivity and develops future leaders.

In harmony with these goals, proper delegation has two distinguishing characteristics: (1) Most of the delegated tasks are a meaningful part of the manager's job and not just drudgery to avoid; (2) subordinates are allowed—even encouraged—to perform the delegated work in their own way, with managers helping only when asked.

In many cases, employees will do a better job than managers on delegated work, even though mistakes may be made along the way. Too often managers assume that, with delegation, quality must be sacrificed for the sake of growth. Not so; with competent hiring practices and under good management, each person tends to find a better way to do something, bringing a fresh viewpoint and without the need to defend past practices.

Indeed, one of the primary benefits of widespread delegation is often overlooked: reduction in turnover. A major cause of employee turnover, especially in R&D organizations, is "five-year ennui." Talented, self-motivated scientists often become bored in four to six years if their jobs and responsibilities remain the same. This seems to be true (although the time frame may vary) even when the technical projects are broad in scope. If this situation continues, people seek employment elsewhere—to get a fresh start. (The grass-is-always-greener syndrome.)

Since opportunities for promotion into management are always scarce, bored employees and their managers are in a quandary. However, if managers and employees work together, and talk about job enlargement a year or two before boredom appears on the horizon, something can often be done about ennui when it comes. Enlarging a scientist's responsibilities, particularly in planning and decision making, without an official change of job may solve the problem for a number of years.

Putting the Theory to Work

Reverse Delegation. One of the best ways to minimize the relegation problem (i.e., that employees perceive the manager dumping only unwanted, routine tasks on them) is for managers to offer to occasionally take some of the employees' drudgery off *their* hands. (If managers are good delegators, they will have time for some extra work.) The employees may refuse the offer, but when they become overstressed, they will very much appreciate the boss lending a helping hand, especially with paperwork. This small time-and-effort investment on the part of management can pay huge dividends, especially in reducing the manager's imperious position.

Case Study: "It's His Case, Senator"

In the movie, *Bullitt*, Police Lieutenant Frank Bullitt is working on a case that happens to be of intense interest to powerful U.S. Senator Chalmers. Chalmers is not happy with the way Bullitt is conducting the investigation, so he pressures Bullitt's boss, Captain Bennett, to force his subordinate to proceed differently. As it happens, Bennett agrees with the senator but refuses to interfere, saying, "It's *his* case, senator."

Planned Delegation. A campaign to delegate works best with forethought and planning. For instance, spending time with the boss planning one's career gives an employee a genuine feeling of worth and importance. This is especially true when employees are given the chance to choose the areas of increased responsibility that are of the most interest. Also, subordinates and managers will function better when they have a mutual understanding of the desired delegation.

While corporate life is not as dangerous as police work (although some corporate raiders might disagree), the same principles of delegation hold true. As a manager, if you delegate only when you are confident that the subordinate will do the job your way, and if you interfere or take over when problems arise, without giving the employee the opportunity to ask for help or to solve the problem independently, delegation becomes a mockery. The employee becomes frustrated and learns little, and the relationship between you two suffers.

In summary, for delegation to work, you need to trust that employees will do the job well, on time, and within the context of broad departmental objectives. You must have confidence that subordinates will come to you for help if serious problems arise. You also want subordinates to succeed. You want this for many reasons, but primarily because you enjoy seeing others do well.

Your employees, on the other hand, need to know that you have confidence in them and will not be looking over their shoulder. The subordinates must also feel that they will be given the freedom to do the job as they see fit and, if difficulties are encountered or mistakes are made, that you will offer help and encouragement rather than criticism. It is important to be aware that your employees want to succeed—because they wish to reward you for having faith in them.

Managers who hire strong subordinates and then encourage their growth through appropriate delegation will be perceived—by peers, subordinates, and superiors—as an especially competent, worthwhile member of the management team. Furthermore, good delegation helps recruiting. As employees grow in responsibility and competence, they become more enthusiastic about working in the department; soon word gets around, both inside and outside the company.

Monitoring Progress in R&D

The task of monitoring others' work is closely connected to controlling, which was discussed in Chapter 8. Managers can be either authoritarian (running a tight ship) or smart. They can foolishly spend much of their valuable time monitoring their operation or they can wisely delegate most of that function to subordinates, thus improving productivity and orderliness, fostering employee growth, and freeing up more time for broader, long-range tasks.

Impetus From Below

In a good work environment, the impetus for monitoring comes from *below*, not from above. This places a positive focus on the process. In other words, managers trust their subordinates and don't feel a need to monitor the operation closely. On the other hand, employees are eager to keep management informed because they sense that the manager is interested in their work and in departmental progress. They also recognize the manager's need to know the general situation, to be informed of major progress or problems. Lastly, they recognize that a manager needs a certain amount of information to do his or her job properly, for the overall benefit of the group. But authoritative monitoring can only yield bad results.

Six Effects of Authoritative Monitoring

In an authoritative work environment, any attempt by a manager to monitor may be interpreted by subordinates as evidence that the boss fears things won't go well unless he or she rides herd on unreliable workers. Detailed monitoring has at least six effects, all of them bad:

1. Subordinates can't help but feel that managers don't trust them—else why would two people do one person's job? Most workers feel, correctly, that it is part of *their* job to monitor progress and deal with problems.
2. The situation is inherently inane, and perceived management inanities are major contributors to employee disrespect and alienation.
3. Many subordinates will lose interest in doing a careful job of monitoring when they see the boss repeating what they do.
4. Management seldom does lower-level tasks well. Subordinates, to whom such tasks are often challenging, are much more motivated and equipped to do them properly.
5. Efficiency and productivity suffer, not only because of the redundancy, but because subordinates are forced to spend time educating the manager about the details. Anyone who has attempted to inform a detail-oriented boss only about the major aspects of a project knows that such an exercise often deteriorates into a frustrating, seemingly endless question-and-answer session. Both parties may become upset—the manager, because he or she feels like a dentist pulling teeth, and the employee, because he or she is forced to give a disjointed account of the project, especially because the individual sees his or her boss getting upset. As is often the case, both individuals are justified in their feelings; it's the basic situation that is the primary culprit.
6. If managers get too involved with minutia, they will meddle in subordinates' jobs. Soup is not the only brew spoiled by too many cooks.

Some managers believe that running a tight ship means more efficiency, fewer mistakes, and better performance. But logic and experience—and management experts such as Douglas McGregor, Peter Drucker, and Tom Peters—say otherwise. When things are working as they should, employees become expert at informing the boss appropriately and sufficiently, leaving them more time for hands-on productive work and allowing the manager to concentrate on long-range planning, contemplation, and innovative thinking.

Reference

Rogers, Carl R. *Carl Rogers on Personal Power*. New York: Delacorte, 1977.

Chapter 10

Advocating and Sheltering

There are two additional tasks that never appear in an R&D manager's job description, yet they are vital to enhancing the culture and environment of an R&D operation: advocating and sheltering.

Advocating

Amid this world of toil and sin, your head grows bald but not your chin.

Burma Shave roadside sign

[The wicked's] ways are always prosperous.

Psalms 10:5

The world is not a fair place. This is not a complaint, it's a statement of fact, and most adults have come to accept it. Occasionally we engage an attorney to represent our interests, but the need for a professional advocate seldom arises because, in a free society, we make most of our own decisions concerning the nonwork portion of our lives.

The situation at work is quite different. There, we all have far less personal control. Management makes most of the decisions; and being under the direct control of another person, to say nothing of the inherent facelessness of company policy, can make us feel helpless and vulnerable to unfair, impersonal treatment. This sense of vulnerability may not surface every day, but if it arises often enough, it can be a significant factor in how we feel about our jobs, our management, and our company. It can affect our performance and, more important, our well-being.

In unionized organizations, the agent or steward serves as the workers' advocate (although R&D scientists are seldom part of a labor union); in nonunion companies, the employee relations department usually fills that role.

Seldom is management viewed as an advocate for workers, and rarely does management perceive itself that way. In fact, employees often consider the boss a powerful adversary—the very reason they need an advocate! Surely productivity, not to mention loyalty and enthusiasm, suffers when workers and management consider themselves antagonists.

The Manager as Advocate

In the well-managed organization, the primary advocate for each employee is his or her immediate supervisor. Not only is that individual in the best position to know and help subordinates, but he or she is the major beneficiary of the increased productivity, loyalty, and enthusiasm that follow. Experience has consistently shown that if workers believe their manager is really for them and wants them to succeed, and if they sense that he or she is there as a helper and a facilitator rather than as an overseer, then there's little they won't do for the manager. In fact, when managers are under great stress or in trouble, the roles become reversed and employees rush to their aid.

Some managers believe that they should be neither advocates nor adversaries but impartial judges. Social science tells us, however, that managers are no more rational or impartial than anyone else; we all labor under a cloud of personal bias. Furthermore, strict impartiality usually results in impersonal treatment, and no one likes being regarded as a nonperson.

Advocacy, like any other managerial function, cannot be practiced in a vacuum. How, then, do managers go about becoming the primary advocate for their subordinates? It is done on two levels: personal advocacy and organizational advocacy.

Personal Advocacy Guidelines

1. Get to know each person as an individual and develop a relationship based on mutual trust, respect, and caring. Only then will employees feel comfortable bringing their concerns to you, and only then will you be able to give them optimum help.

2. Be a perceptive observer of your employees, not to check up on them but rather to pick up subtle signs of possible trouble. For example, if a usually ebullient subordinate becomes very quiet on the job and this persists for a week or two, you may want to say, "I don't want to be nosy, but is there anything wrong? Anything I can do to help?" If he doesn't want to talk, don't force the issue, but keep abreast of the situation.

Showing genuine interest in individuals has a positive effect, even though they may not want to confide in you. When an employee's performance starts to decline and you're sure it's not because of any action or inaction on your part, it's best not to intrude on her privacy too soon; treat her as an adult and give her every chance to work out her difficulties herself.

3. If performance continues to deteriorate, there will obviously come a time when you need to sit down and talk with the employee. But if you have

built a relationship with that individual, he will confide in you long before that point is reached. If you find yourself growing impatient with an employee during a difficulty, try to wait a bit longer; it will usually pay off. People appreciate a supervisor who shows patience and faith in them during times of trouble.

4. When an employee confides in you, refrain from giving advice unless you are really pressed for it. Any troubled individual coming to you needs, first of all, a sympathetic ear and then appropriate reassurance.

5. Even when pressed for advice, you and the employee are best off if you simply outline the options and their advantages and disadvantages. Leave the ultimate decision to the subordinate. If her difficulties involve another employee, any comments you can make concerning that individual (without violating anyone's privacy) may be helpful. If your observations about the other person are negative, take care that you are not vindictive or overly critical. Make your point candidly and matter-of-factly, and move on.

6. Don't try to do too much. If you sense that professional help may be appropriate, a suggestion to that effect or a referral to the company's employee assistance program may be in order.

Organizational Advocacy Guidelines

1. Not all problems are highly personal or greatly troubling. You might be able to use your administrative ingenuity to deal directly with such problems as a temporarily stalled promotion, a continuing problem with another department, tension or a disagreement with a colleague, or resentment over an ill-defined or apparently unfair company policy. The no-advice rule softens considerably when you have some control over the situation. Employees do not expect you to solve *all* their problems, but they do expect you to be committed to try when it's important to them.

2. The advocating manager serves as a bridge between each employee and the general organization. A key girder in that bridge is "loyalty up and down." Your subordinates have to feel that you are truly for them, while *your* boss has to be confident that you are looking out for the company's interests as well. If you have a reputation as a strong advocate for employees, when irreconcilable conflicts arise (assuming no violations of ethics or the law are involved), you can come down on the side of the company without hurting your relationship with your subordinates.

3. As a manager, one of your primary responsibilities is to remove impediments to your subordinates' productivity. This can be viewed as advocacy as well, because such assistance improves your employees' well-being, both emotional and financial.

Although advocacy is a major responsibility of a manager, you should work constantly to make your subordinates as independent as possible. Independence is best fostered by managing with a light touch and by creating a fertile environment in which employees can grow and mature, both as individuals and as a close-knit group. There will, however, always be a need for competent and caring advocacy—because the world is not a fair place.

A relevant story applies here. One day a small boy was trying to lift a heavy stone, but he couldn't budge it. His father, passing by, stopped to watch his efforts. Finally he said to his son, "Are you using all your strength?"

"Yes, I am," the boy cried, exasperated.

"No," the father said calmly, "you're not. You haven't asked me to help you."

Sheltering Laboratory Workers

From actual experience, I can assure R&D managers that sheltering employees is one of the most important and, when done with perseverance and imagination, most effective ways a manager can create and maintain a competent, productive, enthusiastic R&D department. The before-and-after difference will astound both you and your subordinates.

What do I mean by sheltering? No matter what the weather outside, the roof of the house, and its siding, insulation, windows, doors, and heating or cooling system provide a hospitable, safe environment for its occupants. So, too, managers need to create an optimum work atmosphere by sheltering their employees.

Shelter them from what? Swirling about any organization are tensions, antagonisms, organizational red tape, and inanities—unpleasantness and distractions. For example, perhaps your boss—a tense, caustic individual who is uncomfortable with the deliberate pace of research—is constantly berating you to speed things up and increase productivity. The strong tendency in such a situation is to translate at least some of that unpleasantness and pressure down to your employees—kick-the-dog syndrome. With this response, not only are you relieving some of your own frustrations and resentments, but you are convincing yourself—and trying to convince your boss—that you are a team player and are bottom-line oriented.

However well-intentioned and justified, such a reaction seriously damages a group's environment and is most likely to reduce, not enhance, performance. This is especially true in R&D, since innovation and creativity require a positive, fertile atmosphere. Robert Sampson, in *Managing the Managers*, says, "Anxiety is highly contagious—the anxious suffer, and they make others suffer." Equally important, there's a strong chance that employees will start to view you as an inconsistent, unprincipled stooge for upper management—someone only too willing to sacrifice his or her employees' well-being for personal advancement. Such an individual is often derided by subordinates as "all style and no substance," "all sail and no anchor," or (out West) "all hat and no cattle."

To avoid such debilitating problems, you need to prevent disruption of your R&D group's productive, relatively tranquil work environment by absorbing as much of the pressure and unpleasantness as possible. By taking most of that burden on your own shoulders, you will protect your group from contamination by poor management practices elsewhere in the organization. Two simple analogies emphasize the concept:

1. The manager as an umbrella, with obvious implications
2. The manager astride a fault line, damping the rumbling beneath his feet so that what he holds in his hands remains safe and tranquil

This does not mean that legitimate pressures and emergencies should not filter down; employees can and will respond with vigor and enthusiasm to such emergencies, especially when the crisis is viewed as a challenge to the entire group. Furthermore, if the work environment is characterized by the qualities described in Chapter 2, subordinates will be eager to help their manager in times of stress.

Sheltering Can be Subtle

Sheltering your employees can take many forms. For example, some official company policies may be out of date, rigid, or no longer appropriate. Some may seem to antagonize employees or fly in the face of common sense. Some of these detrimental policies can be overturned, and it is a manager's responsibility to put consistent, appropriate pressure on "the system" to change.

Even when the system can't be changed, subtle managerial sheltering can be beneficial. For example, when employees complain about an unfair policy and you agree it's unfair, you should say so. But then you should quickly point out that, in general, yours is a high-quality company and every organization has its faults. Furthermore, there may be good but nonobvious reasons for the policy, and you should endeavor to uncover those reasons. When subordinates see that you understand their point of view, most of their resentment and frustration will disappear; we all feel better when our feelings are validated by others.

Your success at sheltering is highly dependent upon the level of mutual trust, respect, and confidence within the work group. If there's a strong, caring sense of family, then intense sheltering is unnecessary because intrusions from the outside have minimal effect. If, however, the group atmosphere is already poisoned by dissension and mistrust, sheltering becomes a contradiction; instilling trust, raising spirits, and repairing relationships within the group must then be first priority.

Quality sheltering requires that you get out of your office and see what's going on in your department. If you have no sense of your group's day-to-day moods, it's difficult to detect rising patterns of tension or indifference. Also, employees are more apt to call problems to your attention if they perceive you as interested, friendly, and accessible.

The five most important personal qualities required for good sheltering are these:

1. *Strength*—because you need to swim against a strong current (i.e., the system or an unreasonable, autocratic boss).
2. *Courage*—because there is risk for the manager who stands up for his or her people against superiors or the system.
3. *Stamina*—because sheltering is a never-ending task.
4. *Ingenuity*—because deflecting a rushing stream (again, the system) usually works better than constructing a dam.
5. *Tact*—because diplomacy usually makes deflection acceptable to the system.

Case Study: Sheltering From a Bad Boss

Jane, an R&D manager, differed with Sheldon, her boss, on just about every facet of management. Nevertheless, for many years the two were able to "work" together under an uneasy truce. Both were strong-willed and stubborn, but the department's consistently high productivity prevented Sheldon from taking any drastic action. Knowledgeable observers were amazed that the group could maintain an excellent work environment that was 179 degrees from the philosophy and personality of the "big boss." For example, Sheldon was disagreeable, authoritative, and rigid while Jane was friendly, flexible, and delegated extensively. Department members recognized and appreciated Jane's great talent for sheltering, while she gratefully acknowledged each employee's essential contribution to the group's success.

Managers who are strong advocates and provide effective shelter for their employees will succeed, both with their subordinates and with their bosses.

Reference

Sampson, Robert C. *Managing the Managers*. New York: McGraw-Hill, 1965.

PART III

Developing a Productive R&D Team

The new manager who enters Alice's Looking-Glass World is likely to find a confusion of responsibilities and procedures. Part II talked about basic management functions. In Part III, we concentrate on the skills and techniques that promote a harmonious, productive environment for R&D work on all levels. Following this path will lead managers and their groups through the looking-glass maze to ultimate success.

R&D Productivity Stems From Creativity

It should be obvious that R&D managers must be concerned with creativity, since it is the means for greater productivity. Innovation is important because new products are the lifeblood of any technical corporation. However, seldom do managers feel the need or have the opportunity to study how to be creative.

Before commencing this part's survey of managerial skills, it is important to assess the manager's role in fostering creativity. The fact is, an R&D manager plays a major part in determining the degree of creativity within the group. As John Steinbeck wrote, "Ideas are like rabbits. You get a couple and learn how to handle them, and pretty soon you have a dozen."

Here are some of the primary contributions of R&D managers:

1. Demonstrating enthusiasm and excitement for new ideas
2. Managing with a light touch, allowing laboratory scientists the freedom to grow in their own way and at their own pace, and to explore new territory
3. Encouraging employees to take risks, and being there with encouragement rather than criticism when they fail
4. Being flexible and secure, and creating a work atmosphere with the same characteristics
5. Being committed, not just to today's and this year's comfort and well-being, but to the long-term health of the organization and its employees
6. Hiring competent, innovative scientists

The literature is replete with writings on creativity, including books, a newspaper column, general reports, a specific technical article, and feature issues of two national magazines (see References). But my favorite is from Charles Kettering, the inventive genius. In an article in the old *Collier's* magazine, Charles Kettering tells the story of a young colleague who didn't believe him when he said he could drive from Detroit to Dayton in four and one-half hours. So the inventor took the young man with him on his next trip, and arrived within that time. The coworker objected because Kettering didn't stay on the main road, Route 25, but the inventor reminded him (and reminds us R&D managers): "A great challenge lies off the traveled highway. Half a world of opportunity is on either side."

R&D managers cannot, by force of will, cause their subordinates to be creative. Like most other managerial accomplishments, creativity emerges from a group when the manager manages in the manner described in Part II and in the chapters that follow here.

Tips for Encouraging Creativity

1. "Two heads are better than one" is not just a cliché. A person's ideas are often enriched through discussions with other people.

2. Brainstorming sessions involving multidisciplinary groups often produce marketable ideas. The cardinal rule of brainstorming is that no expressed idea is evaluated during the session, since the threat of evaluation inhibits the free flow of ideas.

3. Managers should refrain from making judgments on employee ideas. It's best to ask workers to "research" their concepts with the help of their colleagues (e.g., R&D, Marketing) and then evaluate their value themselves. This usually produces the best decisions without constricting creativity—that is, employees do not get "turned off" by management's rejection of their suggestions.

Case Study: Let the Neophytes Do It

In the 1950s, Professor Dale Wurster of the University of Wisconsin School of Pharmacy (in cooperation with the Wisconsin Alumni Research Foundation) introduced the pharmaceutical industry to air-suspension coating of particles and tablets as an improvement over conventional rotating-pan methods. While not a panacea, air-suspension techniques often produced shorter and more quantitative and efficient processes as well as a higher-quality end product. In addition, air-suspension coating and granulating led to a proliferation of drug-delivery technology—for example, controlled release of medication. Many firms assigned development work to veteran pan coaters, but those companies often lagged behind competitors who assigned responsibility to relatively new scientists who had limited experience with pan coating.

4. When innovation involves replacement of old technology, R&D management tends to entrust development of the new technology to old-technology experts. At times this succeeds, but more often than not the effort fails because these veterans have too much intellectual and emotional investment in the old way. It's often best to assign development of new technology to competent but relatively inexperienced scientists because they are likely to take a fresh, unencumbered approach to the problem.

5. Formal suggestion systems can be beneficial, but management must guard against their calcification, where the suggestions nourish the bureaucratic system instead of the other way around.

Case Study: An Idea-Quenching System

A major corporation had a suggestion system wherein employees were rewarded monetarily on the basis of the idea's estimated contribution to the company's bottom line. At first the system worked well, but as the years went by the process became inundated with administrative rules and tracking procedures, and program administrators became more concerned with the workings of the system than with seeing ideas bear fruit.

Susan, a new program administrator, met with the R&D managers to get their suggestions for improvement. First she introduced new, more complex forms designed to help her tout *her* performance to top management. When Maryellen, an R&D manager, asked Susan if she thought the suggestion system had too much paperwork or not enough, Susan quickly replied, "not enough." Maryellen told Susan that most of the people in the room thought otherwise, whereupon Susan became angry and defensive. The meeting stumbled on for another half-hour or so, ending on a sour note. Under Susan's smothering stewardship, the idea system degenerated logarithmically and was soon abandoned by the company.

---

6. "We need to look for the opportunity in every difficulty instead of being paralyzed at the thought of the difficulty in every opportunity."—M. Cole

As Peter Drucker has said, "Ideas are like babies. They are born small, immature and shapeless. They are promise rather than fulfillment." The R&D managers' role is to nurture those ideas in a productive environment. The chapters that follow ensure that environment. Chapter 11 discusses how to achieve a cohesive research group—the essential characteristic of a productive department. Chapter 12 explains how important it is for a manager to communicate effectively with subordinates to ensure a creative and productive atmosphere. Chapter 13 considers the problems of recruitment and how to attract good, productive employees. Chapter 14 looks at motivation, while Chapter 15 gets more specific about fostering employee growth, and Chapter 16 defends the value of praise and reassurance as management techniques for increasing innovation. Chapter 17 gives tips on evaluating performance, while Chapter 18 delves into the controversial matter of performance reviews. Chapter 19 explains how to deal with unsatisfactory work, while Chapter 20 concludes this part of the book with information on promotions.

Suggested Readings

Books

Argyris, Chris. *Organization and Innovation.* Homewood, Ill.: Richard D. Irwin, 1965.
Bennis, Warren G. *Changing Organizations.* New York: McGraw-Hill, 1966.
Drucker, Peter F. *Innovation and Entrepreneurship: Practice and Principles.* New York: Harper & Row, 1985.
Gardner, John W. *Self-Renewal: The Individual and the Innovative Society.* New York: Harper & Row, 1964.
Kanter, Rosabeth Moss. *The Change Masters: Innovation for Productivity in the American Corporation.* New York: Simon and Schuster, 1983.
Peters, Thomas J. *Thriving on Chaos.* New York: Alfred A. Knopf, 1987.

Newspaper Column

Peters, Thomas J. "Resisting Change: A Routine That Must Be Broken." *Chicago Tribune,* February 1, 1988.

General Reports

Peters, Thomas J. "The Mythology of Innovation: A Skunkworks Tale." *Chemtech,* vol. 16 (May 1986).
Tucker, Robert. "Ten Proven Methods for Hatching Brilliant Ideas." *Republic* (October 1985).

Technical Report

Oliveira, Robert J. "Better Hearing Instruments Through Chemistry." *Hearing Instruments,* 39, no. 10 (1988).

Feature Issues

"Innovation: The Global Race." *Business Week,* Special Bonus Issue, June 15, 1990.
"Innovation in America." *Business Week,* Special Bonus Issue (June 16, 1989).
"The Innovators." *Newsweek,* October 2, 1989.
Kettering, Charles F. "Get Off Route 25, Young Man." *Collier's Magazine,* December 3, 1949.

Additional Articles

Abbey, Augustus, and John W. Dickson. "R&D Work Climate and Innovation in Semiconductors." *Academy of Management Journal* 26, no. 2 (June 1983).

Agee, William. "CEOs Can Influence Innovation." *Chief Executive,* 23 (Spring 1983).

Badawy, Michael K. "How to Prevent Creativity Mismanagement." *Research Management* 29, no. 4 (July-August 1986).

———. "Managing Those 'Tech' Whiz Kids." *Industry Week* 238, no. 10 (May 15, 1989).

Barr, Vilma. "The Process of Innovation: Brainstorming and Storyboarding." *Mechanical Engineering* 110, no. 11 (November 1988).

Bergen, S. A. "The Creative Catastrophe." *R&D Management* 12, no. 3 (July 1982).

Cassidy, Robert. "The Blood, Sweat, and Years of Developing a Product." *Research & Development* 31, no. 9 (September 1989).

Ebadi, Yar M., and James M. Utterback, "The Effects of Communication on Technological Innovation." *Management Science* 30, no. 5 (May 1984).

Edson, Lee. "R&D: General Electric's Man in the Crow's Nest." *Across the Board* 24, no. 5 (May 1987).

Gilder, George. "You Ain't Seen Nothing Yet." *Forbes* 141, no. 7 (April 4, 1988).

Glassman, E. "Managing for Creativity: Back to Basics in R&D." *R&D Management* 16, no. 2 (April 1986).

Jacobson, Gary. "Carlson's Timeless Lessons on Innovation." *Management Review* 78, no. 2 (February 1989).

Johnson, Alicia. "3M: Organized to Innovate." *Management Review* 75, no. 7 (July 1986).

Johnstone, Bob. "A Patent on Creativity." *Far Eastern Economic Review* 147, no. 5 (February 1, 1990).

Long, Carl F., and John P. Collier. "Education for Technological Innovation at the Thayer School." *Technovation* 1, no. 3 (February 1982).

Lovelace, R. F. "Stimulating Creativity Through Managerial Intervention." *R&D Management* 16, no. 2 (April 1986).

Lowe, E. A., and W. G. K. Taylor. "Creativity in Life Sciences Research." *R&D Management* 16, no. 1 (January 1986).

Luckenbach, Thomas A. "Encouraging 'Little C' and 'Big C' Creativity." *Research Management* 29, no. 2 (March-April 1986).

McDermott, Kevin. "An Inventive Mind." *D&B Reports* 35, no. 4 (July-August 1987).

Niles, Howard. "A Novel Approach to Nuclear Fusion." *Dun's Business Month* 123, no. 5 (November 1983).

Price, Derek deSolla. "The Science/Technology Relationship, the Craft of Experimental Science, and Policy for the Improvement of High Technology Innovation." *Research Policy* 13, no. 1 (February 1984).

Rabinow, Jacob. "We Have to Keep Inventors Inventing." *Research Management* 25, no. 6 (November 1982).

Reid, T. R. "Tracing the Roots of the Microchip." *Computerworld* 20, no. 15 (April 14, 1986).

Roberts, Edward B. "What We've Learned: Managing Invention and Innovation." *Research-Technology Management* 31, no. 1 (January-February 1988).

Roman, Mark B. "Renegades of the Year." *Success* 35, no. 1 (January-February 1988).

Ryssina, V. N., and G. N. Koroleva. "Role Structures and Creative Potential of Working Teams." *R&D Management* 14, no. 4 (October 1984).

Schmitt, Roland W. "Where Is Tom Edison Now That We Need Him?" *Research Management* 26, no. 5 (September-October 1983).

Slutsker, Gary. "To Catch a Particle." *Forbes* 143, no. 2 (January 23, 1989).

Smeltz, Wayne, and Barrington Cross. "Toward a Profile of the Creative R&D Professional." *IEEE Transactions on Engineering Management* EM-31, no. 1 (February 1984).

Stahl, Michael J., Thomas W. Zimmerer, and Anil Gulati. "Measuring Innovation, Productivity, and Job Performance of Professionals: A Decision Modeling Approach." *IEEE Transactions on Engineering Management* EM-31, no. 1 (February 1984).

Stookey, S. D. "The Pioneering Researcher and the Corporation." *Research Management* 23, no. 1 (January 1980).

Thamia, S., and M. F. Woods. "A Systematic Small Group Approach to Creativity and Innovation: A Case Study." *R&D Management* 14, no. 1 (January 1984).

Valery, Nicholas. "Japanese Technology: Thinking Ahead." *Economist* 313, no. 7631 (December 2, 1989).

Warner, Ed. "Astrophysicist Arno Penzias on Making R&D Pay Off." *High Technology Business* 9, no. 7 (July-August 1989).

Westwood, Albert R. C., and Yukiko Sekine. "Fostering Creativity and Innovation in an Industrial R&D Laboratory." *Research-Technology Management* 31, no. 4 (July-August 1988).

Whittingham-Barnes, Donna, Deborah Hairston, Vira Jones, and Frank McCoy. "Architects of the Future." *Black Enterprise* 20, no. 7 (February 1990).

Williams, Charles. "Future Developments and Planning Implications: The Issue." *Managerial Planning* 32, no. 5 (March-April 1984).

Wolff, Michael. "How to Find—and Keep—Creative People." *Research Management* 22, no. 5 (September 1979).

———. "Managing Large Egos." *Research Management* 15, no. 4 (July 1982).

Wyeth, Nathaniel C. "Inventing the PET Bottle." *Research-Technology Management* 31, no. 3 (May-June 1988).

Zachary, William B., and Robert M. Krone. "Managing Creative Individuals in High-technology Research Projects." *IEEE Transactions on Engineering Management* EM-31, no. 1 (February 1984).

Chapter 11

The Cohesive
Research Group

Psychologist Carl Rogers (*On Becoming a Person*) provides this insight into the nature of leadership and its beneficial effects:

> *We know how to establish, in any group, the conditions of leadership which will be followed by personality development in the members of the group, as well as by increased productivity and originality, and improved group spirit. . . .* [I]f the leader is acceptant, both of feelings of group members and of his own feelings; if he is understanding of others in a sensitively empathic way; if he permits and encourages free discussion; if he places responsibility with the group; then there is evidence of personality growth in the members of the group, and the group functions more effectively, with greater creativity and better spirit.

All organizations involve group effort, but effective groups are especially important in R&D because of the inherent complexity and interdependence of science. Because of continuous advances in every technical field, no one person or scientific discipline can supply all the answers. The only recourse is to work in groups, whether formal or informal. In this chapter we discuss the formal team of a manager and his or her subordinates; other groups—for example, R&D management committees and project teams—are addressed in Part IV.

A Cohesive Research Team Is Productive

An R&D team's effectiveness depends heavily on strong group cohesiveness. While each team member is ultimately responsible for the group's togetherness, the R&D manager must set the tone.

In Chapter 2, I discuss the characteristics of a fertile work environment. Group cohesiveness emanates directly from many of these attributes. For instance:

1. *Respect.* When a manager has and shows respect for each employee— respect as a person and as a highly valued, contributing member of the group—everything else falls into place.

Case Study: Respect Breeds Productivity

An R&D work group had low morale and even lower productivity; peevishness, discouragement, and lethargy permeated the air. Ralph, one of the company's troubleshooting supervisors, was asked to remedy the situation; his most valuable personal traits were a healthy respect for other people and an uncanny ability to convey it. Within a short time, group members began to sense that respect and to feel better about themselves. As their self-esteem improved, so did their performance and their relationships with one another. Within six months, the group was a close family and its excellence was recognized throughout the company; most observers could only watch with wonder what was happening.

The effect was most dramatic on Wendy, a quiet, unassuming laboratory technician. She had been the lowest rated performer for years. Shown respect and given increased responsibility (e.g., she became group safety coordinator and was in charge of a refurbishing project in the general laboratory area), within ten months she was rated outstanding and promoted to the next laboratory level.

---

2. *Trust.* When employees feel respected, they begin to trust their manager and each other. As trust increases, defensiveness and the need for self-protection decrease, so that energy can be focused on useful work and cooperation.
3. *Sense of Purpose.* A group needs clearly understood, unequivocal, common goals.
4. *Commitment, Enthusiasm, Loyalty.* Members of a close group throw their heart, soul, and energy toward attaining the group's goals.
5. *High Competence and Dedication.* When group members experience an atmosphere of high competence and intense dedication, the air is filled with elation, confidence, expectation, and comradeship.
6. *Urgent but Reasoned Goal-Focused Activity.* Employees need to be busy and experience steady progress toward their goals.
7. *Involvement and Recognition.* Involvement means teamwork, and when people are recognized for their contributions to the group, they feel even closer to their teammates.
8. *Caring.* When employees sense that their leader is interested in their personal well-being, they also care about the manager and each other, creating supportive interdependence.

9. *Acceptance.* According to Rogers, the essence of acceptance is "warm regard."
10. *Civility, Friendliness, Thoughtfulness, and Genuineness.* These add up to day-to-day sustenance for a group.
11. *Honesty, Candor, Openness.* These guard against an invasion of secrecy, uncertainty, and suspicion.
12. *Cooperation.* In a cohesive group, cooperation eclipses competition. In an article in *Working Woman* (April 1989), management professor and consultant Rosabeth Moss Kanter decries competition and calls it "cowboy management."
13. *Effective Communication.* Unless people communicate their respect, trust, and caring to each other, those attitudes are, for all practical purposes, nonexistent.
14. *Independence, Interdependence, and Deference.* Independence is a prerequisite for healthy interdependence, and deference strengthens interdependence by minimizing "turf" considerations.
15. *Pride.* Being appropriately proud of the group, one's colleagues, and oneself is a major quality in a cohesive organization.

Cohesiveness is not, however, a characteristic that comes automatically. Robert Sampson, in his book *Managing the Managers* (see References at end of chapter), suggests six basic conditions for establishing a cohesive group:

1. *Time.* People need months of working together before they can feel comfortable as a team and discover how best to get along with one another.
2. *Compatibility.* While some diversity—both professional and personal—is desirable, "people must like each other, want to help each other, [and] have open communications in a trusting atmosphere with relaxed working relationships" (p. 231).
3. *Mutual Support.* Each person must feel necessary—that is, that he or she is making an important contribution to the group. At the same time, group members must want to associate with and be dependent upon one another.
4. *Relative Capability.* If individual competence, creativity, intelligence, and motivation vary excessively within the group, envy will soon displace mutual respect and admiration. [Thus group cohesiveness relies heavily on the manager's ability to recruit high-quality people, transfer or terminate poorly performing group members, and help everyone grow in competence.]
5. *Group Goals.* The first four conditions are necessary for a cohesive group, but it may be emotionally cohesive *for* or *against* the manager and the organization. Under adverse conditions, a group's goals may be mutual protection and mutual expression of hostility toward the manager. (Herman Wouk's *The Caine Mutiny* is a classic example of a cohesive crew hellbent on (1) survival and (2) doing in a reviled leader.

As often happens, the group prevailed.) Cohesiveness will be a positive force when the group identifies itself with and supports the manager.

6. *Acceptance of the Boss.* Supervisors are welcomed as group leaders when there is mutual trust and respect, and when they willingly acknowledge *their* dependence upon the group. However, they are rejected if they are perceived to be a threat to the group's well-being.

A Circle, Not a Pyramid

An R&D manager can optimize group spirit, cohesiveness, and performance by presenting the team as a circle, not a pyramid. Most organizations are structured as pyramids, with the leader at the apex and all other individuals below in decreasing order of responsibility and authority. This organization of duties has a certain orderliness and serves many useful functions; however, it also has disadvantages. It gives rise to such terms as "superior" and "subordinate" and tends to propagate the idea that people's wisdom and intelligence, as well as their contributions, are measured only by how far up the pyramid they rise.

While the pyramid may be appropriate and necessary for corporate structure, an R&D manager is involved with well-trained, highly motivated technical employees, and should consider the group as a circle. In a circular structure, power and responsibility are dispersed among *all* members of the group rather than concentrated with the manager. Also, each member of the team is unique and has something significant to contribute to the group, its performance, and its welfare. All members are equally responsible for the long-term health of the team, and they constantly look for ways to improve themselves and the group.

In a circle, the manager is simply one member of the team. He or she has a particular set of talents and responsibilities, but those are not more important than the work performed by others. For example, most accounting systems regard the manager's job as overhead, while others produce the results.

A good test of a group's adherence to the circle is whether the members are truly glad the manager occupies his or her position. Can they say, "We're glad to have her as our manager; she really pulls her share of the load and helps us accomplish our goals!"? Managers need not worry that a circle structure will cause people to forget who's boss. The corporate way of life constantly reminds employees about who has the ultimate authority. But the manager uses authority for the benefit of the group.

Does Competition Spur Performance?

Internal competition is the mortal enemy of group cohesiveness. Some say rivalry is good, that it motivates individuals to higher performance, but a closer examination says otherwise.

Bil Gilbert ("Competition: Is It What Life's All About?") discusses the value and limitations of competition.

The fuss over competition is a revival of some older conceits about the survival of the fittest.... The idea is that competition is the behavioral equivalent of gravity, a force that makes the world go 'round.... Indeed, it all sounds as if it has a lot to do with the realities of evolution and zoology, but it does not. The trouble with the theory of direct, unrelenting competition as a long-range force in nature is that such a scheme always has fewer winners than losers.

Thus the win-or-drop-dead, tennis-tournament model of competition is at odds with the fact that, through the aeons, life-forms on Earth have become increasingly numerous and various. The multitude of species reflects the evolutionary drive to find a small edge—a niche, zoologists call it—that enables creatures to go about their business without always fighting with others with the same appetites. Humans have long had a high regard for niches, which allow us to occupy positions in which competition is completely eliminated or greatly reduced.

As a practical matter, cooperation is the tactic most commonly used to get what we want.... So, while we may in principle praise the virtues and joys of head-on competition, we are much less enthusiastic about it in practice. Getting what we want by taking it from somebody else in an overt contest is usually for us, as for other species, a last resort.

Similarly, people in R&D work groups will be happier, healthier, and more productive to the extent that managers successfully create an atmosphere that minimizes competition and optimizes cooperation. Group theory experts David W. and Frank P. Johnson (*Joining Together*, pp. 124–125) agree:

In a cooperative group, achievement will be higher than in a competitive one.... A cooperative orientation leads to increased cohesiveness and greater group productivity.... A considerable body of research shows that when a situation within a group is cooperatively structured, relevant information is communicated openly, accurately, and honestly. In a competitively structured situation, however, communication is either lacking or misleading....

The very nature of competition, in which one works to gain an edge toward winning and fears the possibility of losing, promotes a great deal of defensiveness among group members.... Competition is inevitably accompanied by defensive behavior. And defensive people, even if they work on the group's tasks, devote a lot of energy just to defending themselves. They think about how they look to others, how they may win over or dominate their peers, how they may impress their superiors, how they may keep from losing, and how they may protect themselves from anticipated attacks.

As Bil Gilbert mentioned, competition clearly implies there will be winners—but also losers; and any work situation in which most employees are labeled losers is not good. Charles Schulz's Charlie Brown cartoon character illustrates the point. In one frame, Linus tells Charlie about watching a great football game which ended with members of the winning team and their fans jumping for joy after a miraculous last-second winning touchdown. In reply, Charlie muses, "I wonder how the other team felt?" Competition can be emphasized only at the expense of cooperation, and work groups in technology-intensive industries do especially poorly in a noncooperative environment.

The idea of a group of people living and working in a relatively noncompetitive environment is not farfetched. According to Riane Eisler in her introduction to *The Chalice and the Blade*:

> Underlying the great surface diversity of human culture are two basic models of society. The first, which I call the *dominator* model, is what is popularly termed either patriarch or matriarch—the *ranking* of one half of humanity over the other. The second, in which social relations are primarily based on the principle of *linking* rather than ranking, may best be described as the *partnership* model. In this model . . . diversity is not equated with either inferiority or superiority.
>
> [Nonviolent, nonhierarchical civilizations predate competitive societies by thousands of years.] The original direction in the mainstream of our cultural evolution was toward partnership but . . . following a period of chaos and almost total cultural disruption, there occurred a fundamental social shift . . . from a partnership to a dominator model.

In reality, and certainly among R&D work groups, cooperation, not competition, makes the world go 'round. When the right atmosphere is created, competition among employees almost disappears—replaced by a pervasive family-type spirit of cooperation and helpfulness.

Case Study: Cooperation, Not Competition

An R&D department was composed of Cosmo, a veteran scientist, and a host of neophytes. The work environment was remarkable, largely because of Cosmo's unselfish behavior. He was very competent and knowledgeable but also extremely helpful and patient. No request for assistance or advice was rejected, and his unassuming manner guaranteed that someone else would get the credit. He was truly respected—even beloved—by everyone in the group. As a result, the atmosphere was essentially devoid of competition.

Cosmo's helpfulness and unpretentiousness were diffused throughout the department, and young scientists beginning their industrial careers grew rapidly by learning from each other. The manager's primary contribution was to stay out of the way.

Managers can help construct a cooperative environment by setting a noncompetitive example. For instance, they can (1) maintain a low profile, (2) let subordinates represent the department in multigroup meetings, (3) publicly recognize subordinates' quality and accomplishments as often as possible, and (4) emphasize the importance of group accomplishment and group welfare. Managers get their satisfaction vicariously, although direct recognition of their contributions will come when others begin to connect the excellence and harmony of the group with their performance.

There are sound psychological reasons for the success of cooperation over competition. The highest level of human motivation is self-actualization, the drive within each of us to become the very best of which we are inherently capable. When people are motivated in this way, they are most efficient; they make the most progress with the least expenditure of energy.

More important, people are not in competition with others (which can lead to envy, hostility, and discouragement). Rather, they are in competition with *themselves*, creating a psychologically healthy situation. For example, a child learning to walk is only interested in staying vertical while moving (mostly) forward; he doesn't care whether he can walk faster than his older brother. In that same vein, competitive employees need not—and should not—change and become passive. Instead, they can set aggressive goals for themselves and then work toward attaining them.

In summary, R&D managers who foster cooperation and minimize competition among their employees will optimize group cohesiveness, personal growth, and productivity.

References

Eisler, Riane. *The Chalice and the Blade: Our History, Our Future*. San Francisco: Harper & Row, 1988.

Gilbert, Bil. "Competition: Is It What Life's All About?" *Sports Illustrated*, May 16, 1988.

Johnson, David W., and Frank P. Johnson. *Joining Together: Group Theory and Group Skills*, 2nd ed. Englewood Cliffs, N. J.: Prentice-Hall, 1982.

Kanter, Rosabeth Moss. "Why Cowboy Management Is Bad for American Business." *Working Woman*, April 1989.

Rogers, Carl R. *On Becoming a Person: A Therapist's View of Psychotherapy*. Boston: Houghton Mifflin, 1961.

Sampson, Robert C. *Managing the Managers*. New York: McGraw-Hill, 1965.

Chapter 12

Effective Communication

"Out of sight, out of mind," when translated into Russian by computer, then back again into English, became "invisible maniac."

A. Calder-Marshall

We have two ears but only one mouth, for obvious reasons.

Jokes about communication abound, but in industry—and especially in R&D, where the exchange of knowledge and information must reign supreme—the widespread problems in communication are no laughing matter. Managers must be able to communicate effectively. The best way to emphasize the importance of good communication is to give two examples of *non*communication. The first:

"Shut up!" he explained.—Ring Lardner

The second is the following case study (all case studies in this book are true, but this one strains credulity):

Case Study: Noncommunication

William was a directive, detail-oriented, technically competent R&D group leader whose subordinates were both competent and independent. He held weekly meetings to plan the group's activities, and each session followed the same procedure.

William would outline what he thought the group ought to do, then he would say, "But I want this to be a participative planning session, so let me hear your opinions." After the group members expressed their strong views (often disagreeing with their leader), William would say, "Then it's all agreed: We'll do this and this"—and the "agreement" would always be what he suggested at the start! He consistently ignored any recommendations that were contrary to his preconceived notions.

After the meeting, William's subordinates would go into their laboratories and, for the next week they did what they thought was best and completely ignored William's directives, just as he had ignored their recommendations. For whatever reasons, William never chastised his subordinates for their actions, and they were content to live with the charade.

Now that you've learned how *not* to communicate, let's look at the key to effective communication.

Effective communication is the creation of understanding. Carl Rogers and F. J. Roethlisberger (*Harvard Business Review*, vol. 30) marvel that communication *ever* occurs, because people do not see and assume the same things, nor do they share the same values. The writers suggest two quite different assumptions that people have about communication:

1. The goal of communication is to *persuade* the listener to agree with the speaker. In this case, one gives little thought to the other's position.
2. The purpose of communication is to *create understanding*. Here the emphasis is on listening, accepting differences of opinion, and freely expressing feelings.

Hearing vs. *Listening*

The primary cause of poor communication is a failure to listen to the other person. Most of us do not appreciate the important difference between hearing and listening.

Many sounds in our lives (street noise, small talk at a party) are assimilated through a process of hearing. This is primarily a physical phenomenon, with only a small mental element and virtually no emotional component. We tend to take such hearing for granted, like breathing, and in many situations this is appropriate.

But when people try to communicate to us something they consider important, hearing becomes inadequate; instead, we need to *listen* to what they have to say. Now the process requires three components— physical, mental, and emotional—and becomes more complex. Unfortunately, often we fail to distinguish between hearing and listening, and we assume we know, with little effort, exactly what another person is saying or means. Similarly, when we think people have misunderstood what we have just said, we usually assume they were "not listening"; how else could something go wrong with such a simple process?

To minimize problems in listening, we need to appreciate the complexities involved. There are four components to communication, or the creation of understanding:

1. The sender
2. The receiver
3. The message
4. The feedback (closing the loop)

Barriers get in the way of accurate communication. A useful analogy is the red appearance of the sun at sunset; the sun's rays are refracted so that "things are not as they appear." Similarly, communication is "bent" by—

▲ the atmosphere (bad vibes between the sender and the receiver);
▲ intellectual differences between the two speakers;
▲ language differences (different languages or dialects);
▲ use of jargon (especially scientific and organizational);
▲ identity or status (e.g., a tendency not to listen to a technician in the same way we listen to a vice-president);
▲ limited clarity of expression (inability to explain accurately);
▲ limited attention span of the receiver;
▲ distractions in the environment (e.g., noisy manufacturing area);
▲ culture from which each person comes;
▲ preoccupation of sender and (especially) receiver;
▲ limited perceptiveness of sender and (especially) receiver; and/or
▲ past experiences, especially between sender and receiver.

Let's look at the communication process in detail: A speaker's thoughts and feelings spring forth from a unique mental-emotional-experiential network and join together in a complex, ill-defined process to form an idea. He then utters words to express the idea, but the words he chooses and the tone or inflection in his voice depend greatly on his—

▲ verbal language skills;
▲ mental state (alert or confused);
▲ inherent degree of congruence (the harmony among his feelings, his awareness of those feelings, and his willingness or ability to communicate those feelings to the receiver);
▲ relationship with the listener (boss, subordinate, close friend, antagonist);
▲ emotional state (angry, excited, or calm); and
▲ perception of the other person's emotional state.

Add to this the basic language, cultural, and scientific differences common in multinational, multicultural, and multidisciplinary R&D organizations, and we begin to see why his ideas may not reach his listener.

The listener hears the speaker's words, but how accurately he assimilates them depends on all the factors listed above, as applied now to him rather than to the speaker. The listener then processes his understanding of the speaker's words through his own mental-emotional-experiential network and forms a general opinion of what the speaker has said or meant to say.

The situation is further complicated by the following:

▲ Sometimes the listener is not interested in what the speaker has to say.
▲ The listener is often busy deciding what *he* intends to say next as soon as he gets a chance.
▲ The two people involved view reality differently.

Persuasion vs. Creating Understanding

Earlier in this chapter we noted that people communicate either to persuade or create understanding.

The persuasion vs. creation of understanding concept is discussed in detail by Gary Combs in the *1981 Annual Handbook for Group Facilitators* (p. 113): "Much of our time as teachers, parents, and workers is devoted to social influence. We attempt to modify the views of others and move them to action; others attempt to do the same with us."

Thus much of our communication is devoted to converting others to our point of view on a variety of subjects; this propensity for debate and the desire to have our opinions confirmed by others seem to be especially characteristic of scientists. Combs emphasizes that the usual prescriptions for effective communication are to "speak clearly and thoughtfully, avoid stereotyping, maintain an

---

Case Study: Jordan v. Zastrow

For example, let's suppose Mary Jordan, representative of a pharmaceutical company's regulatory affairs department, is talking to Herman Zastrow, director of quality control. Mary is dissatisfied with the format of QC information that is regularly included in the company's new drug applications (NDAs). In fact, she has already told her boss that she will work to upgrade all sections of the company's NDA submissions. Unfortunately, adopting Jordan's suggestions for improvements in the QC format would cause Zastrow's people considerably more work; besides, Herman says, the present system is on computer and works just fine the way it is.

Jordan is well prepared for Zastrow's objections and responds patiently and politely, emphasizing that her suggested changes could reduce FDA response time by several months and are well worth the effort. Herman is also polite but firm. He replies that the QC section is the best-organized part of the company's submissions, and he doubts that the FDA would respond faster if it were changed. He suggests that Jordan concentrate on the real problems—the clinical and manufacturing portions of the NDAs. Mary, a persistent and dedicated employee, assures Herman that she is working on those areas, but she continues to press her point.

attentive posture, be honest and timely, listen carefully, and repeat for emphasis and retention."

Although these points are important, they are several orders of magnitude less so than the interpersonal climate that exists between two individuals, especially while they are attempting to communicate. As Combs says, "*supportive* climates promote understanding and problem solving; *defensive* climates impede them."

In the defensive-communication climate, the primary goal is control. We want to persuade our listeners—to win them over to our side, and to compel them to do what we think is best. This is not shameful behavior; we all do it often, with honorable intentions. But the results are twofold: ineffective communication and deterioration of the relationship.

Reread the case study on page 97. What is happening to the climate between these two individuals, and what is the likely outcome? If the QC director continues to question the validity of Jordan's request, and if Mary refuses to abandon her contention that the QC format needs to be improved, both will become entrenched in their point of view. They almost certainly will become critical of the other person. They may hide their feelings, but tension will escalate. Soon each will come to regard the other as stubborn and unreasonable, if not stupid.

As the conversation proceeds, both will spend more and more time preparing rebuttals, and will listen less and less to what the other person is saying. According to Combs, "Energy will be focused on winning and overcoming rather than on listening and problem solving." Eventually, each individual will begin to feel superior to the other, in both intellect and dedication to the company's best interests.

Both parties will subconsciously solidify their positions; all tentativeness will disappear because moderation will be seen as a sign of weakness. In the end, either the problem will be "kicked upstairs," one of them will have to capitulate, both will sulk and lick their wounds with the basic issue unresolved, or a grudging compromise will be reached. Whatever the outcome, the Jordan-Zastrow relationship will be significantly damaged, understanding of the other's position will be minimal, and any compromise will receive, at best, tepid support from both individuals.

Sound familiar? Is this the way you want to do business? Combs and others (see, e.g., Carl Rogers and F. J. Roethlisberger) believe there's a better way. It involves developing a supportive climate and listening long enough to understand, not just long enough to disagree.

Let's go back to the beginning of the Jordan-Zastrow conversation. This time, one of the individuals (it doesn't matter who, but someone has to break the defensive chain and start moving things in the right direction), instead of trying to persuade and instead of concentrating on "making myself clear," first focuses almost exclusively on trying to *listen* to the other individual and then attempt to *understand* his position. Let's assume Mary Jordan takes that initiative and seeks, as Combs says, "to establish a dialogue, to listen, and to appreciate and explore differences of opinion."

Mary, *listening* to Herman's objections and also to his comments on the clinical and manufacturing sections of the NDA, assumes that he, too, has an interest in improving the overall quality of submissions and asks for his help on her project. Talking—and *listening*—further, she learns that Zastrow worked at the FDA for twelve years before coming to the company and has some definite ideas about what the agency wants. He agrees to help her organize a small task force composed of representatives from relevant disciplines within the company. He nominates his most innovative, energetic subordinate as the QC member and promises to keep an open mind on any recommendations that the group may generate, including those regarding the QC format.

Thus, when Herman perceives that Mary recognizes his expertise and appreciates his position, he feels *understood* and *respected*. He no longer needs to defend himself; he begins to *listen* and understand her point of view.

As Combs explains, as each person becomes more "open and responsive, less energy will be focused on strategic rebuttal. Both will be able to concentrate on what is being said, and each will feel free to express her/his own thoughts and feelings." The task force idea will probably result in a win-win, collaborative program, not a lose-lose compromise.

Carl Rogers (*On Becoming a Person*), supports Comb's general position on communication. Rogers believes that the principal barrier in interpersonal communication is our natural tendency to *evaluate* what the other person is saying. The more intense our feelings about the subject under discussion, the more evaluative we tend to be. In his *Harvard Business Review* article with F. J. Roethlisberger (vol. 30), Rogers explains: "The stronger our feelings, the more likely it is that there will be no mutual element in the communication. There will be just two ideas, two feelings, two judgments, missing each other in psychological space."

For Rogers, the key to effective communication is listening with understanding, especially with empathic understanding: "To see the expressed idea and attitude from the other person's point of view, to sense how it feels to him, to achieve his frame of reference." He suggests that this can best be done by repeating what the other person says (not verbatim, but in essence) until he agrees that "you've got it."

We can quickly check whether we are merely hearing or are *listening* by asking ourselves: Am I trying to *convince* the other person of my point of view or am I trying to gain a better *understanding* of his?

In short, effective communication demands that we learn to prize others, to value them as unique individuals and to respect them and their opinions as we want to be respected. As Plachy says, "The classic failure in interpersonal communications is the failure to recognize the other person's right to believe in the good sense of his point of view."

Listening to others is hard work and involves, among other things, learning to concentrate on what the other person is saying, not on what we are planning to say next. More important, we need to listen empathically—that is, gain a sense of what the person is feeling as well as what he is saying. Only then can we begin to *understand*.

When we speak, we need to express ourselves in nonthreatening ways. For example, rather than saying, "You misunderstood me," it is better to say, "I'm sorry I didn't make myself clear." We also must observe the other person's reactions to what we are saying, because much of communication is nonverbal. For example, Peter Drucker (*Management: Tasks, Responsibilities, Practices*) emphasizes the importance of hearing what *isn't* said.

If the other person appears to be taking umbrage, we need to stop and say, "I sense that I've said something that upset you; if I did, I apologize. I'd appreciate your telling me where I went wrong." At the same time, we need to be candid. If we find ourselves angry at something the other person said, we should say so, but then emphasize that perhaps we've misunderstood and ask him to restate it.

Obviously we must be honest and forthright in our communications. Dishonesty and deceit are not only wrong, they require a better memory than most people have. And, most important, we need to be genuine. The more authentic we are, the healthier our relationships will be. Learning to communicate effectively is not easy, but the path is clear: Listen with empathic understanding and be supportive. Remember, "There is none so deaf as the person who does not listen."

Communication Within the Organization

Generalizations aside, we now need to look at how communication skills apply to an R&D manager and the work group. To begin, a manager needs to communicate to employees the kind of person he or she is. Good working relationships—the cornerstone of good performance—depend on people getting to know one another. It is the manager's responsibility to initiate and encourage the communication process that brings about that understanding of one another. There are specific actions managers can take to reduce the communication gap between themselves and their subordinates. They can—

▲ meet semiannually with each employee for an hour to find out how things are going, personally and on-the-job, and what's right and what's wrong with the general work environment;

▲ always refer to the group as "our" department, never "my" department;

▲ when introducing a subordinate to someone else, always say, "He works *with* me," never, "He works *for* me";

▲ encourage being called by their first name, as formality tends to disappear when people are on a first-name basis; and

▲ try to be the first one at a department meeting. Too many managers wait until everyone else is assembled and then walk into the room. This is often because the leader is busy, but making people wait is an inherent sign of disrespect, intended or not. Even worse, a manager walking in on an assembled group is in danger of giving the impression that she considers herself a "royal" figure.

Such actions are not gimmicks as long as they represent a sincere effort by managers to communicate to others that *everyone* in the group is important.

Case Study: Regular Meetings With Individual Employees

Bryce, a middle manager in R&D, was promoted to vice-president and became responsible for a group of about 100 people. One of his highest priorities was to meet individually with each employee for an hour; this practice was continued annually. While it took a great deal of time (both his and the employees'), Bryce realized that it was the best time investment he ever made:

1. He became well acquainted with each employee and, equally important, they became much better acquainted with him.
2. Employees felt respected as individuals because the vice-president took an interest in them.
3. Bryce created a valuable early warning system; because of his candor and trustworthiness, employees felt comfortable speaking their minds. Thus he was able to detect subtle signs of impending trouble within the organization and could take steps to solve small problems before they became major crises.

Keeping Employees Informed

One of the major complaints employees have is that they feel they don't know enough about what is going on within the organization. This lack of communication tends to alienate employees from management, demean and frustrate workers at all levels, and create overall confusion. It is especially harmful in R&D organizations involved with complex technology.

Poor corporate communication also has other ill effects, especially on motivation. Psychologist Abraham Maslow (*Motivation and Personality*) emphasizes that secrecy threatens *all* our basic needs. Secretive managers are always forcing their subordinates toward their lower-level needs, where they operate less efficiently and less productively.

To minimize such problems, managers need to disseminate information accurately. The following case study shows the importance of keeping employees informed.

Case Study: Bulletin Boards

Mary Beth Saunders, an R&D manager, felt she was adequately informing her subordinates by circulating appropriate (by her definition) memos and notices throughout the department. However, an annual employee survey revealed that group members felt the flow of information was a case of "too little too late." Not only was some information not circulated, but it took weeks, or even months, for memos to reach the entire department.

To correct the situation, someone suggested that the manager and secretary post all nonconfidential memos and notices on a bulletin board. Group members enthusiastically endorsed the suggestion and agreed to be responsible for checking the board frequently. To accommodate the huge flow of paper, a jumbo bulletin board was installed with areas designated for "urgent," "new," and "old" information. Mary Beth agreed to update the display weekly; she took that responsibility (about twenty to thirty minutes per week) because she could best decide when items should be moved from one category to another and whether to discard or file the old information. (Note: Since Mary Beth posted *all* nonconfidential pieces of information, the *employees* decided what they wanted to read or ignore.)

Department members found the bulletin board to be a rich resource; it also became a prime source of information for members of other departments. But when Mary Beth left the department, she neglected to tell her successor, Esther, about the bulletin board. Esther inadvertently let it "go to seed," and the employees soon stopped looking at it; it was messy and out of date. Fortunately, within a few weeks someone brought the problem to Esther's attention, and the bulletin board again became a primary source of information.

Poor Managerial Communication

When managers don't communicate effectively with employees, it has a pronounced negative effect on morale and, therefore, on performance. For example, when people are kept in the dark, they inevitably feel that management does not trust them—so why should they trust management? Likewise, excessive secrecy on the part of management makes subordinates feel unimportant and disrespected, thus threatening their sense of identity, individuality, and belonging.

When managers emphasize rather than diminish the distance between themselves and their employees, they are, in effect, telling them, "We consider ourselves to be different from and better than you." That creates resentment and antagonism (a "we-they" mentality), both of which erode worker loyalty. This seems a very high price to pay for the marginal benefit of segregation, which is primarily the inflation of managerial egos.

The family-type group cohesiveness so important to a good R&D work environment depends heavily on the manager's being part of the group, and this requires communication. If a manager is a chronically poor communicator, employees will give up on the situation and become lethargic, discouraged, and alienated.

▲▲▲▲▲

In summary, when you listen carefully to what an employee has to say, you validate that person as a human being of considerable worth. As one social scientist says, "If you fail in communication with one of your employees, look upon it as you would a power failure: You don't jump to the conclusion that there's no more electricity; you merely assume that there's something wrong with the connection."

Effective communication is the foundation for all other management tasks. In the chapters that follow we discuss recruiting, motivating, helping, and assessing employees' work, but in each of these activities, good communication skills are essential.

References

Combs, Gary. "Defensive and Supportive Communication." In *The 1981 Annual Handbook for Group Facilitators,* ed. John E. Jones and J. William Pfeiffer. San Diego: University Associates, 1981.

Drucker, Peter F. *Management: Tasks, Responsibilities, Practices.* New York: Harper & Row, 1974.

Maslow, Abraham H. *Motivation and Personality,* 2nd ed., ed. Wayne G. Holtzman and Gardner Murphy. New York: Harper & Row, 1970.

Rogers, Carl R. *On Becoming a Person: A Therapist's View of Psychotherapy.* Boston: Houghton Mifflin, 1961.

Rogers, Carl R., and F. J. Roethlisberger. "Barriers and Gateways to Communication." *Harvard Business Review* 30 (1952).

Sampson, Robert C. *Managing the Managers.* New York: McGraw-Hill, 1965.

Chapter 13

Recruiting Technical People

It is the special task of R&D management to hire competent, innovative, independent, self-reliant, self-starting people, and then *work like hell* to keep organizational restrictions from doing them in. Most managers of R&D are involved with recruiting, but not enough are committed to this important task.

What's the difference between being *involved* and being *committed*? It's like a plate of ham and eggs. The chicken was involved, but the pig was committed. Identifying and hiring people is one of management's most crucial responsibilities. When competent subordinates are hired, a manager is almost guaranteed good results, but with inadequate employees even a brilliant leader is in serious trouble.

One of the major reasons for this lack of commitment is that too many managers consider the recruiting and hiring process to be an unwelcome interruption of their real job, running the organization. As a result, inappropriate or barely adequate candidates are hired, only to be terminated later when they don't work out or—worse—to become long-term problem employees. Equally bad, too often the best candidates slip away because either their quality goes undetected or they sense they are interruptions in a manager's busy day. Feeling undervalued and underappreciated, these prospects join another organization.

Not everyone can shine as a recruiter, but we can all hone our skills and thereby improve the quality of the people we hire, no matter what their level of education* or training.

The Search for Candidates

Effective recruiting first depends on good management of the people you already have. This is your best way of attracting good candidates. If employees

---

*The emphasis here is on recruiting M.S.s and Ph.D.s, but most of the principles can be applied to hiring technical people in general.

are motivated, enthusiastic, loyal, and committed to the organization, this will be evident to visiting prospects. Without being asked to do so, subordinates will try hard to convince candidates that theirs is a super organization in which to work; most people are eager to share such positive feelings about their jobs. Furthermore, when a manager develops a good reputation within R&D—not only for managing well but also for emphasizing employee growth—word gets around. Soon people from other departments and from other companies, as well as those coming directly from graduate schools, start queuing up for employment in the group.

The two major steps in recruiting are (1) identifying quality candidates and (2) bringing them to the organization for in-depth interviews. In the search for candidates, if possible start the process by beating the bushes—that is, with regular visits to graduate schools. R&D managers who never leave the office and rely instead on their own networking system or on professional search firms surrender a huge advantage to competitors who visit the universities. Consider:

▲ Since almost everyone looks good on a résumé, a half-hour conversation with a graduate student on his or her turf provides a wealth of additional information and gives impressions that otherwise could not be obtained.

▲ Showing genuine interest in students, faculty, and the university fosters a close relationship based on mutual trust.

▲ Visiting the universities, even when you're not hiring, demonstrates your commitment to education and to the scientific field.

▲ Students benefit greatly from these contacts with industry.

It's important to involve as many of your department members as possible in the recruiting process, although some selectivity is necessary when planning visits to graduate schools. Company representatives should have a high degree of competence and be able to project a genuinely enthusiastic image of the organization. During in-depth departmental interviews, talking to too many people can confuse and overload the interviewees, but involving members of your group in the hiring process will help you find the best candidates and will also encourage the members to feel responsible for the welfare of the group.

Involving subordinates in the recruiting process also offers candidates a larger sampling of the people with whom they would work. In addition, it ensures that better hiring decisions will be made. If your opinion differs from those of your subordinates, especially when they are united in their opinion, you might do well to go with their judgment. Not only are subordinates likely to be right, but they will be more committed to making the new relationship work if their choice is honored.

Recruiting trips are an important growth opportunity for subordinates because the visits hone their interviewing skills and judgments and expose them to graduate schools, faculty, and students around the country. Whenever possible, two people should be sent on any given visit. Pairings for these trips should be given considerable thought because neophytes can learn from veterans, and vice versa. Also, this experience can draw the two individuals closer together, which has a surprisingly strong, positive impact on their future work relationship. Furthermore, talking to ten to fifteen students a day is tiring; with two interviewers, breaks can be taken. This is important because the last student to be interviewed deserves the same careful attention as the first.

Characteristics to Look For

What should you look for when evaluating potential technical employees? This is a complex question, prone to oversimplification, but the inherent risks in hiring can be minimized by answering the following questions:

Competence:	Is the candidate basically competent? This question can be largely answered by having her present a seminar on her graduate work to the group.
Productivity:	Does the candidate like to work? How productive is he?
Genuineness:	Is she psychologically honest with herself and with others? Does she appear to be genuine and relatively free of façades?
Growth:	What is his capacity for growth? Is he likely to bloom under good management?
Flexibility, Open-Mindedness:	Related to growth, is she open-minded? How flexible is she? In complex technical businesses, there usually are many ways to reach a goal. Also, working in industry is quite different from the graduate school experience, and adjustments must be made.
Cooperativeness:	How well does he work with others? Is he tolerant of them and of their opinions? Does he treat other people with respect and as individuals? Does he present the same face to everyone, or is he deferential to the faculty, argumentative with his peers, and imperious to technicians, secretaries, and the supply room staff?
Deference:	Related to cooperativeness, does she defer to others when appropriate (e.g., when they know more than she does)?
Communication:	Is he a good communicator? How well does he speak before a group? How well does he write? Can he clearly present his ideas to others? Most important, how well does he listen?

Selfishness:	To what degree is she self-centered? Will she tend to look out for herself at the expense of the welfare and the accomplishments of the group?
Self-Confidence:	Does he have a healthy self-confidence, a strong but realistic sense of self-esteem?
Arrogance:	Is she arrogant? Can she easily admit when she's wrong? Does she take herself too seriously?
Motivation:	Is he a self-starter? Is he likely to perform, under good management, at the self-actualization level of motivation?
Thoughtfulness:	Is she considerate of others? Is she a giver or a taker?
Ethics:	Does he have a strong set of basic values, or does he drift with the prevailing winds, all sail and no anchor?
Independence:	How independent is she? Can she think for herself?
Commitment:	If management shows commitment to employees, is he likely to reciprocate?

We should not expect anyone to be perfect, of course, but these considerations are relevant to whether a candidate is likely to become a high-quality, productive worker. Personal characteristics* are important because employees are individuals, not interchangeable gears in the corporate machinery. Furthermore, industrial R&D's complex projects demand group effort, and a scientist's success depends as much on interpersonal and communication skills as on technical competence. Even a farmer who is about to purchase a team of horses (if farmers still do that) will ask how well they pull together.

Not every graduate program and not every adviser is of equal quality. Generally, the personal qualities of the individual should be weighed about 80 percent when making a hiring decision. But if a student comes out of a mediocre program convinced that he has had the ultimate in education and has little more to learn, it's probably best to look further.

You cannot adequately answer the many questions about a candidate in a half-hour interview at the school or even during in-depth sessions in the department. However, there are four specific sources of information you can use to ensure success.

---

*The question is not whether you should embrace psychology or, as an amateur, keep your distance. Because you deal with people and because psychology is concerned with human motivation and behavior, the real question is: Are you going to practice poor amateur psychology—based on conscious, planned ignorance and neglect—or are you going to try to perform as competently as possible despite the complexities involved? Besides, if you manage with a light touch, you needn't worry much about overstepping your expertise in the strange, looking-glass world of social science. Peter Drucker, in *Management: Tasks, Responsibilities, Practice,* says that the main purpose of psychology is to acquire insight into, and mastery of, oneself.

1. *Major Advisers.* For graduate students, the obvious primary source of information is the major adviser. This person knows his or her people best and is in a position to answer questions about a student's productivity and capacity for growth. This is especially important if one candidate has peaked while the other is just hitting her stride.

2. *Primary Faculty Contact.* In each graduate school there is usually at least one faculty member who is highly professional and has a strong interest in students. He or she can recognize a high-quality person and will be candid about what he or she thinks. Try to find this person.

3. *Former Classmates.* Get the opinion of former graduate students who were one or two years the candidate's senior. Although they may be personally biased to some extent, they can offer the best view of a candidate's ability to get along with peers and can say whether he presents one face to the faculty and another to fellow students. In some cases, talented individuals who were highly rated by the faculty were regarded by former peers as arrogant, competitive, and noncooperative.

4. *Formal References.* Ask the candidate's references as many of the afore-mentioned questions as appropriate. Also give the references time to tell their views without your steering the conversation in a particular direction.

All of these sources usually provide valuable information upon which to make a judgment, but only if you have established a reputation for honesty, fairness, and discretion, and have shown a genuine concern for the students' welfare. Then people will feel comfortable enough to speak candidly.

Presenting the Job and the Company

Although proper evaluation of each candidate is critical, recruiters should spend equal time presenting an accurate, candid picture of the job. Be sure to explain the following:

▲ *What Is Expected.* What's the job? Few students, unless they have previously worked in industry, have a clear picture of what their responsibilities will be.

▲ *Opportunities for Growth and Advancement.* Be prepared to answer, honestly and candidly, the following questions:
— How well does the dual-ladder system work in your organization, if you have one?
— How crowded is the roster of employees who are interested in and who qualify for scarce managerial positions?
— What is your personal commitment to the growth of subordinates? (No lip service, please.)
— What are your company's policies and practices concerning in-house education, internal transfers, promotion from within, job posting, external publications, attendance at professional meetings, and external education and training?

▲ *Advantages and Disadvantages of Your Corporation.* Large or well-established organizations have many mentors for new recruits; smaller, newer companies may not be able to provide this particular learning opportunity, although in a smaller company there may be more time for one-on-one teaching. A new employee will get in on the ground floor at a small, budding company and will experience less organizational red tape. However, large companies usually— but not always—provide a more secure financial base. Recruiters who extol only the virtues of their organization are doing interviewees a disservice and will eventually be viewed negatively by the students.

▲ *The General Work Atmosphere in Your Group.* Encourage candidates to ask pertinent questions of your employees and urge your employees to give candid, forthright answers. How do the workers feel about themselves, their group, their jobs, their management, and their company? Are they content, happy, and challenged, or are they just putting in their time as they look for a way out?

The advantages of painting a true picture for interviewees should be obvious, but one important and perhaps more subtle advantage is that there will be few unpleasant surprises later on, either for the new hire or for the company. This should result in better selection and lower turnover. When a new employee leaves after a year or so because the job or the organization were not as they were presented, the company loses money, its reputation becomes slightly tarnished, and the employee gets off to a bumpy start in his career.

Handling the Process

Take detailed notes during each interview and write your recruiting report as soon as possible after your visit (preferably during the plane ride home). After talking to ten to twenty students, your impressions of them as individuals soon blur, especially after you get back to the work that has piled up on your desk. See Figure 3 for a representative completed on-site interview form, Figure 4 for an example of a trip report, and Figure 5 for a completed evaluation form after a candidate's visit to the organization.

Send copies of your interview trip report to appropriate personnel department people and to relevant R&D departments. This gives the students more job opportunities within your company and helps the overall R&D organization meet its needs.

Easing the Pain

As a representative of a corporation and as an ethical professional, your first concern should be for the well-being of the students you consider as candidates. They often are naïve and vulnerable, and are heavily dependent on your commitment to act in good faith. If you lose a candidate, you simply go on to the next one. If a candidate doesn't get a job or makes the wrong choice,

Figure 3. Completed on-site interview form.

UNIVERSITY Excel U.   **INTERVIEWERS** Brown/Oz **DATE** 9/8/91

NAME Mary Jones   **PHONE: B-** 222-222-2222   **H-** 333-333-3333

HOME ADDRESS 9876 Student Drive, Collegetown

	SCHOOL	YEAR	GPA	MAJOR	MAJOR ADVISER
B.S.	Winfred U.	1989	3.7/4.0	Chemistry	None
M.S.	Excel U.	1991	3.5/4.0	Physics	Williams
Ph.D.	Excel U.	exp.1995	3.9/4.0	Physics	Williams

THESIS SUBJECT Effect of gamma rays on thixatropic suspensions

PROFESSIONAL INTERESTS & CAPABILITIES Any areas of industrial physics; has worked with variety of instruments.

PUBLICATIONS & RELEVANT EXPERIENCE Dean's List, 3 publications; spent summer at Physics, Inc.

MISCELLANEOUS Is an expert mechanic (Williams told us that his car broke down on the freeway while transporting some students to a seminar and Mary got under the car and fixed it on the spot).

FACULTY RATING & REMARKS Top 10% of graduate students; started slow but is a fast learner. Williams' best student;

INTERVIEWER'S RATING & REMARKS A winner: A- to A; personable, smart, alert, good communicator; bring in when she's ready to start interviewing.

Figure 4. Sample interview trip report.

Trip Report by Brown & Oz, Excel U., 9/8/91

We interviewed 14 Ph.D. candidates at various stages
of development. Two should be brought in for in-depth
interviews. Excel U.'s program continues to be
strong; good crop of students.

<u>Mary Jones:</u> BS Chem '89 Winfred U. MS '91 Excel U.
in physics under Williams. PhD expected '95 in phys-
ics/Williams. GPA consistently over 3.5 out of 4.0
Thesis: Effect of gamma rays on thixatropic suspensions. Prefers industry. Spent summer at Physics Inc.
Smart, alert, personable, good communicator. Williams' best student. Was a slow starter but has grown
rapidly in recent past. We rate her A or A-. Bring
her in.
<u>Sandy Watts:</u> BS mechanical engineering '88 Castle U.
PhD expected '93 in M.E. under Tibbs. Above average
grades. Excellent lab worker. May prefer academic
position. Good communication skills. Above average
but not the clear winner Jones is. Deserves a chance
to show his stuff, so will bring him in for interview
early November. Tibbs gave strong recommendation. Has
tough thesis problem. We rate B+.

---

it can have a negative impact on his or her career and perhaps even on his or
her life.

Interviews understandably are stressful times for students, so it's important that you help them relax as much as possible. Not only does this help the
candidate but it also gives you the best chance to see the real person. The more
hospitable, courteous, and respectful you are toward interviewees, and the
more genuine interest you show in them, the better your chances will be. At
this stage of their careers, most students are short on self-confidence, at least
during the job-hunting process. If they feel really wanted by your group, that's
the direction toward which they will lean.

Here are specific steps you can take to make a candidate feel genuinely
wanted:

▲ When an individual flies in for an interview, meet his plane at the gate
   instead of letting him find his own way to the hotel.

Figure 5. Completed candidate evaluation form.

CANDIDATE: Sandy Watts **INTERVIEWER** Joe Watson **DATE** 11/14/92

COMMENTS ON SEMINAR:

Excellent. Complex problem but his approach was sound and
he's done a great deal of high quality work. Excellent
presentation skills. Was well acquainted with his field.
Answered questions well and gave good answers to
hypothetical "What if?" queries. Seemed a bit nervous at
first but that disappeared in 5 minutes.

STRENGTHS OF CANDIDATE:

Good training, good communicator (once he got going),
knows his thesis subject and his technical area in
general. Showed interest in broad areas of research.

WEAKNESSES OF CANDIDATE:

Not sure what he wanted to do with his early career. Seemed
shy and somewhat withdrawn at first.

GENERAL COMMENTS:

Said he may take academic position.

RANKING (10 BEING HIGH)   1 2 3 4 5 6 7 8 (9) 10

WOULD YOU RECOMMEND HIRING? (YES) NO LOOK AT OTHERS
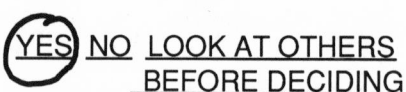
                                            BEFORE DECIDING

- ▲ If appropriate, invite the candidate to your home.
- ▲ Take him back to the airport when the interview is over; that's an ideal time to have a wrap-up conversation.
- ▲ After an interview trip, write the candidate a letter of acknowledgment and appreciation for taking the time to talk with you. Obviously, the letter should be personalized, not a form.

During interviews at a graduate school, encourage students to do most of the talking. Otherwise you learn little about them, and they may feel cheated out of a chance to present themselves and their qualifications. You can get your message across about the organization and about some of its scientific work by presenting a seminar. However, unless you take the time to prepare and do a first-class job, such presentations can do more harm than good.

The Best Match

Most students can be placed in three categories: (1) those who are obvious winners, (2) those in whom you definitely are not interested, and (3) those who deserve a chance for an in-depth interview. It's relatively easy to deal with the first two groups; the third category tends to get short-changed. Invite these students to your company for in-depth interviews and give them a fair opportunity to demonstrate their quality. It's usually a good investment.

If you're sure of the candidate, offer the job before she leaves; don't wait weeks or months unless it's absolutely necessary. Taking time to deliberate has its advantages, but every day's delay sends a subtle message to the candidate about your confidence in her ability. Of course, you should poll your subordinates near the end of the interview day, but if their opinions are unanimously positive, there's no need to wait unless you have more candidates for the same position. The main beneficiaries of hospitable, courteous, and respectful behavior are not the recipients, but the people who practice it. You grow and become a better manager—a better person—when you develop such habits.

If you see a poor fit because you can't offer what the candidate apparently wants, say so. If he is of modest quality and would, in your opinion, fit best in a company that is less technically oriented, tell him that (not necessarily about the quality, but at least about the fit). Candor and genuine concern usually elicit candor and appreciation in return. In one case, a candidate who didn't fit at the time of her original interview was encouraged by the recruiter's complimentary remarks and reapplied several years later. She was then accepted, to the benefit of all.

Starting Salaries

Managers often try to hire new employees at the lowest possible salary. To me, this is a serious mistake because it sets a "we-they" tone to the relationship. In contrast, if the neophyte sees her manager striving to get her as high a starting rate as possible, the stage is set for trust and positive motivation.

Some managers use the excuse that aggressive starting salaries are unfair to established employees, but there are three pieces of logic that refute such a contention: (1) minimizing starting rates places *not one extra nickel* in the pockets of veteran workers; on the contrary, (2) increases in starting salaries create pressure to make equity adjustments for established employees; and (3) the higher a person's initial rate, the less pressure there will be for his first merit increase. This, in effect, enlarges the size of the merit-increase pie for all employees.

For example, if a manager starts a new technician at $15.50 per hour rather than $15.00, there will, in effect, be 50 cents more to "play with" come merit-increase time—to the benefit of all department members. Obviously, starting salaries cannot run amok, and a manager must pay close attention to the interworker fairness issue.

The Long Haul

A snowball effect applies to recruiting, particularly when the scientific discipline is underpopulated. As you gather a cadre of high-quality people from strong programs, especially when they are enthusiastic about their jobs, your chances of hiring more of the same improve considerably. However, try to recruit from a variety of schools and disciplines, because diversity of backgrounds is important.

Considering the shortage of graduate students in many scientific disciplines, R&D managers must convince *their* management of the need for a long-range recruiting program. In many fields, top candidates receive numerous offers six to twelve months before graduation. In some years, the crop is lean; in others, the harvest may be bountiful. This necessitates flexibility in budgeting and hiring practices.

When you call graduate schools to set up an interviewing schedule, emphasize that you want to talk to as many students as possible, not just those who are about to graduate. A cornerstone of any long-range recruiting program is to get acquainted with individuals early in their graduate careers.

▲▲▲▲▲

If possible, resist the temptation to hire someone about whom you're less than enthusiastic but whom you need because you are getting desperate. The good ones are worth waiting for; a mismatch or mediocrity means big trouble down the road for all concerned.

Remember also that for candidates with a family, you are recruiting (and therefore responsible for) the entire family, not just the candidate. Does the spouse need a job in your geographical area? Are they parents and therefore concerned about the quality of the school system? Are there any special housing concerns (a reputable real estate agent and financial institution)?

The personnel department of your company can provide valuable assistance in the process of recruiting and hiring, and wise managers will develop a close working relationship with these professionals. They can be especially helpful in the areas of corporate regulations and legal fine points, and usually can find shortcuts in the hiring system when you're in a hurry. Some managers involve corporate recruiters in visits to graduate schools, while others feel that their presence makes student interviews less personal and more formal, official, and intimidating.

▲▲▲▲▲

Recruiting is a tough, frustrating, and demanding activity, but if you believe that your success as a manager is achieved through the efforts of your people, you have no choice but to be committed to this vital task. As Henry Kissinger said, "The absence of alternatives clears the mind marvelously."

Reference

Drucker, Peter F. *Management: Tasks, Responsibilities, Practices*. New York: Harper and Row, 1974.

Chapter 14

Motivating Your Employees

We know nothing about motivation. All we can do is write books about it.

Peter Drucker

In a sense, Peter Drucker is right: there are more misconceptions than accurate perceptions about what motivates people, especially among managers. For example, Kenneth Kovach ("What Motivates Employees?") describes how thousands of supervisors (including those in R&D) listed, in order of descending importance, what they thought motivated their employees. The results were as follows:

1. High wages
2. Job security
3. Promotion
4. Good working conditions
5. Interesting work
6. Personal loyalty of supervisor
7. Tactful discipline
8. Full appreciation for work done
9. Help with personal problems
10. Feeling of being in on things

However, when their employees were asked the same question, the list looked quite different:

1. Interesting work
2. Full appreciation for work done
3. Feeling of being in on things
4. Job security
5. High wages
6. Promotion
7. Good working conditions
8. Personal loyalty of supervisor
9. Tactful discipline
10. Help with personal problems

Clearly, as managers, we need to learn more about motivation and what is important to the people who report to us.

In spite of Drucker's apparent disdain for books about motivation, we cannot throw up our hands just because the topic is complex. It *is* important and it *is* relevant. We can begin by reading what social scientists have to say, then try to integrate that information into our behavior as managers, and do the best we can.

For example, Harold Leavitt, in his book *Managerial Psychology*, offers three generalizations with which most experts agree:

1. Human behavior is not random, it is caused.
2. Behavior is internally motivated.
3. Behavior is always directed toward some goal.

Strictly speaking, managers do not and cannot motivate subordinates. The best they can do is provide the stimuli to which employees react, driven by their own internal motivation. However, since each person is a unique, complex individual, the idea of managers stimulating employees into desirable performance (with a nondiscriminating supervisory cattle prod, if you will) strikes a discordant note. Instead, you need to create a fertile work atmosphere—one that will allow each worker to capitalize on his or her unique motivational make-up, thus ensuring optimum freedom, growth, and productivity.

In his book *Motivation and Personality*, psychologist Abraham Maslow hypothesized a hierarchy of needs that classifies human motivation. Arranged according to priority, they are:

1. Physiological (hunger, thirst)
2. Safety (security, stability, predictability)
3. Belongingness and social integration (companionship, being part of a group)
4. Esteem (self-respect and recognition and respect from others)
5. Self-actualization or self-fulfillment (each person's drive to move toward being the very best of which he or she is inherently capable).

The list is an oversimplification, of course. Our needs are not so clearly separated; they overlap and intertwine. Also, some needs fall between categories: the need to know and understand is not always necessary for safety, but knowledge and understanding can make threats to one's security seem less dangerous.

According to Maslow, our most basic needs—the physiological ones—are the most important; but once satisfied, they no longer motivate and the next higher set becomes operative. Love means little or nothing to a starving person, but a recently sated individual who is assured of the next meal clearly is not motivated by more food.

Because most technically trained employees are not starving or threatened by anarchy, the motivations with which R&D managers should be primarily concerned, according to Maslow, are (1) belongingness or social needs, (2) esteem; and (3) self-fulfillment (although job security becomes very important during hard times). This is supported by Kovach's study as well. The top three employee concerns were interesting work (self-fulfillment); full appreciation of work done (esteem); and a feeling of being in on things (belongingness). Furthermore, it is in the best interests of both the organization and its employees to have people operating at their highest possible motivational level. Social science experiments have shown that people operating at higher motivational strata work more effectively and efficiently.

How does a manager create an organizational environment wherein employees' higher-level needs will be met? Let's look at each.

Case Study: The Management Picnic

For many years, the collective management of an R&D organization sponsored an annual weekend picnic for employees and their families. Each management person was assessed his or her share of the cost, and management made all the arrangements. Nonmanagement employee involvement was only in planning the games and bringing a covered dish. Attendance steadily declined over the years, especially among the technicians. What was the problem?

1. Lower-level supervisors resented the levying of an assessment without having a choice.
2. Lower-level employees felt patronized and left out of the planning.
3. A cordial, family-type outing was in stark contrast to the environment at work; management was directive, arrogant, and separated from laboratory workers.

A perceptive employee explained the technicians' lack of interest: "They are made to feel essentially worthless on the job; why should we expect them to come to a picnic—on their own time, yet!—and be further demeaned in front of their spouses and children?"

Several years later, after significant changes in management, all employees began to feel like first-class citizens. Planning for the picnic was turned over to a workers' committee, with only a few management people participating (attending as members of the group, not as management representatives). Members of management were no longer assessed for cash contributions. Since employees now felt this was *their* outing, interest and participation soared.

Social Needs

Managers can facilitate a strong group spirit by emphasizing the importance of group accomplishments and cooperation, as opposed to concentrating on individual achievement, which encourages competition. More important, if managers shine the spotlight on subordinates rather than on themselves, and if they subjugate their own needs to those of their employees, they will be setting a "giving" tone in the department rather than a "taking" one—and giving brings people together. In addition, managers can encourage group social events such as luncheons, picnics, and award ceremonies. But let the employees plan and execute these social events; otherwise their value may be lost (see the case study on the facing page).

The Need for Esteem (Recognition)

Everyone needs and wants respect, both as a person and as a contributing member of a work group. A good technical manager will make sure that all employees are recognized for their *efforts*, as well as for their accomplishments, because of the many disappointments characteristic of research. Furthermore, in an R&D group, managers must recognize that technically trained people (no matter what their educational level) are less likely to regard themselves as subservient to management—a justifiable view, considering the extent of their training and education.

This point of view need not be a source of contention; rather, it should be viewed as a positive situation calling for mutual respect. The wise R&D manager will have respect—and show it—for *all* employees, no matter what their station. Respect leads to increased self-confidence, which translates into growth, improved performance, and reciprocal respect and trust.

In addition to esteem from others, people also need self-esteem. Although recognition from others fuels self-esteem, there's more to it than that. Self-esteem comes from a sense of independence, uniqueness, and accomplishment; it was best defined by Anne Bernstein ("Feeling Great (about Myself)") as an "accumulated sense of competence." People's basic sense of self-worth stems from their childhood, especially from their relationship with their parents and other significant people. Children develop self-esteem if they: are valued for *who they are*, not just for *what they do*, and if they feel understood as individuals.

Psychologist Carl Rogers (*On Becoming a Person*) supports this view for adults as well as children. If employees feel that their manager values them for who they are and is not always sitting in judgment of them, self-confidence, growth, and productivity will be high.

The Need for Self-Fulfillment

Although this is the most nebulous and complex human need, it is the level at which people perform best. Managers seeking excellence should focus particular attention here. Actually, the task is not as intimidating as it may seem, because in a healthy, supportive work environment this drive tends to become naturally dominant. Because self-fulfillment, by definition, cannot be directly stimulated by someone else, the key here is for managers to allow employees considerable control over their jobs as well as their pace and direction of growth. Once again, it means managing with a light touch. It is an especially fruitful area for R&D managers because scientists, having already demonstrated considerable drive in getting an advanced education, usually move easily into this motivational category, given half a chance.

▲ ▲ ▲ ▲ ▲

These needs are particularly interdependent. For example, the more self-fulfilled people feel and the more respect from co-workers they sense, the better they will feel about themselves. Such individuals will tend to be more concerned about others, will be more social, and will be more focused on group welfare. The manager who is successful in helping employees feel good about themselves will see a strong family-type spirit develop month by month. In many respects it is like watching a garden grow.

Creating a motivating environment is not a simple task; it takes talent, determination, ingenuity, dedication, and stamina. Why? Because giving subordinates more responsibility and (especially) more freedom usually involves (1) resisting a natural tendency to overcontrol and (2) "bucking" the traditions and systems inherent in most organizations.

Neither of these is easy. Still, leaders who seek excellence have little choice because they cannot change their employees. Psychologists aver that a person's basic personality is in place by age 6 or 7! Thus Harold Leavitt (*Managerial Psychology*, p. 3) reminds us, "Managers, unlike parents, must work with used, not new, human beings—human beings whom other people have gotten to first." Little wonder that leaders who strive to improve productivity are advised to tinker with the work environment, not with subordinates.

Abraham Maslow once said that "when the only tool you have is a hammer, you tend to see every problem as a nail." Managers who rely only on their organizational authority to "motivate" employees will be no more successful than a carpenter who tries to build a house with only a hammer. The world of R&D management is a complex Looking-Glass World full of complex people; there is more than just nails out there. In the two chapters that follow, we look at some of these complexities and how R&D management, with an understanding of people's needs, can motivate workers to achieve personal and professional growth.

References

Bernstein, Anne C. "Feeling Great (about Myself)." *Parents Magazine*, September 1982.

Kovach, Kenneth A. "What Motivates Employees? Workers and Supervisors Give Different Answers." *Business Horizons*, vol. 30 (September-October 1987).

Leavitt, Harold J. *Managerial Psychology: An Introduction to Individuals, Pairs, and Groups in Organizations*. Chicago: University of Chicago Press, 1978.

Maslow, Abraham H. *Eupsychian Management: A Journal*. Homewood, Ill.: Irwin-Dorsey, 1965.

———. *Motivation and Personality*, 2nd ed., ed. Wayne G. Holtzman and Gardner Murphy. New York: Harper & Row, 1970.

McGregor, Douglas. *The Human Side of Enterprise*. New York: McGraw-Hill, 1960.

Rogers, Carl R. *On Becoming a Person: A Therapist's View of Psychotherapy*. Boston: Houghton Mifflin, 1961.

Chapter 15

Fostering Employee Growth

Life is more than just reaching our goals. As individuals and as a group we need to reach our potential. Nothing else is good enough.

Max DePree, *Leadership Is an Art*

The purpose of learning is self-improvement. It qualifies a man to do his present task with continually wider vision, continually increasing competence, and continually rising demands on himself.

Peter Drucker, *Management: Tasks, Responsibilities, Practices*

Fostering the growth of their subordinates is a crucial responsibility of R&D managers. It not only fulfills a primary duty to the organization by increasing productivity and developing future leaders, but also discharges one of the manager's major obligations to society and to the individuals. Indeed, Tom Peters, in an article in the *Arizona Daily Star* (April 4, 1989), lists "lifelong learning and development for every employee" as one of management's survival requirements for the 1990s.

R&D managers have a special obligation, because so many of their subordinates, by obtaining a college education, have demonstrated both a high capacity and a strong desire for growth. Furthermore, since most technologies are characterized by rapid change, the viability of a technical organization rests heavily on new products and new technology, the development of which depends on growing, innovative employees.

How do managers foster the growth of their subordinates? Certainly this is a complex, if not mystifying, task. As popular author Robert Fulgham (*All I Really Need to Know I Learned in Kindergarten*) cautions us, "Remember the little seed in the plastic cup. The roots go down and the plant goes up and nobody really knows how or why, but we are all like that."

Managers who strive for excellence in nurturing subordinates must (1) understand people so that their efforts will harmonize with the realities of human nature; (2) understand the learning process in order to ensure the optimal rate of growth; and (3) apply that understanding on the job with diligence and patience. Let's examine these three components.

Understanding People

What human characteristics are most relevant to the learning or growing process?

▲ *Desire to Grow.* People are, in many important aspects, the same. In each of us, there is an inherent tendency to move toward psychological health and maturity. As psychiatrist-author Willard Gaylin (*Rediscovering Love*) has said: "Human beings have innate pleasure in a sense of growth and improvement." We all want to learn and grow, to try new things, to experiment with life. But if change is forced upon us, especially at too rapid a rate, we resist it. If external pressure to change persists, we become disoriented and retreat to a less advanced psychological state, seeking shelter in familiarity. We also regress when we perceive that we are in a hostile atmosphere—for example, if we are constantly criticized by others, especially by our boss.

▲ *Personal Freedom.* All adults prefer to be in control of their own situation as much as possible; this is especially true in the workplace. The more we have to say about what we do, about how and when we do it, and about the direction and pace of our personal growth, the better we feel about our situation and the faster and surer we progress. There are obvious limitations to this freedom on the job, but most experts agree that management errs too often on the side of controlling others.

▲ *Uniqueness.* People are very different from one another. We are all unique individuals, as varied as our fingerprints. We each have different needs and distinct ways of satisfying those needs. We vary greatly in the intensity and direction of our motivation and interests, in our skills and abilities, in our capacity for growth, and in the rate at which we grow. The human organism is extremely complex; each adult personality reflects a unique combination of heredity and environment.

Furthermore, we treasure our individuality and strongly resist attempts by others to depersonalize us. Managers who attempt to be fair and impartial by treating all subordinates alike deprive them of their uniqueness. Much worker belligerence toward management can be characterized as—to borrow a phrase from Herman Wouk—"assertion of a threatened identity."

Harold Leavitt (*Managerial Psychology*, p. 11) has said it well: "People are different to the extent that they are subject to different kinds of stimulation, that they vary in kinds and degrees of motivation, that they behave in many different ways to achieve many different goals, and that they have different sizes and powers in their physical equipment."

Understanding the Learning Process

What does an R&D manager need to know about the learning process?

▲ Learning can be *cognitive*, as in memorizing multiplication tables or the date World War I began; or *experiential*, as when riding a bicycle or working effectively in groups. Most learning is a combination of the two, especially in technical organizations, where cognitive scientific knowledge must be integrated with a wide variety of experiential skills.

▲ Personal growth is best achieved experientially. Carl Rogers, in *Freedom to Learn for the 80's*, defines the elements involved in experiential learning as (1) primarily self-initiated, involving the entire person, physically, intellectually, and emotionally (simply put, we learn best when we are ready and want to learn); (2) pervasive, making a difference in the attitudes and behavior of the learner; (3) self-evaluated, in that the learner is the one who decides whether the learning experience is meeting his or her needs; and (4) comprehensive, so that total (intellectual and emotional) meaning is experienced by the individual.

David Johnson and Frank Johnson (*Joining Together*, p. 7) agree with Rogers, stating:

> You learn best when you are personally involved in the learning experience. . . . Knowledge has to be discovered by yourself if it is to mean anything to you or make a difference in your behavior. . . . A commitment to learning is highest when you are free to set your own learning goals and actively pursue them within a given framework. . . . Experience alone is not beneficial; you learn from the combination of experience and the conceptualization of your experiences.

Applying That Understanding

How can R&D managers go about creating a fertile environment for their subordinates? The analogy Abraham Maslow (*Eupsychian Management*) uses is of the farmer:

> The good farmer simply throws out seeds, sets up good growing conditions, and then gets out of the way of the growing seeds most of the time, helping them only where they really need help. He doesn't pull up the sprouting seed to see if it's doing all right; he doesn't twist it, or train it or shove it around or put it back in the soil, or whatever. He just leaves it alone, giving it the minimum necessary help. . . . The good leader is . . . like the farmer, not so much in training or molding or forcing or shaping people, but in offering them good growing conditions and in either supplying them with seeds or bringing out their own inner seeds and then permitting them to grow without too much interference.

Managers have the responsibility of following their own experiential pathways, depending upon the kind of people they are and the type of organization they are in. However, here are general guidelines:

1. *Manage with a light touch.* Because of the complexity and individuality of people, the only way to ensure that each person moves in a positive direction—and at an optimum rate—is to entrust responsibility to the individuals themselves to the greatest extent possible. Albert Einstein said it well: "This delicate little plant [the holy curiosity of inquiry], aside from stimulation, stands mainly in need of freedom; without this it goes to wrack and ruin without fail." Managers need to avoid overmanaging. The social science data (see Rensis Likert) shows persuasively that loosening the managerial reins results in increased productivity and growth. Some managers are concerned that a light touch will result in chaos; not so. If you trust your subordinates, the result is more—not less—orderliness.

2. *Set a good example.* The value of a role model in experiential learning cannot be overestimated. If managers conduct themselves with honor and dignity; if they accept others as they are rather than try to change them into what they think they ought to be; if they treat others with trust, respect, decency, and civility; if they display thoughtfulness and concern; and if they are genuine, committed, candid, encouraging, and amiable; then they will find their employees growing a great deal—learning from a splendid teacher without ever realizing they are "in school."

3. *Get to know subordinates as individuals.* What are their strengths and weaknesses, their dreams and desires? What is their background—where are they now and where do they want to go in their careers? This takes time and effort, but managers cannot treat people as individuals if they don't know them individually.

4. *Involve employees as much as possible.* Ask employees to take part in decisions about their work environment and their future within the organization. Don't be like the boy scout who helped an elderly man across a busy street, only to find that he didn't really want to go!

5. *Encourage risk taking and creative thinking.* Reward those who innovate and avoid criticizing mistakes. As the saying goes, one word of encouragement during a failure is worth a whole book of praise after a success.

6. *Don't underestimate your employees' potential.* I have a reputation as a manager who sets high performance standards for myself and my group. Likewise, I have high expectations (in the good sense) for each of my employees. In spite of my inherent optimism about people, I have often been surprised by the extraordinary growth and achievements accomplished by many individuals. I thought they were *really* good, but they proved to be even better than I imagined. So, *never* assume employees have gone as far—personally and professionally—as they can go. Always assume they can be even better; encourage them to try, then do your damnedest to help them succeed. You'll seldom be disappointed, and often you'll be pleasantly surprised.

7. *Consider overall personal growth.* Chris Argyris (*Personality and Organization*) emphasizes that when people learn a new skill or ability, it needs to be integrated into their "already existing personality make-up"; otherwise, the

skill "will never be effective and will always be a source of tension and anxiety." Thus, management cannot demand changes by fiat. Employees cannot be trained in new skills if those skills don't ultimately harmonize with their basic interests. Thus, as part of the hiring process, management must pay attention to a candidate's capacity for growth and flexibility.

8. *Expect setbacks.* There is, in all human beings, a dynamic balance between growth and regression. Sometimes we move ahead, sometimes we slip back. Abraham Maslow (*Motivation and Personality*) says that anything that increases fear and anxiety tends to push us back. Consequently, a manager can foster growth by minimizing fear and anxiety in the workplace.

Good R&D managers do not try to change their subordinates in order to improve performance; rather, they tinker with the work environment, which in turn enables people to improve themselves. A sculptor twists, chisels, and shapes an image while a farmer just plants seeds, provides good growing conditions, and enjoys the fruits of that labor. For managerial excellence, the message is clear: be a farmer, not a sculptor.

The Manager as Helper

Keeping psychologist Abraham Maslow's words about the farmer and the good leader in mind, it is natural to ask, What is the minimum necessary help a manager should give an employee? When should he or she give it? The answer to the first question is complex, since it depends on the situation, the employee, and the manager. Let's take a look at each in turn:

▲ *The Situation.* What are the likely outcomes of the situation? What will be the impact on the employee, the department, R&D, and the corporation? If the consequences of failure are dire and irreversible, the manager should intervene and provide more help earlier. But if this is not the case, the employee can be given more leeway. No one enjoys being called on the carpet for a subordinate's failure, but in the long run allowing occasional small-to-moderate mistakes for the sake of growth increases efficiency, productivity, and creativity, and also provides a much higher chance of success.

Managers should resist their natural tendency to become involved in every situation. If they seldom criticize and develop a reputation for trust, helpfulness, and good communication, the subordinates will welcome—even initiate—frequent interaction. This tends to reduce the overall incidence of mistakes and failures without hindering employee initiative and growth.

▲ *The Employee.* Obviously there is a difference between an employee who is a neophyte and one who is a veteran: the latter is given more freedom. In addition, the subordinate's talent and desire for independent action, along with the quality of his or her judgment, should be considered. Managers must likewise consider the present emotional state of their employees. If employees are over their Plimsoll* line, any attempt to coach or teach should be post-poned.

As Robert Sampson (*Managing the Managers*) asks, "How do you help another most effectively? . . . You accept him for what he is and what he wants to do in developing himself. You identify with him and understand his viewpoint, respect his individuality, and help him grow."

▲ *The Manager.* Managers need to determine how sure they are that their employees really need their help. Are they capable of giving the employee the particular help he or she needs, or would someone else be of more use?

Some managers lack the self-confidence and flexibility to allow mistakes; they are directive and detail oriented. This approach may, at first glance, reduce minor errors, but it will stifle growth, creativity, and productivity. Jacques Lemaire, former coach of hockey's Montreal Canadiens, said, "We had guys [who were afraid] of making a mistake because it might put them on the bench. But any player who's afraid of making a mistake isn't going to want the puck. And not wanting the puck is the biggest mistake of all."

Likewise, insecure managers are usually poor helpers, since they see people as threats. True superstars (but not always the average professional) in sports and the arts usually help others because they are not afraid of being overshadowed by a neophyte. Julius Erving, Chris Evert, Walter Payton, Beverly Sills, and Helen Hayes come to mind. Don't be afraid to share your knowledge.

When to Help

While it is difficult to determine what the minimum necessary help should be, deciding when a manager should give help is simple: wait until you are asked. This approach works beautifully because it is based on a universal truth about human nature: people are most likely to accept, benefit from, and appreciate assistance when they *desire and perceive a need for help*. Contrast this to the usually strong resistance and resentment that comes when it is manage-ment who decides a person needs assistance.

Waiting to be asked for your help, however, may be very hard to act upon—or, rather, to *not* act upon. It takes a great deal of self-discipline to refrain from helping when you perceive a subordinate is having a problem. It is natural for you to want to help, but it is even more natural for the employee to prefer doing it himself.

If you exercise sufficient self-restraint in such situations, you will be rewarded four ways:

1. Subordinates will grow more rapidly and thus perform better.
2. You will gain their respect and confidence.

---

*The Plimsoll line is a mark on the side of a ship above which the vessel cannot be loaded or it will capsize with the first strong wind. A person over his or her Plimsoll (or "Plim") line is overstressed and in disequilibrium—a sign for management to lighten the load or at least handle with care.

3. You will find them asking for your help much more often because it will be their idea, a profound difference.
4. You will move closer toward managerial excellence.

For those situations where a manager perceives that an employee needs help but does not request it, the best approach is to offer but add quickly, "You decide what to do and whether or not you want my help." Then be willing to shrug off rejection if necessary. In the right work environment, employees will feel comfortable rejecting or accepting your offer because they know it was made out of concern for them (a desire to see them do well) and *not from a lack of confidence in them*. Furthermore, employees will be certain that you will not take the rejection unkindly, because they know that you prefer subordinates to be as independent as possible. The irony here is that by not forcing help on your employees you actually provide maximum assistance, helping them to become more mature and independent.

Figure 6 is a simple analogy involving concentric squares and circles. The innermost square represents an employee's present capabilities, the smallest circle depicts her present operational space, and the outermost square represents the best she can possibly be. As she grows, it is your responsibility to enlarge her job and her operational freedom to the next level so that she never feels crammed or restricted but still operates within her "safe" zone. Success here necessitates that you become adept at estimating your employees' capabilities and matching them with current and proposed projects, but remember, we all tend to underestimate the potential of others. How well this process works is a valid measure of your competence as an R&D manager. After all, it

Figure 6. Employee capability and potential.

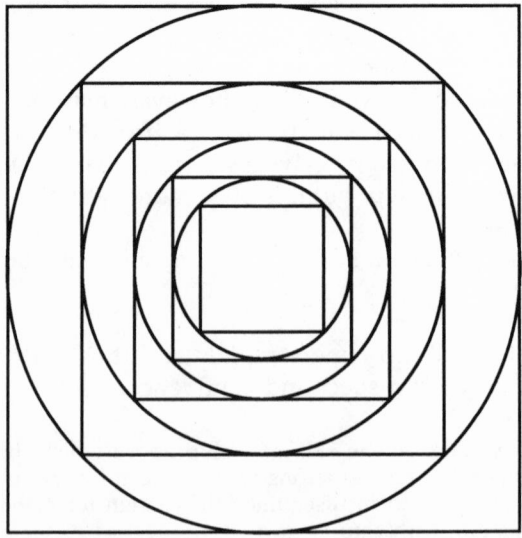

is in the company's best interests to develop each employee to the limit of his or her abilities, and managers should be partly judged on how well they develop people.

Help Via Proactive Management

In some situations, an R&D manager should become more proactive as a helper. For example, you can stimulate employees to learn by enthusiastically supporting their efforts to improve themselves, including taking courses or even working toward advanced degrees in science or management. You can go further and encourage those with less initiative to take advantage of educational opportunities so long as that encouragement stops well short of becoming pressure.

An R&D manager can also become active at the other end of the spectrum and press the corporation for significant financial support for external education. You can also institute informal sessions to discuss interpersonal subjects as well as how to improve the work environment. These sessions should *not* be lectures; they should be entirely voluntary, open to employees at all levels within the group. In addition, you can encourage advanced-degree scientists to give in-house technical courses for technicians on company time, if possible. Again, attendance should be voluntary.

The Manager as Teacher

The R&D manager should create a "helping" atmosphere—one where group members are comfortable admitting they need help, willing and eager to help each other, and not afraid to refuse help or make mistakes. When management frowns on mistakes, they tend to inhibit helping, learning, and growing actions.

For any teaching to be effective, you need to know *what* to teach (so that you don't just pass along shopworn theories or misinformation) and also *how* to teach.

What to Teach. In addition to the technical or functional factors associated with a particular R&D job, the manager's primary agenda for instruction ought to be such things as individual and organizational growth or improvement and the necessity for continuous learning. In such matters you are the role model, the tone-setter. It's crucial that all employees improve their interpersonal skills; performance failures in technical organizations are caused more often by interpersonal problems than by technical deficiencies.

How to Teach. It's best to have laboratory employees (rather than yourself) instruct others on the technical or functional factors of an operation. This fosters the growth of both teacher and pupil, increases their sense of community, and reduces their dependence on management—all desirable outcomes. Furthermore, employees are more qualified than management to do technical teaching since they are more up-to-date scientifically and more familiar with operational details.

This leaves you free to concentrate on personal and organizational growth. One-on-one and group discussions are helpful, especially the former. But since personal growth primarily occurs experientially, a manager can best teach such things by example and by creating and maintaining a fertile work environment.

All attempts to coach or teach should place major emphasis on the learner, not the teacher. Winston Churchill once said, "Personally, I am always ready to learn, although I do not always like to be taught."

Effective managers will probably experience periods of discouragement, as their subordinates need and want less and less of their help. But take heart, because that proves your employees are growing and becoming more independent.

In any group, the first person in need of an education is the leader. At minimum, managers need to learn about themselves, about others, and about the intricacies of interpersonal relations—no small task. But if they are interested in excellence, they must learn much more than the minimum; they need to become lifelong scholars. Helping, coaching, and teaching will not be effective without continual managerial learning—on the job, at seminars, and through management and social science literature.

References

Argyris, Chris. *Personality and Organization*. New York: Harper & Brothers, 1957.

DePree, Max. *Leadership Is an Art*. East Lansing, Mich.: Michigan State University Press, 1987.

Drucker, Peter F. *Management: Tasks, Responsibilities, Practices*. New York: Harper & Row, 1974.

Fulgham, Robert L. *All I Really Need to Know I Learned in Kindergarten*. New York: Villard Books, 1988.

Gaylin, Willard. *Rediscovering Love*. New York: Viking Press, 1986.

Johnson, David W., and Frank P. Johnson. *Joining Together: Group Therapy and Group Skills*, 2nd ed. Englewood Cliffs, N.J.: Prentice-Hall, 1982.

Leavitt, Harold J. *Managerial Psychology: An Introduction to Individuals, Pairs, and Groups in Organizations*. Chicago: University of Chicago Press, 1978.

Likert, Rensis. *New Patterns of Management*. New York: McGraw-Hill, 1961.

Maslow, Abraham H. *Eupsychian Management: A Journal*. Homewood, Ill.: Irwin-Dorsey, 1965.

———. *Motivation and Personality*, 2nd ed., ed. Wayne G. Holtzman and Gardner Murphy. New York: Harper & Row, 1970.

Peters, Tom. "Firms May Be Dancing Last Macho Tango." *Arizona Daily Star*, April 4, 1989.

Rogers, Carl R. *Freedom to Learn for the 80's*. Columbus, Ohio: Charles E. Merrill, 1983.

Sampson, Robert C. *Managing the Managers*. New York: McGraw-Hill, 1965.

Chapter 16

Building Subordinates' Self-Confidence

If I am not for myself, who will be for me?

Hillel

I thought I was actually fighting for my own self-worth; that is why I so desperately wanted people to like me. I thought their liking me was a comment on me, but it was a comment on them.

Hugh Prather, *Notes to Myself*

Self-Confidence Leads to Higher Productivity

One of my daughters had an interesting behavior pattern as a child. If told she had five minutes to get ready for something, it would take her a half-hour. But if informed that she had a half-hour, it would take her five minutes. The explanation? Under severe time pressure, she became flustered and, not knowing what to do first, would stumble over herself in haste. With adequate notification, however, she was able to quickly do what had to be done.

▲ ▲ ▲ ▲ ▲

Red squill is a plant extract once used as a rat poison. It was considered relatively safe around children because its local emetic properties caused humans to void the poison if accidently ingested before any damage to health occurred (rats cannot vomit).

Some African cultures used red squill to determine the guilt or innocence of accused wrongdoers and, simultaneously, to punish the guilty. The suspect was handed a single pill of red squill to ingest. According to legend, the innocent would survive the poison but the guilty would die.

The apparent magic was actually pharmacologically sound and philosophically clever. Since all members of the tribe believed in the infallibility of this judicial system, if the person was in fact innocent, he would swallow the entire dose at once, confident that he would be vindicated. If guilty, the culprit apprehensively nibbled at the deadly threat. The innocent individuals, thanks to the sudden and severe challenge to their stomachs, safely vomited the pill, while the guilty slowly accumulated a lethal systemic dose because small bits do not cause emesis.

▲ ▲ ▲ ▲ ▲

Warren Bennis tells this story: A teacher asked an eight-year-old what he was doing. The student responded, "I'm drawing a picture of God." The teacher replied, "But we don't know what God looks like." And the student explained, "We will when I'm finished."

▲ ▲ ▲ ▲ ▲

What do a flustered offspring, a rat poison in the hands of African tribesmen, and an eight-year-old artist have to do with managerial tasks? The common thread is *self-confidence*. Given a half-hour to get ready, my daughter moved about confidently and efficiently. The eight-year-old was confident that God's likeness would be known once his drawing was completed. Most dramatic, the innocent African's confidence in his own righteousness ensured his survival.

One of management's basic responsibilities is to help subordinates gain self-confidence. This task is closely allied with fostering the growth of employees and with helping and teaching, which were discussed in Chapter 15.

Realistic Self-Confidence

Helping other people feel good about themselves is a fundamental responsibility for all of us, in the workplace or outside of it. However, why is it so important to management? Here are some reasons:

1. Self-confident employees perform better because they are decisive rather than tentative. Being relatively free from worry and fear, they are better able to focus their energies on the job at hand. They are confident things will go well, and they almost always do, Murphy's law notwithstanding.

2. Social scientists say there is a basic difference between coping behavior and expressive behavior. Simply put, *coping behavior* is trying to catch up when we are behind; *expressive behavior* means we are ahead and pulling away. Self-confident people are risk-takers; they exhibit expressive behavior. They are not afraid to try new things and thus are able to learn, grow, and innovate. Risk-taking is especially crucial for technical organizations, whose lifeblood is new products and new technology.

3. When people feel good about themselves they are better able to help others do the same. When workers feel respected, they are more likely to

respect others; when they are trusted by their colleagues and management, they reciprocate.

In an article in *Parents* magazine (Sept. 1982), Anne Bernstein helps us understand the roots of self-confidence: "Children will come to value themselves as they have been valued by the significant people in their lives." Bernstein goes on to emphasize that the beginnings of self-esteem reside in early infancy. When a baby cries and gets a response from his or her environment (a feeding of milk, a changed diaper, a warm embrace), he or she develops a feeling of *efficacy*: "The experience of being able to make things happen, to obtain relief through one's own efforts. . . . leads to an accumulated sense of competence." An accumulated sense of competence is an excellent definition of self-confidence.

Self-confidence is not sufficient, however; it must be *realistic* self-confidence. Only when people have an accurate perception of their abilities and potential will major errors be kept to a minimum while they try new and challenging tasks. Authentically confident individuals will stretch themselves but will seek help in strange and potentially harmful waters. This promotes cooperation and harmonious group effort—critical factors in the complex world of industrial science.

What can R&D managers do to foster realistic self-confidence among subordinates? The most relevant managerial tasks are accepting, praising, appreciating, encouraging, and reassuring.

Accepting People as They Are

We like the hardness of a rock when we need one to pound tent stakes in the ground while camping; we are far less enchanted if one is in our shoe while hiking. We are delighted with the wetness of water when we are thirsty, but we despair if a sudden shower ruins our best clothes. It is no different with people: A person's good and bad habits stem from the same basic qualities. For example, my friend's courage of conviction becomes my enemy's intransigence. Just as we have learned to accept a rock's hardness and water's wetness, so must we try to accept people as we find them.

Managers need to accept their employees by valuing them for *who they are*, not just for what they do. If you develop an acceptant attitude toward subordinates, experience shows that they will grow in both performance and self-confidence. When employees feel valued, rather than as if they are constantly "on trial," they feel safe and secure. This fosters innovation, allowing them to make mistakes without fear of retribution. A sense of security also helps people develop a realistic self-confidence because, feeling safe, they are not afraid to admit their deficiencies to themselves and to others.

Although accepting is, by definition and intuition, primarily passive, there is an active component, too. Almost every day someone does something that a manager doesn't like, or at least that he would do differently if he were doing it. At that moment a natural urge surfaces, tempting the manager to criticize or tell the employee to change (a.k.a. "my way is better").

Instead, the first part of this scenario should be the manager's conscious decision to keep quiet. He then engages in an intellectual-emotional process whereby he reminds himself that: (1) everyone is different; (2) if he were the employee, he would appreciate being allowed to do it his own way; (3) by allowing the employee to do as he chooses, the manager is confirming the worker's worth and individuality—thus he is more likely to grow both in competence and in self-confidence; and (4) by adopting this attitude and behavior, the manager is becoming a more competent and more mature person.

This experiential learning process—developing an accepting attitude toward others—is slow, hard work. In time, however, progress can be made, and the manager grows and matures in *attitude*, apart from any conscious act of will.

▲ ▲ ▲ ▲ ▲

Workers perform better—working people *are* better—when they feel good about themselves as responsible, contributing members of their work group. Toward that end, it is a manager's basic responsibility to create an organizational environment wherein employees feel accepted (prized, valued) for who they are and for what they can and do contribute to the goals of the organization.

Praising People for What They Do

The philosopher William James tells us, "The deepest principle of human nature is the craving to be appreciated." Yet most of us are very reluctant to praise others. Why should this be? It must be human nature. Many parents seldom praise their children. We hesitate to compliment our spouses and friends. And many managers find it hard to commend subordinates. Perhaps, as some have said, managers fear the net effect will be negative—that is, employees will expect wages higher than the organization is willing to pay. Certainly managers don't want to admit that they did such a poor job of hiring and are doing such a poor job of managing that their subordinates' performance is not praiseworthy!

A more likely answer is that managers are too insensitive, too busy, and too concerned with their own egos. In Kenneth Kovach's study (discussed in Chapter 14), when supervisors were asked what they thought motivated their employees, "full appreciation of work done" was eighth out of ten (but it is ranked second by employees)! But wise managers will listen to their employees, take the time to get outside themselves, and become concerned with the self-esteem of their subordinates.

Why managers keep praise to a minimum is one of the true mysteries in management, considering how simple it is to do and do well; how effective it is in improving morale, productivity, employee self-confidence, and managements' relations with subordinates; and how good it feels to be praised (managers must certainly be aware of this unless they have *never* been complimented themselves—which is difficult to believe).

Five Rules to Praise By

1. Praise *must* be genuine (deserved) or it will be detractive.
2. A spontaneous compliment tends to be the most genuine.
3. In light of rules 1 and 2, *never* suppress the urge to praise.
4. Compliments should be specific. "You did a good job in that meeting" is clearly inferior to "Your presentation in that meeting was especially clear; I never really understood that issue until then."
5. Specific praise can be expanded to laudatory (but genuine) generalizations. "That memo was especially persuasive; you surely have a way with words."

Dictionaries define praise as the act of expressing approval or admiration. The most common methods of praising are verbal and written, but if your basic attitude toward subordinates is one of "prizing" or "valuing," then nonverbal praise (showing approval) takes place any time you are together. This explains why people feel so good—so warm and safe—in the company of others who think highly of them, even when no verbal compliments are expressed.

Giving Recognition. Giving recognition is a particularly effective form of praise. There are many forms of recognition for individuals and groups, such as verbal, written, plaques (e.g., "scientist/technician/secretary of the year"), formal company awards, pictures or articles in company and local newspapers, presentations to corporate management, dinners (especially with spouses), co-authorship of internal and external publications, being picked to represent the company at special outside technical meetings, and encouragement to participate in national scientific societies. If a group has problems with recognition, it's usually because the manager hasn't creatively pursued the many available options.

Appreciating Others. Appreciation is closely related to praise, but with a slight difference that makes additional comments worthwhile. While the value of praise depends upon whether the recipient feels the compliment is deserved, it is the donor who largely determines the value of appreciation.

Case Study: Memo of Appreciation

Louis, an R&D scientist, told Martha, his manager, about the consistently fine job Rebecca, a statistician in a different department, was doing in support of their group's effort. The two agreed that a memo of appreciation to Rebecca's manager was in order. A few days later, Rebecca called Louis and Martha, saying, "It's the first time this has ever happened to me! You really made my day!"

Case Study: "Thanks for Your Help"

The duplicating department of a large corporation was efficient but understaffed. Over a period of six weeks, a user department made great demands on the duplicating staff during an important crash project. When the uproar subsided, the manager and secretary of the user department sent the duplicating staff a large box of candy, along with a formal memo of appreciation to their manager. In the past, the two had received good service, but from then on they were showered with duplicating favors.

Verbal praise and appreciation are important, but written expression has even more impact and can be kept and savored over and over. Also, copies of written acknowledgement can be sent to upper management or home to one's spouse. Of course, managers should show appreciation when it is due, not primarily to increase productivity or to gain favors from recipients but because it is the right and proper way to treat people. Otherwise, *managing* is in danger of becoming *manipulating*.

Additional Ways to Build Worker Self-Confidence

Managers can help employees become more self-confident by doing a good job of hiring—that is, by hiring competent, self-confident people who are well matched with their positions in the organization. Likewise, managers can increase group confidence by transferring or terminating poor performers. This increases group spirit, performance, and enthusiasm, because every member is a full contributor to the effort. Remember, self-confidence is an essential ingredient of good performance and personal well-being. Although it is impossible to quantify, the intensity of people's reactions to perceived threats to their self-esteem is inversely proportional to their level of self-confidence. As Anne Bernstein concludes, "Acceptance leads to self-acceptance, respect to self-respect . . . responsibility to self-reliance and cooperation."

Appreciation is Reciprocated

The following are examples of notes of appreciation received by managers. They are included here to illustrate that self-confident subordinates express their feelings to their boss, and to emphasize the tremendous impact good management can have on employee attitudes, careers, and lives:

> *"To a Terrific Boss:* You have constantly (every day for five years) challenged me to do better—you've worked hard at understanding me, what I've done, what I want to and can do. You've given me ever increasing amounts of responsibility and independence. This . . .

is something you do better than any boss I've ever had or even observed. You've contributed to something I never thought I had enough of in school, i.e., learning how to learn... while working for you, I've changed from wishing I didn't have to work (but scared not to) to really enjoying work and looking forward to planning for changes, development, and variety in my career.... Thank you for so many things."

"It's been such a joy working with you; you have a real talent for making people feel good about themselves and their work."

"Words cannot express what you've been and what you are to me. You were there when I took on my first managerial job of substance; you talked, you listened, you advised, you contended, you accepted me for what I was, you picked up on me where I was at, you taught, and carried me beyond. For the rest of my life I will remain in your debt for such a gift."

"I was sad when you left. You are truly an inspiring manager and person. You left behind a good working environment that has maintained itself. That truly says something about you. Some of my fondest memories will always include you. Thanks for everything you have done for me."

"Your management approach has resulted in a general improvement of the quality of life within and outside [name of company]. Thanks for improving the opportunities for further personal development."

"With great appreciation for your genuine human concern and the guidance, encouragement, trust, and respect you freely gave to each one of us. Thank you for enriching our lives."

In summary, employees do best if they are realistically self-confident and management helps sustain and improve their self-confidence.

Encouragement, Not Criticism

If praise and appreciation are appropriate managerial responses to a job well done, then criticism would seem to be the logical alternative when things go poorly. No so. For the wise R&D manager, the alternative to praise is not criticism but encouragement. Encouragement is especially important in an R&D organization because research, by its nature, usually involves more setbacks than successes. "One word of encouragement during a failure is worth a whole book of praise after a success."

Criticism Is Destructive

Criticism, especially when levied by one's supervisor, is *inherently* destructive, and therefore it is not an appropriate managerial activity. In fact, hypercritical managers are disappointed mostly in themselves.

An employee under constant criticism is forced to expend great amounts of emotional energy on being defensive, struggling with self-esteem, and dealing with anxiety; that energy is unavailable for productive work. Indeed, under unpleasant, critical management, the major motivation for a subordinate becomes the avoidance of pain. In addition, criticism endangers risk taking and creativity. Employees become tentative and conservative because they fear mistakes will get them in trouble with the boss.

Setting aside until later the counterargument that people want to know where they stand and therefore desire criticism (as well as praise) from their boss, the only conceivable justification for a manager criticizing a subordinate is that "constructive" criticism improves performance and fosters personal growth.

Faultfinding, especially when the critic is one's supervisor, is perceived by the recipient as external pressure to change. Yet Carl Rogers (*On Becoming a Person*) emphasizes repeatedly that external pressure to change has a decidedly negative effect: the person feels threatened and may regress, or retreat to a less advanced state. This is not to say that every time a healthy adult is criticized, the person goes into a blue funk. Rogers is talking about the *direction of change*—growth or regression—and he believes that criticism moves an individual toward regression.

If the most likely consequence of faultfinding is regression, then how can one contend that a manager should criticize subordinates for mistakes or bad qualities in order to improve their performance and stimulate growth? This is analogous to a mathematician saying that 1 multiplied by 0 is not 0, or a grade school math teacher informing his young charges that 1 plus 1 equals 3! People who insist that criticism is good for you bring to mind humorist/philosopher Josh Billings's comment, "The trouble with most folks is not so much their ignorance, as knowing so many things that just ain't so." In short, "constructive" criticism is a contradiction in terms.

External Criticism

Because managers are human, we find it difficult to abstain from criticizing, as do parents and spouses, but at least we need to recognize why we do it. The primary motivation would seem to be a self-serving, mostly subconscious one: it serves to release tension, relieve frustration, make us feel superior, and put pressure on the recipient to do things *our* way. However, as a manager you must avoid falling into the trap of thinking that your promotion into management conveys upon you a special wisdom whereby you know the best way for another human being to be or to do things.

Most faultfinding arises not from a caring, sincere desire to help the other person but from the critic's own emotional needs. The faultfinder feels better at the expense of the recipient. How, then, can you assign altruistic motives to criticism, even managerial criticism?

The primary benefit of recognizing the emotional, self-serving roots of criticism is that it will help you become more proficient at swallowing the urge to find fault. If this proficiency is accompanied by a growing appreciation of the worth of each of your subordinates, growth will occur among your subordinates as well as for you. Although swallowing that urge requires an expenditure of psychological energy (because you are internalizing something your psyche would prefer to air), you should eventually reap emotional profit from that investment as you begin to view yourself as a strong, mature leader who willingly sacrifices your own psychological comfort to help another person improve.

There will be occasions when you need to talk to a subordinate about a problem, but if your impetus is a genuine concern for the employee, and if your relationship with that person has essentially been devoid of criticism, then the subordinate, feeling psychologically safe, will most likely consider your comments as caring feedback. This case study provides an example.

Case Study: Caring Feedback, Not Criticism

Tim, an assertive, competent worker, had a tendency to antagonize coworkers because of his insensitivity and tactlessness; and this reduced his and the group's effectiveness. The problem was so severe that several veteran employees complained to Harry, Tim's manager. Harry had a close, trusting relationship with Tim, so the next time they were having a private conversation, Harry raised the subject in this way:

"Tim, something has come to my attention, and I'm sure you'd want me to pass it along to you. Evidently you're rubbing some of your coworkers the wrong way—mostly, I understand, by being too blunt and hypercritical. Tim, you and I get along fine, and you know how highly I think of you; you're a key individual around here. I know you want to be as effective as possible. I also know you'd prefer to get along well with your colleagues. I'm sharing this information—this feedback—with you as a friend, simply because I think you'd prefer to know about it."

Although he couldn't help being mildly defensive, Tim appreciated Harry's candor and concern. While Tim could not become a different person, he worked hard and was able to reduce the problem to a manageable level.

Psychologists emphasize that if one person has consistently bad feelings about some specific behavior on the part of another, keeping totally silent tends to put emotional distance between the two. This is especially true if the silent person's discomfort is sensed by the other (as it often is). In such cases, it is clearly best for their relationship if the two can discuss the problem candidly. However, progress is most likely if the complainant, rather than criticize the other person, tries to describe how he or she feels about the situation. In general, the more two people can share their feelings with each other, the better their relationship will be.

Self-Criticism

In spite of the logic, the discussion of criticism can't end at this point; faultfinding is too much a part of our lives to be dismissed out of hand. Fortunately, psychologists have supplied the answer. For example, Carl Rogers (*On Becoming a Person*) says that, in light of the realities of human nature, criticism *can* stimulate growth and improve performance, but primarily if it is *self-generated*.

In most work situations, overt self-criticism is the exception rather than the rule, so the R&D manager striving to improve performance and the work environment needs to reverse that trend. How is that done? Here are two thoughts to consider:

1. Members of a group are most likely to engage in self-criticism when they have confidence in themselves and when they feel safe and secure—when they are among friends who think highly of them. Thus decreasing external criticism creates conditions favorable to self-criticism.

2. Frequent faultfinding by the leader tends to generate defensiveness, alibis, and lower self-esteem among members of the group, as well as increased finger-pointing. Thus, a decrease in managerial criticism, coupled with an increase in managerial praise and encouragement when appropriate, should boost self-confidence and lower incidences of group faultfinding and buck passing.

Some managers will scoff at this, pointing out that their own subordinates seldom engage in self-criticism. Such skeptics reveal themselves as leaders who probably find fault so frequently that their employees have little choice but to defend themselves by circling their psychological wagons. Remember, criticizing is not a managerial responsibility but a human foible.

Some managers will argue that employees actually welcome criticism from their boss because they prefer to know where they stand. Consistent personal experience says otherwise; this reasoning seems akin to suggesting that people like to sit on tacks because it feels so good when they get up. Social scientists dispute that people *really* want to hear a litany of their faults, but the best rebuttal is that, under good management, employees *do* know where they stand: they are highly valued and, as responsible adults, they have the responsibility for criticizing themselves.

It should be emphasized that whenever I discuss mistakes in this book, I am referring to errors other than life-threatening or corporation-threatening ones. Mistakes of this latter magnitude require more drastic measures to prevent or correct, but should be dealt with individually. Even then, managers must remember that they are dealing with the realities of human nature.

Encouraging Words Produce Results

Nothing captures the essence of high-quality, person-oriented management quite so clearly as the substitution of encouragement for criticism. Managers know they have a caring, acceptant, prizing attitude toward others when their automatic response to mistakes is one of empathy or sympathy followed by words of encouragement, as opposed to anger and then criticism.

Encouragement is the proper way to treat other human beings. It also makes sense pragmatically for four reasons:

1. Managerial encouragement leads to a psychologically safe work environment.
2. An atmosphere of encouragement leads to more self-analysis by all group members, *including the manager*.
3. In a safe, fertile work environment, self-analysis leads to self-criticism, and self-criticism leads to self-improvement.
4. Self-improvement leads to greater productivity and stronger group morale.

To summarize, the R&D management task is to encourage (defined as "inspiring with courage, spirit, and confidence"). Wise, caring, person-oriented R&D managers want their subordinates to do well, mostly for the employees' sake (although managers have a stake in employees' success too). In that same vein, they grieve for the employees when they do poorly or when they are struggling; and they want to do *something* to lift their spirits and give them heart. The most effective "something" is encouragement, along with help if the employee so desires.

Encouragement is one of the more poignant and uplifting words in our language—poignant because it exhorts people to have courage, as if life were a struggle (and for many of us it is), yet uplifting because the encourager is reminding the disheartened one that the struggle need not be faced alone.

More than any other managerial activity, encouragement comes in a broad range of intensities since, in most people's lives, troubles come in all sizes. However, the magnitude of the encouragement offered should be inversely proportional to the size of the difficulty. Someone in deep trouble is not yet ready to climb mountains, so encouragement has to be dispensed softly and gently; mild, empathic encouragement is most compatible with the modest expectations that are an inherent part of intense discouragement. Encouragement can be much more exuberant if the recipient is only slightly discouraged, because there are still mounds of self-esteem with which to fuel yet another foray.

The Power of Reassurance

In his book *Uncommon Friends*, James Newton describes an incident that serves as a perfect example of the power of reassurance:

> When Thomas Edison was working on improving his first light bulb, he handed a finished bulb to a young helper, who nervously carried it upstairs, step by step. At the last moment, the boy dropped it. The whole team had to work another 24 hours to make another bulb. Edison looked around, then handed it to the same boy. The gesture probably changed the boy's life. Edison knew that more than the bulb was at stake.

Reassurance is defined as, "restoring to assurance or confidence," and the justification for including it as a managerial task is supplied by Robert Tannenbaum (Berkeley Report 137) and Robert Sampson (*Managing the Managers*). In a study involving business executives, Tannenbaum found that two-thirds to three-fourths of the executives revealed feelings of personal inadequacy and doubt; Sampson reports similar results in his work. These were successful people by any corporate standard. If top management is in need of reassurance, why not the rest of us?

Despite Tannenbaum's and Sampson's research, one may think that mature adults ought to be able to go through life without requiring constant reaffirmation of their basic worth, without needing continual reminders of others' regard. However, social science experts and our own experience tell us differently. We *all* need as much reassurance as possible from those around us—family, friends, co-workers, and especially supervisors. Although different individuals have different needs, the more reassurance a person receives, the more secure and confident he or she will be, translating that confidence directly into greater personal growth and better performance on the job.

Anyone who doubts the need for continual reassurance should think of a wedding. In our society there is no more overtly expressed personal commitment than marriage. Yet what spouse, no matter how self-sufficient, would long be content with a single "I love you" on that wedding day, never to hear those words uttered again? On the contrary, successful marriages exist on daily reassurances, verbal and nonverbal.

The more important someone is to us, the more frequently we need signals from that person that all is well in our relationship. In the workplace, the immediate supervisor is by far the most important person, so it follows that reassurance from that person is a very important managerial task—especially in R&D, where disappointments often outnumber successes.

While reassurance overlaps other managerial tasks already discussed (praise, appreciation, and encouragement), it is also different. In fact, people wanting to improve all of their relationships would do well to concentrate on giving others increased reassurance, especially when a strong need is perceived. And when is that? Whenever that other person appears discouraged, upset, angry, anxious, distant, or unsettled. The universal antidote for bad vibes is reassurance, no matter what the cause of the difficulty and no matter how complicated the situation. This may be an oversimplification, but not by much.

Rules to Reassure By

Reassurance is not only a tool for strengthening a relationship, it makes the recipient feel better, and that should be reason enough to use it. Remember, however, that if overdone, the beneficiary may feel patronized. Here are some tips:

1. To be effective, any particular managerial activity must be part of a consistent behavior pattern. This is especially true of reassurance. An isolated burst of activity, especially when it is incongruous to the relationship *as the employee perceives it*, is likely to be received negatively.

2. The reassurance should be realistic. For example, if an employee's sense of well being is seriously threatened by a personal disaster (e.g., the death of a spouse), trying to convince him that everything will be all right is obviously inappropriate. At such a time, he needs sympathy, understanding, and caring; reassurance comes later when he is in a better position to accept it.

3. Reassurance is most effective when it addresses the recipient's area of anxiety. For example, in Toscanini's later years, a woman performer approached him after a concert and said, "Maestro, how handsome you looked tonight!" which pleased him greatly. Toscanini was well aware of his ability as a conductor, so perhaps a compliment in that area would have been far less effective than one involving his personal appearance.

4. People like to be praised for what they do well, but they *need* reassurance in areas where they have doubts. Either tell them that they are making progress toward minimizing a deficiency or else indicate that it is of little consequence (nobody is perfect).

5. Reassurance is best done empathetically—when you can see things from the other person's point of view and can identify with those feelings.

6. The ability to give reassurance depends heavily on developing an attitude of forgiving—with good humor—the mistakes of others and of substituting a sympathetic pat on the back for a disapproving frown.

7. To give reassurance, you must be a mature, secure person.

Reassurance Works Wonders

The next time your boss is upset with you, try substituting reassurance for defensiveness; you will be pleasantly surprised by the result. Here reassurance consists of an apology: "I'm sorry I erred" or, at least, "I'm sorry you're upset." Couple that with a nondefensive attitude and other appropriate verbal reassurance.

The apology reassures because it acknowledges your boss's right to be upset. A nondefensive attitude reassures because it tells your boss that your relationship is healthy enough to handle his or her anger without a similar response from you. Finally, verbal reassurance might include a pledge to learn from the experience.

Some managers fear that if their response to most errors is limited to reassurance and encouragement, employees will get the impression that mistakes are of little consequence. There are two replies to that justifiable concern:

1. People's normal tendency is to feel too guilty when they err. As Abraham Maslow (*Eupsychian Management*) says, "Even the normal member of our culture feels unnecessarily guilty or ashamed about too many things." Thus, in a safe environment, the chances of employees taking their mistakes too lightly are small.

2. If people do not recognize the severity of their mistake, they *should* be informed; that's basic courtesy on the part of the manager. But it should be done in a reassuring manner, for example: "Yes, it was a serious error, but I'm sure the foundations of the corporation will survive. Besides, if you were perfect, you'd make the rest of us look bad."

The following two case studies prove the effectiveness of reassurance.

Case Study: Concerned About Me, Not the Machine

John Crowell was an R&D technician who performed assays on an expensive piece of equipment. Soon after being trained he made an error in setting up the unit, causing several thousand dollars worth of damage when it was turned on. His manager, Herbert, heard about the incident and made a point of dropping in on John at his laboratory. "John," Herbert began, "I know you're feeling bad right now, but try not to worry too much about the accident; I'm just glad you weren't hurt." He then proceeded to describe a similar incident that happened to him many years earlier. By the time Herbert was finished, John was obviously touched—his eyes had misted over—and he said, "Herbert, you seem to be more concerned about my feelings than you are about the machine."

Case Study: How Could I Be So Stupid?

Norman, a mature, confident R&D scientist, was not overly sensitive to criticism. However, when a top executive showed displeasure at one of Norman's errors during a meeting, the latter became defensive and tried to explain, making matters worse. Later, his mentor, who was present at the meeting, took him aside and counseled, "Norman, I discovered long ago that the best way to deal with criticism is to say, 'You're right; how could I be so stupid?' As soon as I say that, the other person stops being upset, says, 'Oh, it's not *that* bad,' and immediately tries to make me feel better."

References

Bernstein, Anne C. "Feeling Great (about Myself)." *Parents Magazine*, September 1982.

Kovach, Kenneth A. "What Motivates Employees? Workers and Supervisors Give Different Answers." *Business Horizons*, vol. 30 (September-October, 1987).

McGregor, Douglas. *The Human Side of Enterprise.* New York: McGraw-Hill, 1960.

Maslow, Abraham H. *Eupsychian Management: A Journal.* Homewood, Ill.: Irwin-Dorsey, 1965.

Prather, Hugh. *Notes to Myself.* Moab, Utah: Real People Press, 1970.

Rogers, Carl R. *On Becoming a Person: A Therapist's View of Psychotherapy.* Boston: Houghton Mifflin, 1961.

Rogers, Carl R., and Barry Stevens. *Person to Person: The Problem of Being Human.* Lafayette, Calif.: Real People Press, 1967.

Sampson, Robert C. *Managing the Managers.* New York: McGraw-Hill, 1965.

Tannenbaum, Robert. "New Approaches to Stresses on the Job," *University of California Institute of Industrial Relations, Berkeley Report # 137,* 1964.

Chapter 17

Evaluating Professional Performance and Potential

The words *criticizing* and *evaluating* are considered synonyms in the dictionary; both imply analyzing for merits as well as for deficiencies. However, in common usage, *criticizing* has donned a negative cloak while *evaluating* has retained its relative neutrality. If I'm evaluating you, the jury is still out, but if I'm criticizing you, I've already decided you're guilty.

The managerial task of evaluation involves four interrelated functions, listed below in decreasing order of importance and effectiveness.

1. *Evaluation of the manager by subordinates.* The inclusion of this, especially as the first priority, may come as a surprise. However, as stressed by Douglas McGregor, in his book *The Human Side of Enterprise*, "any individual's performance is, to a considerable extent, a function of how he is managed." Also, managers have more control over themselves than over others. Consequently, improving managerial performance by having employees candidly assess their boss is the most productive use of this managerial task. (For example, 3M once had formal evaluations of managers by their boss, their peers, and their subordinates. A comparison of the three sets of perceptions can be particularly valuable.)

2. *Self-evaluation by the manager.* Former U.S. Senate Chaplain Peter Marshall's prayer is sufficient comment here: "Lord, when I am wrong, make me willing to change. When I am right, make me easy to live with."

3. *Helping subordinates to evaluate themselves.* This assumes they will ask their manager to help, and in a trusting environment they will.

4. *Evaluation of subordinates by the manager.* This is of value, but only if the above three are given higher priority.

Let's discuss these four activities in greater detail.

Evaluation of the Manager by Subordinates

Most employees are understandably reticent to criticize their bosses, especially face-to-face. Therefore, as manager of an R&D department, call the group together and say,

> "My boss reviews my performance each year, but the best judges of how well or how poorly I do my job are sitting in this room. Only you *really* know how effective or ineffective a manager I am. Just like you, I am interested in improving myself, but to do that I need your help. Let me suggest one way; if you think it unwise, or if you can think of a better approach, please speak up."

Then follow this simple procedure:

1. Ask them to comment, in writing, on (1) what they like about their job, (2) what they don't like about their job, and (3) what they feel you, as manager, can do to improve the work situation.
2. Have them submit their comments to the department secretary, who then will combine the answers (including the secretary's) and give the collated results to you. It's vitally important to preserve anonymity.
3. Review the comments, then call another meeting to discuss the results. Ask the employees to help you decide priorities and how best to implement their suggestions. Encourage everyone to enter the discussion. If possible, decide on a time frame for the changes to emphasize their importance.
4. Implement as many of the improvements as possible. *This is the most important step of all.* If you do little or nothing, the entire exercise will have a negative impact.

Assuming success, expand the procedure the next year to include all departmental supervisors (including laboratory scientists who supervise a technician), provided they wish to be evaluated. Encourage workers to comment on any departmental supervisor, even though they don't report directly to that person; this increases the breadth and quality of the feedback and helps ensure anonymity. It's important that the secretary give comments on a particular supervisor only to that person. Stress that you consider their evaluations as their business, and that you don't want to see them unless the individual wants you to.

In subsequent years, more detailed questions can be added. For example:

> "Do you see any unfair situations in our group? Please list them, in decreasing order of importance."
> "Do you have adequate growth or advancement opportunities?"
> "How would you rate your work environment: excellent, good, fair, or poor? Why?"

"Are you treated with respect and courtesy?"

"Are you given clear directions as to what is expected of you?"

"Does your supervisor show interest in you as an individual?"

"Does your supervisor take advantage of you to advance his career?"

"Do you get proper recognition for your efforts and accomplishments?

"Does your supervisor share the credit and glory with you, or do you hear only about the failures?"

"Does your supervisor criticize you often? How fair or unfair is he or she in this respect?"

"Is your supervisor pleasant to you most of the time?"

"Do you feel you are an important, integral part of the organization or just a pair of hands doing someone else's bidding?"

"Does your supervisor and management in general keep you informed about what's going on?"

"Do you have enough interaction with your supervisor? If not, how can this best be remedied?"

"Does your supervisor listen to your point of view and give serious consideration to your ideas?"

"Please add any other comments and concerns."

How well this attempt at upward evaluation succeeds depends on the maturity of the managers and supervisors and on how much employees trust their management. If the first attempt goes poorly because group members are not candid, that's a clear sign that an evaluation of management is badly needed. This exercise is guaranteed to increase trust as long as management makes a sincere attempt to respond to employee concerns. A hidden benefit of such a survey is educational: It starts group members thinking about these important matters.

When management is thus evaluated, it is the employee *perceptions* that matter; whether those perceptions are accurate is less important. In contrast, in downward evaluations it's the *accuracy* of the manager's perceptions that is important. Note that in both cases the manager holds the power. That is—

▲ In upward evaluations, managers are most concerned with subordinates' perceptions; this helps them use their power *wisely*.

▲ In downward evaluations, managers are most concerned with the accuracy of their own perceptions; this helps them use their power *fairly*.

Self-Evaluation by the Manager

A major goal of every organization is improvement of managerial performance. Since management is, by definition, a human relationship (a manager with no one to manage is not a manager), it follows that one major route toward improving managerial performance is for R&D supervisors to become more proficient in human relations. To do this, we need to learn more about ourselves and others to find out why we do the things we do. Being better informed, we can then deal with the realities of a situation.

A major problem in business is that managers often pressure others to change into what they would like them to be; equally bad, they pretend they are something they are not. As Peter Drucker (*Management: Tasks, Responsibilities, Practices*) says, "Above all . . . managers need to know much more about themselves, for most managers are action-focused rather than introspective." As the saying goes, "Thinking is like loving and dying. Each of us must do it for himself."

Management self-evaluation is important because when managers improve their leadership skills, they also improve group performance. Likewise, when subordinates see a manager concentrating on self-evaluation and self-criticism instead of worrying only about subordinates' performance—when they observe him striving for his own excellence rather than just preaching excellence to them—that really becomes contagious. This process requires continual self-examination, but each manager's improvement is under his or her direct control. Experiencing self-improvement is at least as satisfying as observing it in others—usually it is more so.

This story, which actually came to me in the mail, is appropriate:

> On the executive floor of a major company is a curious room. In it is a comfortable chair. That's all. No desk. No telephone. No computer. The emptiness of this room might lead one to conclude that nothing of any great importance happens here. To the contrary, its one and only function is vital: This is a "quiet place" where people come to *think*. Well thought-out judgments rarely come from a mind caught in a whirlwind of activity. It's difficult to keep a balanced perspective on where we are and where we're going if we allow everyday pressures to absorb every moment of every day.

Although most of us regard quiet time as nonproductive, we all need time to contemplate, to put everyday events into long-range perspective. This reflection relates closely to the managerial task of planning. Here are some questions to ask yourself during the process of self-evaluation:

"Are my short-range objectives compatible with the R&D organization's and the corporation's long-term needs?

"Are my long-range goals still appropriate, or should they be modified?"

"Am I still hiring the right kinds and mixes of people?"

"Do my employees feel challenged, or do they see themselves as burned-out and dead-ended?"

"Is the laboratory equipment becoming obsolete?"

"Is the department's reputation and morale beginning to suffer from experimental failures?"

"How is the group doing in the overall scheme of things? Is it on the cutting edge, or is it in danger of becoming irrelevant?"

"Am I proactive or reactive?"

Positive personal development on the part of managers depends greatly on their ability to increase their awareness, understanding, and acceptance of themselves and others. Every manager needs to continually assess his or her performance and progress. Here are some additional questions; you can add your own as needed:

"Am I taking things too seriously?"

"Am I getting outside myself enough so that I can concentrate on the needs of my subordinates?"

"What did I do wrong in that meeting yesterday—the one where several people read me the wrong way?"

"Am I a good communicator? Do people grasp what I'm saying or am I often misunderstood? More important, do I *really* listen to others?"

"Am I starting to sacrifice my basic principles in order to make points with the "top brass"? If so, what must I do to get back on track?"

"Now that I've been promoted, am I more distant from my subordinates?"

"Do I like myself as a vice-president as much as I did as a first-line supervisor?"

"How do I appear to friends and colleagues in my new position? Do they still respect me and value my opinions or do they feel that this promotion has caused me to inflate rather than grow?"

"Am I spending too much time on the job?"

"Am I biased toward old friends in the group to the detriment of newer workers?"

Case Study: Self-Evaluation Reveals a Pattern

On occasion, Sallie, an R&D manager, had considerable difficulty dealing with tough personnel matters; at other times she did very well. In those sessions where difficulties arose, her subordinates seemed overly defensive and less cooperative than usual. At these times, the topic under discussion was seldom resolved and the situation often worsened.

One day, while struggling with this puzzle during a quiet, reflective moment, Sallie realized that every one of the problem sessions occurred in the late afternoon. She had recognized for some time that she was a "morning person"—during college days she always did her best studying in the early morning hours—but she had never connected that phenomenon with her work situation.

Following this insight, Sallie began to schedule such meetings in the morning, and she also suggested to her subordinates that they would find her more pleasant and receptive if they deferred heavy subjects until the following morning when feasible. The problem with her subordinates, *which was really her problem*, essentially disappeared.

"Do I challenge the conventional wisdom often enough? I don't want to get caught in the trap described by Civil War historian Bruce Catton, concerning a wasted battle in Charleston Harbor for Morris Island: 'a place of no consequence, lying at the end of one of those insane chains of war-time logic in which men step from one undeniable truth to another and so come at last to a land of crippling nonsense.'"

Instead of trying to determine exactly where you are concerning a particular characteristic (e.g., impulsiveness vs. spontaneity), it's best to look at the two extremes and determine at which end ("too impulsive" "not spontaneous enough") you usually fall. Then in a specific situation, you're probably better off choosing the option further from that extreme.

Helping Subordinates to Evaluate Themselves

Self-evaluation by subordinates is the next priority. This is much less threatening—and therefore much more effective in fostering improvement—than external evaluation by the boss. Psychologist Carl Rogers (*On Becoming a Person*) avers, "Moral or diagnostic evaluations are always threatening." In fact, self-evaluation might be what employees really want when they ask where they stand. They want their manager's help in determining for themselves where they are as a person and as a performer. However, this activity works only if the employees are confident that their manager is on their side and is not trying to trap them into confessing their sins.

In stark contrast to the usually harsh, adversarial, and judgmental tone of an external evaluation, this shared exercise can be pleasant and supportive. The manager does what he or she can to reassure the subordinates and, if invited, helps the employees gain additional insight into themselves and their performance.

The major reasons self-evaluation works far better than external evaluation are:

1. People are constantly evaluating themselves. That's basic human nature; it's part of our attempt to grow, improve, and feel good about ourselves.
2. If a manager negatively assesses a person in a way that is significantly removed from that individual's self-image, such an assessment will be rejected forthwith, with adverse consequences for the relationship.
3. If a manager's assessment of a deficiency is consistent with the employee's self-image, then by definition the employee is already aware of the problem.

If managers offer understanding and encouragement rather than criticism during the self-evaluation session, subordinates will have more emotional energy available for making personal improvements. Managers can also contribute by reinforcing the positive items in a subordinate's self-evaluation and giving the employee additional feedback and insight on both positive and negative items.

Like many complex managerial tasks, "stimulating" subordinates into self-evaluation is difficult. Probably the most effective way to do so is to let subordinates see you trying to improve your own performance—self-evaluation then becomes contagious. Increasing your praise and reassurance of subordinates is another way to create an atmosphere conducive to self-evaluation. But perhaps the most direct stimulation blossoms as a sidelight, when manager and subordinate are sitting quietly and discussing how things are going. By assuming the role of interested helper/advocate and asking soft, supportive, and helpful questions during a relaxed, friendly, nonthreatening session, you can often stimulate the subordinate into examining his or her attitudes,

---

Case Study: Helping a Subordinate in Distress

Betty, an articulate, friendly, and outgoing intellectual, had been with her organization for about six months. She was an energetic, capable individual who had excellent rapport with Horace, her manager. One day Betty dropped in to see Horace and confided that she was in considerable distress. Hard as she tried, she felt estranged from her co-workers, and the more she attempted to mend fences, the more antagonistic they became. Did he have any words of wisdom for her?

Horace replied as follows:

"Betty, let me share with you what I had to learn the hard way. For the first several years, I was always trying to convince the others that I was a quality person, a good performer, and therefore belonged in the group. I think I came on too strong, and it was a long time before I really felt accepted as a bona fide member of the group.

"In retrospect, I realize that, instead, they needed affirmation from me that I regarded *them* as quality individuals. I'm sure I would have done better had I concentrated more on *their* needs rather than on my own. But remember, you and I are different people, so you'll have to decide for yourself if this might work for you. I'd appreciate hearing how it all comes out."

Betty, realizing that she was making the same mistake Horace had made years ago, tried essentially the same remedy Horace suggested, and, thanks to her considerable energy and interpersonal talents, soon became an accepted member of the group.

feelings, and behavior concerning the issues being discussed—*but only* if you are genuinely trying to improve the employee's situation and insight into himself. In other words, if a helpful and caring attitude comes through, the process works; but manipulation doesn't.

Any attempt at evaluating must prove *helpful* to the employee, to the manager-subordinate relationship, and to the group; otherwise, the attempt is a wolf in sheep's clothing and something is fundamentally wrong with the situation.

Evaluation of Subordinates by the Manager

This final phase of evaluation flows directly from the first three—that is, as an R&D manager, you first need to learn how employees view you so that your evaluations of them are put in proper context. Second, after you have carefully looked at yourself you will be able to empathically and accurately evaluate your subordinates. Third, in the process of assisting your employees with their self-examination, you will learn a great deal about them, enabling you to do a better job of evaluating them yourself.

There are four primary reasons why you need to continually assess the performance, capabilities, and interests of your subordinates:

Case Study: Placing an Employee in a More Appropriate Job

Rocco, a scientist, was rated average by two successive supervisors. Most of his assignments were short range and involved tight, companywide timetables. The quality of his work was usually high, but his reports were often late. He definitely was the weak link in the otherwise smooth flow of multidepartmental projects.

When Audrey, a new manager, arrived she quickly recognized that Rocco's slow, deliberate style was quite incompatible with the timing demands of his duties. She also noticed that time pressures tended to unsettle him, occasionally causing the quality of his work to suffer.

With Rocco's enthusiastic concurrence, Audrey assigned him a different set of responsibilities in the group's basic research area; because of his technical excellence, she asked him to consult for other groups within the R&D organization. Protected from the tyranny of the clock and encouraged by Audrey's high regard for him, Rocco's innovative talents and scientific soundness blossomed. Within five years he was earning outstanding ratings and had advanced to the highest job category available to scientists within this major corporation. Rocco thanked Audrey for her great gifts to him— renewed feelings of self-worth and self-confidence.

---

1. As a supervisor, your primary responsibility is to remove the situational and organizational obstacles that prevent employees from doing their best, and your ability to do that job well depends heavily on an accurate assessment of each individual.
2. Most individuals have contributions to make that go well beyond the specific responsibilities of their jobs. Productivity and overall group excellence will soar if you and the group can identify and take advantage of these additional talents.
3. One of your basic obligations—to both subordinates and the corporation— is to look for and then take advantage of promotional opportunities for your subordinates or, as sometimes happens, to solve a performance problem by skillfully placing an individual in another position that will be more harmonious with his capabilities.
4. Accurate evaluation is, obviously, an integral part of any formal performance review. Performance reviews are discussed in more detail in the next chapter.

It should be evident that the evaluation process is a circular rather than a linear stream. Accurate, thorough, and caring evaluation of subordinates can help managers evaluate themselves (what is my culpability, if any, in the performance problem this employee seems to be having?) as well as help them do a better job of assisting their subordinates with their self-evaluation (how can I best help this person see for himself what I have just learned about him?). Evaluation is best viewed, not as two people sitting down together and consciously examining one another's merits and deficiencies, but rather as a gradual process—a getting-to-know-one-another relationship; a gentle, amiable proceeding that flows out of working together in a respectful, trusting environment.

References

Drucker, Peter F. *Management: Tasks, Responsibilities, Practices.* New York: Harper & Row, 1974.

McGregor, Douglas. *The Human Side of Enterprise.* New York: McGraw-Hill, 1960.

Rogers, Carl R. *On Becoming a Person: A Therapist's View of Psychotherapy.* Boston: Houghton Mifflin, 1961.

Chapter 18

Formal Performance Reviews

Moral or diagnostic evaluations are always threatening.

Carl Rogers, *On Becoming a Person*

You cannot strengthen a man's weaknesses, for too often they are the result of anxiety or limited capacity, and all you will do is add to his anxiety.

Robert Sampson, *Managing the Managers*

The typical formal performance review is similar to a trip to the dentist: There is apprehension before, pain during, and a sense of relief after the session. This is true for both the reviewer and the reviewee.

It doesn't have to be that way. When done well, performance reviews can be a pleasant, enjoyable, rewarding, and productive experience for both individuals. The interaction a manager has with a subordinate should improve the latter's well-being and performance; if it doesn't, something is seriously wrong. Let's first look at what's wrong with traditional performance reviews and then see how to conduct them properly. Throughout this chapter, notice that empathy is the manager's most valuable asset.

The Argument Against Performance Reviews

Douglas McGregor (*The Human Side of Enterprise*) questions the value of formal performance appraisals as they are usually structured and conducted. Following are his specific objections and then my comments, some illustrated with a case study. Since quotations out of context can distort meaning, McGregor's remarks should be consulted in the original source as well.

Administrative Use of Performance Reviews

Performance appraisals are used for administrative purposes—to determine "salary administration, promotion, transfer, demotion, and termination."

1. Different Values and Styles

McGregor:	"The answer given by an appraisal form to the question: 'How has *A* done?' is as much a function of the superior's psychological make-up as of the subordinate's performance."
Comment:	We all tend to look at a completed appraisal form as the ultimate basis for judging the quality, performance, and potential of an individual. But McGregor's point is that the personality, values, management style, and competence of the reviewer affect the report every bit as much as the reviewee's performance! This is unavoidable, and we need to remember it when we are evaluating a subordinate.

Case Study: Different Values and Styles

Dana, a liberal-thinking veteran R&D manager, was rated average by his supervisor, Maria. Two years later, with a new boss, Audrey, but still in the same position and performing essentially the same, Dana was rated outstanding, three levels above average. The most likely reason? Maria was rigid, conservative, directive, and controlling, and she strongly disapproved of Dana's easygoing (but effective) style. In contrast, Audrey was flexible, liberal, and managed with a light tough; she viewed Dana's approach to management (and therefore his performance) as highly positive.

---

2. An Unrealistic Picture

McGregor:	"[Data from appraisals] can create a pretty picture, but one which has little relation to reality."
Comment:	For a variety of reasons, including malfeasance of duty on the part of management, the quality and performance of an individual may be misrepresented for many years.

Case Study: What Planet Were They On?

Dino, a first-line R&D supervisor, had above-average performance reviews over the years. He made no waves, followed orders, did the required paperwork, and sleep-walked his way through corporate life for about ten years. When Dino began reporting to Vince, a highly competent manager, the latter quickly recognized Dino's essential incompetence and pressed for his demotion, transfer, or termination. This caused a great uproar because the "record"—a decade of innocuous, relatively positive performance appraisals by a variety of supervisors—painted an entirely different picture.

---

3. Managers Affect Subordinates' Performance

McGregor:	"The problem of judging performance for administrative purposes is further complicated by the fact that an individual's performance is, to a considerable extent, a function of how he is managed."
Comment:	Most of us have seen ham-handed managers affect, even destroy, the well-being and performance of subordinates. Accurate judgments usually cannot be made about a problem employee's quality unless he has worked in different situations and under different supervisors (see case study next page).

Appraisals Used as Feedback

Performance appraisals are often used to tell an employee how he or she is doing.

1. Criticism Begets Defensiveness

McGregor:	"It is characteristic of human beings that they find it difficult to hear and accept criticism. Judgments which are positive can perhaps be communicated effectively, but it is rather difficult to communicate critical judgments without generating defensiveness."
Comment:	Carl Rogers (*On Becoming a Person*) emphasizes that evaluative judgments are inherently threatening; this is especially true when the judge is a person's supervisor, who holds a great deal of power over the employee.

Case Study: Poor Performer? No, Poor Management

Karen, a mid-level laboratory scientist, was in deep trouble. Termination was a distinct possibility. She made frequent errors on mundane but rush projects (her only assignments) and had a reputation for laziness. Maurice, Karen's new manager, discussed the situation with her. Karen readily acknowledged her responsibility for some of the difficulty but explained that past inactivity was partly due to a lack of assigned work and to being overweight. Her current mistakes on urgent projects were caused by her impression that speed was of prime importance and by her panic over possible termination. Karen's comments made sense to Maurice, especially because of the matter-of-fact, nondefensive way she spoke during the conversation and because she accepted her share of the blame.

After confidential discussions with others who were well acquainted with Karen's qualifications and potential, Maurice realized that the clumsy, harsh, but well-meaning style of his predecessor was a significant contributor to the problem. Karen was given a fresh start and plenty of encouragement. Maurice gave her a challenging workload of meaningful projects and told her not to worry about mistakes—just to do the best she could. Feeling valued by Maurice and no longer under ominous pressure, Karen performed enthusiastically and well; her transformation amazed her co-workers.

2. The Inverse Law of Criticism

McGregor: "In attempting to communicate criticisms to a subordinate the superior usually finds that the effectiveness of the communication is inversely related to the subordinate's need to hear it. The more serious the criticism, the less likely is the subordinate to accept it."

Comment: The inverse law of criticism makes sense from a psychological standpoint because healthy people have a positive self-image. As Robert Sampson (*Managing the Managers*) emphasizes, preservation of self-image is the fundamental motive in human behavior. When our boss criticizes us severely, he is attacking our self-image. Likewise, Chris Argyris (*Personality and Organization*) emphasizes that whenever our positive self-image is attacked, we are compelled to defend ourselves vigorously. Thus the more serious our deficiency, the more trouble we have when we are reminded of it.

Case Study: Personal Experience

Here the reader can supply his or her own case study. Aren't McGregor's comments consistent with your experience in conducting performance reviews? When you have called a subordinate to account for a serious performance deficiency, hasn't the usual reaction been defensiveness, anxiety, sullenness or morosity, and blaming others or citing extenuating circumstances? Have the results been generally positive or negative? Have such experiences brought you and your subordinate closer together or driven you farther apart?

---

3. Insistence Damages the Relationship

McGregor:	"If the superior is insistent enough, he may be able to convey his negative judgments to a subordinate, but when this happens he often finds that he has done serious damage to the relationship between them."
Comment:	All of us have been on either the sending or receiving end of a situation where a manager tries hard to prove his or her point concerning a negative judgment while the subordinate tries equally hard to refute the charge or justify his or her behavior. Invariably, the tension level increases and the conversation becomes more and more shrill; finally, the subordinate lapses into sullen silence.

Case Study: A Damaged Relationship

Patsy, a competent R&D group leader, had developed a good relationship with Neil, a talented, sensitive laboratory technician, during the four years they had been working together. Neil was always given a rating of A or A−, even while going to night school to earn a B.S. degree. Then one year Neil suffered some family setbacks while taking several difficult courses, and this affected his performance. Patsy felt compelled to rate Neil B, but the latter believed his performance was worth B+. The practical difference between a rating of B and one of B+ was inconsequential, but Neil was crushed. For many months he hardly spoke to Patsy, and their relationship remained cool for some time thereafter.

---

4. Dependence Is Accentuated

McGregor:	"[The appraisal interview] accentuates [the employee's] dependence and thus readily arouses latent anxieties and hostilities."
Comment:	Whenever an authoritative boss formally reviews my performance, I feel unsettled. It brings back vivid memories of school days when I was called on the carpet by the principal. When I am reviewing subordinates' performances, I sense their discomfort no matter how much I try to reassure them.

Case Study: Dependence Creates Bad Feelings

If your boss, even though she gives you a good overall rating, usually spends considerable time during your personal performance review chronicling your deficiencies over the past year, what are your feelings as you walk into her office for your next appraisal? Resentment? If not resentment, then discomfort? If not discomfort, then vague anxiety? Another trip to the dentist?

---

5. Do I Really Want to Know?

McGregor:	"It is an open question whether subordinates in general really want to know where they stand. . . . If the individual is not doing well, the interview will intensify [his] anxiety and make it extremely difficult for him to react realistically."
Comment:	Abraham Maslow (*Motivation and Personality*) says that the natural tendency for all of us is to feel too guilty. Therefore we hardly need—or want—reminders of our weaknesses, especially from a "judge" with great power over us. Furthermore, employees want to know where they stand primarily when the manager does *little* communicating with them; here they are trying to relieve vague anxieties by hearing some news, be it good or bad. But if the manager is, for example, a good communicator, a helper, and a reassurer, subordinates will have minimal vague anxieties.

Appraisals Used for Counseling

Performance reviews are also used as a counseling tool.

McGregor:	"To attempt to counsel in a formal appraisal interview is as much a travesty as to attempt bribery of a victim during a holdup."
Comment:	McGregor's strong words make negative case studies difficult and perhaps unnecessary. Experience tells most of us that the formal performance review is the worst possible time to counsel an employee concerning performance deficiencies, because the formality greatly intensifies the discomfort. Equally important, *counseling* is probably not the most effective choice of words for this managerial task. See the comments in Chapters 15 and 16 on helping, encouraging, and reassuring.

Concerning amateur counselors (which is what managers are), Carl Rogers says, "The most they can accomplish is some temporary change, which soon disappears, leaving the individual more than ever convinced of his inadequacy."

Case Study: The Problem Disappeared

Pete was an industrious, capable hourly technician who had a great deal of independence in determining his daily workload and schedule. His supervisor, Sylvia, recognized his competence and was civil, respectful, and deferential in her dealings with him.

There was, however, one vexing problem. In spite of their good working relationship, whenever Sylvia came into Pete's work area with an unscheduled high-priority job, he would become extremely quiet, even sullen. Since Pete always performed well, and since Sylvia was a fledgling supervisor and wasn't quite sure what to do about it, she avoided any mention of the problem for several months.

One day when the two were chatting in Sylvia's office, she mentioned a few things about herself that she wished were different. (This was an entirely innocent conversation on her part; she was not even thinking of the problem at the time). Suddenly Pete interjected,

"It really bothers *me* that I get so upset when you interrupt me with an extra job; I must get it from my dad, because he's the same way." Amiably, Sylvia replied,

"I'm sorry I have to dump those jobs on you, Pete, but they are in your area of responsibility and, besides, you're the one who will get them done

Reprinted by permission of UFS, Inc.

on time. Any ideas on how we can remedy the situation?"

This is a situation where a serious performance or behavioral problem was solved outside the formal performance appraisal process. In fact, the solution involved mostly self-evaluation and self-counseling on the part of the employee!

After Pete admitted he had no suggestions to make, an idea popped into Sylvia's mind, "Let's try this. When I give you an emergency job, why

> don't you decide when, during that day, you'd like to do it? If necessary, take overtime."
>
> With the difficulty out in the open and the situation under his control, Pete's (and Sylvia's) problem disappeared completely! For the next two years there was only one case of overtime—Pete's efficient work habits easily accommodated, as they always had, the occasional extra work.

It's not hard to predict what would have happened if, when the problem first arose, Sylvia had called Pete on the carpet (especially during a formal performance review) to tell him that he needed to change his attitude.

Appraisals Used for Motivating

Performance appraisals are used for motivating purposes.

McGregor: "[When the superior is evaluating performance in the usual manner] the stage is set for rationalization, defensiveness, inability to understand, [and] reactions that the superior is being unfair or arbitrary. These are not conditions conducive to effective motivation."

Comment: This statement speaks for itself.

Appraisals Used for Learning

Performance appraisals are used for learning purposes.

McGregor: "The semiannual or annual appraisal is not a particularly effective stimulus to learning [because] it provides 'feedback' about behavior at a time remote from the behavior itself . . . the likelihood of effective learning [from remote feedback] is small."

Comment: Based on personal experience, it's clear that discussions about behavior occurring six to ten months ago—or even a few weeks before—in an annual formal appraisal commonly result in poorly remembered facts or impressions on the part of the supervisor and a "Why didn't you bring this up at the time?" or an "Are you still holding that against me?" attitude on the part of the employee.

▲ ▲ ▲ ▲ ▲

McGregor concludes, "Certainly, the strategy of management by integration* and self-control is more appropriate for intelligent adults and is more likely to be conducive to growth, learning, and improved performance [than is the strategy behind the usual approach to performance appraisals]."

The Right Kind of Performance Review

I do not advocate doing away with formal performance reviews altogether. This is inappropriate and unrealistic. Nevertheless, the paramount question to be addressed is, How can wise management practices—and the realities of people at work—best be harmonized with an organization's formal system for reviewing performance?

If we consider McGregor's comments, the inherent judgmental nature of a formal performance review, the contention that supportive, nonjudgmental prizing of employees encourages growth and improves productivity; and the belief that the only constructive criticism is self-criticism, then the most realistic answer to this question is:

> Harmony can readily be realized, but only if the formal system is slightly adjusted to the principles and practices of good management, *rather than the other way around.*

Put another way, if most formal systems and their common application are based on erroneous assumptions about people (and McGregor's comments as well as personal experience indicate that they are), then the R&D manager interested in excellence has little choice but to adjust the formal system—

Figure 7. The synergistic relationship among performance review, performance, and work environment.

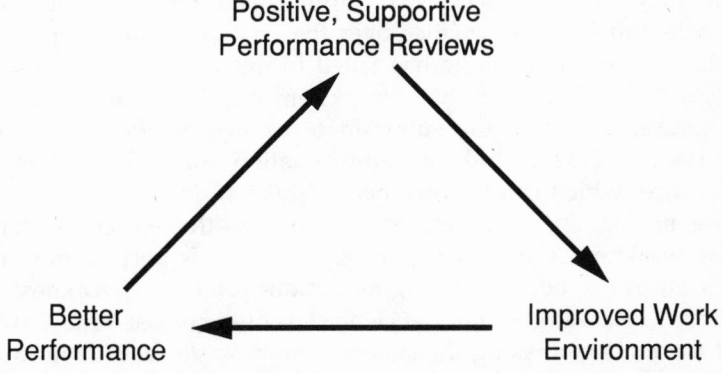

*McGregor defines *integration* as "a situation in which a subordinate can achieve his own goals *best* by directing his efforts toward the objectives of the enterprise."

within corporate rules—to be consistent with the realities of human nature.

After doing hundreds of performance appraisals over the course of thirty years, it has been my experience that the more positive, supportive, and encouraging a manager is, the better the employee's overall performance will be. The manager's primary responsibility to the organization is to optimize performance while helping employees to optimize their growth and fulfillment in the workplace. Conducting performance reviews in the right way helps fulfill both those obligations. It also creates a synergistic triangle, such as the one shown in Figure 7.

Toward that end, the following scenario is offered, not as a checklist for conducting performance reviews but as an illustration of one approach to harmonizing formal systems with the realities of human nature and good management. Like all other managerial tasks, formal performance reviews must be done by each manager within the context of the kind of person he is.

1. Well before the actual reviews, subordinates are reminded that the "system" demands a formal performance appraisal and that certain rituals must, as in the past, be followed.
2. Then the manager reminds them that he has been in close contact with each staff member throughout the year, and that consequently, there will be no surprises during the formal interview.
3. The manager assures everyone that the performance review will be a pleasant experience. (The formal review is not a good time to discuss a performance problem in depth, for reasons outlined by McGregor.)
4. The manager then holds formal reviews only when he is in a relaxed, reassuring mood.
5. When an employee first comes into the manager's office for the appraisal, the latter reiterates points 1, 2, and 3.
6. The manager emphasizes—genuinely—what a good job the subordinate is doing and how glad he is to have her in the department.
7. He then goes into specifics concerning what he likes about the subordinate and her performance over the past year. She is encouraged to add accomplishments he has failed to mention.
8. Next he reminds her that the system requires that he record some negatives and asks the subordinate to suggest what he should say. (Some systems include a self-evaluation form to be filled out in advance, which can be very helpful here.)
9. The manager then reassures—genuinely—the employee concerning any weaknesses she brings up (e.g., no one is perfect, her intentions are always good, her strengths far outweigh her weaknesses). Any further discussion of her deficiencies should consist almost exclusively of the manager asking the subordinate how *she* feels about them and, most important, where he—or her work situation—is deficient in helping her do her best.
10. He then records—honestly—the weaknesses she mentions, but puts them in as positive a light as possible (e.g., "Employee tends to complete some assignments at the last minute, but has a good sense of priorities and is always on schedule.")

11. Then—and this is especially important—the manager asks the subordinate what he can do to help her improve even more. He then sits back and listens in a nondefensive manner, thanking her—genuinely—for her candid feedback. He follows up on her suggestions if possible.
12. He sums up by reemphasizing his appreciation for her contributions to the group's accomplishments and his delight at having her as a member of the department.

When a manager softens (with reassurance) a subordinate's self-criticism during the performance appraisal, the relationship between them takes a giant step forward. This is because, to preserve our self-esteem, we each need to feel that we have good reasons for our actions. When our behavior has been seen as negative, we feel bad and guilty; then it becomes especially important to us that others at least recognize our good motives.

When employees perceive that their manager understands their good intentions, especially during the inherently stressful formal performance review, they feel both *safe* and *understood*. As Carl Rogers says, "To be understood has a very positive value to individuals." Contrast this supportive behavior with McGregor's warning about the wrong way: "If the superior is insistent enough, he may be able to convey his negative judgments to a subordinate, but when this happens he often finds that he has done serious damage to the relationship between them."

In Conclusion

Criticism should be avoided, especially in the formal performance review, where negatives tend to become magnified, because a person's desirable and undesirable characteristics all stem from the same set of psychological drives. Much like a complex mobile (touch one component and all move), a manager cannot attack a subordinate's weaknesses without endangering the individual's strengths. This is why each person is the best judge of what is inherently good for them. The following case study was presented at a management seminar.

Case Study: Leave Well Enough Alone *or* If It Ain't Broke, Don't Fix It

An aggressive, somewhat overbearing but competent worker was responsible for one area of a shipping department. One day the company president came through on a tour and got into an argument with the employee. The president was unhappy with the worker's belligerence (lack of deference to the important personage of a president?) and ordered the employee's manager to "straighten him out." The manager called the worker into his office, told him that he was too pushy and obnoxious, and warned him to shape up or else.

That solved the problem—but not really. From that point on, the

> employee was meek as a lamb on the job, but he also became lethargic in his duties and took no initiative. Needless to say, a short time later the manager needed another session with the troubled employee, this time to discuss his sluggish performance.

I do not suggest that a supervisor ignore orders from top management, nor do I condone disrespectful behavior. But if a supervisor has a good relationship with a belligerent employee, the two can discuss the situation in a nonthreatening manner and solve the problem without creating a larger one.

The approach to formal performance appraisals outlined in this chapter won't solve all the concerns associated with this process but it can minimize them. For example, how can salary administration policies or the need to document unacceptable performance prior to termination be reconciled with such an approach? Here are a few brief examples.

Salary Administration Policies. Personal experience has shown me that under good management, most employees implicitly trust their leader and recognize that person as their strongest advocate. As a result, they accept without much difficulty the unavoidable inequities caused by any salary administration system. Most certainly, we all should recognize that the usual hypercritical approach to performance appraisal does nothing to solve inequities in salary administration except to say to the employee, "Like it or lump it."

Documentation of Unacceptable Performance Prior to Termination. If managers do their jobs competently (hiring quality people and then providing them with a fertile growth environment), the majority of their performance reviews will be positive. Why adhere blindly to a harsh judgmental system that causes unjustified problems in 98 percent of the cases just to accommodate the 2 percent incidence of unacceptable performance requiring termination? That 2 percent can be dealt with on an individual basis (see Chapter 19).

References

Argyris, Chris. *Personality and Organization.* New York: Harper & Brothers, 1957.

McGregor, Douglas. *The Human Side of Enterprise.* New York: McGraw-Hill, 1960.

Maslow, Abraham H. *Motivation and Personality,* 2nd ed., ed. Wayne G. Holtzman and Gardner Murphy. New York: Harper & Row, 1970.

Rogers, Carl R. *On Becoming a Person: A Therapist's View of Psychotherapy.* Boston: Houghton Mifflin, 1961.

Sampson, Robert C. *Managing the Managers.* New York: McGraw-Hill, 1965.

Chapter 19

Transferring and Terminating Unproductive Researchers

> In all of us, rejection is likely to be perceived as an assault on our pride and self-esteem. . . . To be rejected . . . is to feel unsafe as well as unworthy.
>
> Willard Gaylin, *Rediscovering Love*

Transferring or terminating substandard employees is the toughest task in management, but it is basic to improving a group's performance, as well as fulfilling a manager's basic obligation to the corporation, to other group members, and to the transferred or terminated employees themselves.

In addition, the information in this chapter reinforces the legitimacy, if not the primacy, of person-centered management, since it proves to skeptics that this style of management is compatible with the hard decisions that have to be made when employees do not or cannot perform adequately.

Whose Problem Is It?

As suggested in Chapter 18, good hiring techniques and enlightened management techniques should keep employee problems to a minimum. Nevertheless, occasionally situations arise when an employee is not performing as required.

The following describes an approach that has worked consistently, involving many different people in a variety of technical organizations.

1. *Wait and see.* When employees are not performing up to expectations, your first attitude should be "wait and see." This gives subordinates time to iron out the difficulties themselves; they may stem from personal problems outside the workplace and may be temporary. But how long should you wait? That depends on many factors, including the current level of performance and length of service. Certainly workers who have performed well over a period of

ten years and who, even with their current problems, are still reasonably productive deserve more time than six-month neophytes who are doing poorly. Patience out of concern for an employee is laudable and recommended, but once you are convinced the issue requires managerial action, don't procrastinate.

2. *Ask what's wrong.* If the problem persists, the next step is a discussion in which you sympathetically ask if there's anything wrong and if you can help—without mentioning the performance problem. The better the relationship between you, the more candid subordinates are likely to be. At this time, you need to listen empathically and nonjudgmentally—as a friend rather than as a boss. Employees may hesitate to reply, and if their current performance is still acceptable, you should drop the subject by saying—and *meaning*—"I'm sorry; I didn't mean to pry. You seem to be troubled lately and I'm concerned about you." (This gentle approach is recommended because employees *want* to perform well; admonition or premature interference from the boss only increases the pressure and lessens the chances for a quick recovery.)

3. *Discuss the problem.* If subordinates are not successful in eliminating their problems within a reasonable length of time, you now should mention the performance problem in a kindly and concerned way by asking:

Case Study: An Employee Problem

A new supervisor, Ann, noticed that one of her immediate reports, Klaus, was dragging himself around the lab and paying little attention to the work at hand. She went to her manager, Paul, for help. Paul suggested that the three meet in his office. For the first ten minutes Ann and Klaus argued, with Ann saying something was wrong and Klaus steadfastly maintaining that he was working as hard as ever.

Then Paul interrupted, "Klaus, you've always been a good worker. But let's just assume—I'm not saying it's true—that Ann is correct. Can you think of any possible reason for it?" Almost immediately tears came into Klaus's eyes and he said, "You are both aware my father died several months ago. Well, since then I've been helping my mother out in our family store, working four hours every night plus weekends. I'm afraid she can't get along without me."

"Well, Klaus," Paul said, "perhaps you need to talk things over with your mother. We'll certainly give you time to deal with your present situation, but you may eventually have to choose between your job here and the family business." The next day Klaus returned, greatly relieved, and said, "I spoke to my mother and she says she can get along just fine without me; in fact, she apologized for not seeing that I was working too hard." Soon Klaus's lethargy disappeared, and he and Ann quickly developed into a cohesive, productive team.

"Is your perception of this situation similar to mine?"
"Is there anything I'm doing that is causing you problems?"
"Is there anything I can do to help? Can I adjust your work situation?"

Here you are saying, "I perceive a problem; am *I* doing something wrong?" The positive impact of this helpful, nonaccusatory approach is enormous. If there is something about the situation or your behavior that is causing the problem (a distinct possibility), employees will probably give their view and welcome your help—and you will be especially glad you did not start by assuming an employee was at fault.

If, however—and this is another key point—an employee *is* at fault, he or she is much more likely to admit it (first internally and then to you) if he or she perceives you are looking first within *yourself* or the work environment for the cause. Here you are giving the employee a chance to be a responsible adult by not initially forcing him or her into a defensive position.

Once the subordinate starts discussing the problem with you, the two of you are partners rather than adversaries and can usually find a satisfactory solution (most often by altering the work situation, since trying to change people is much more difficult). This approach is illustrated by the case studies shown on these two pages.

The second case study is a classic example of how an employee's reduced productivity was largely due to management's confusion. If Everett had noticed

---

Case Study: A Management Problem

A veteran, conscientious technician, Frank worked hard but generally kept to himself. One day he came to Everett, the new department manager (who had been trying to infuse new enthusiasm into the group), visibly upset, and said, "I've heard you say in department meetings that you want people to take responsibility and initiative. Well, I'm a hard worker, but I need someone to tell me what to do when I work. Now I find that the group leaders aren't giving me any more assignments. Don't you *want* me around here?" Everett was dumbfounded, primarily because the group leaders had been saying that they were short of laboratory technician help. He assured Frank that he was a valuable, needed employee and that he (Everett) would look into the situation immediately.

Everett checked with the two group leaders, and it turned out to be a problem in communication among the department's management, complicated by three weeks of emergency situations. Each group leader thought the other was assigning work to Frank. Alerted to their mistake, the group leaders and Everett apologized to Frank, gave him appropriate reassurance, and corrected the situation.

Frank's inactivity and had admonished him for it without searching for the cause, the situation could have turned out very poorly.

Note that the "simple" solutions in these two cases were possible only because of the strength of the underlying management-employee relationships. Management trusted the employees and assumed they wanted to do a good job. The workers sensed management's trust and also sensed management's desire to help, not judge.

Unfair Labeling by Management

In the following case, one could argue that the employee overreacted to the manager's negative comments and that the manager was entitled to express his opinion without the employee going into orbit. However, a supervisor gets paid to accommodate, as much as possible, the idiosyncracies of workers, especially when such accommodation begets optimum performance. Furthermore, here, the employee proved to be right; her idea was extremely worthwhile.

Case Study: Management's Error Is Reversed

Mary was a competent, creative, dedicated, and hardworking R&D employee, but she had a tendency to be stubbornly resentful when she felt she had been unfairly treated. One day she had a clever idea about monitoring production machines with a simple electronic device to improve product quality and reduce waste. But Jack, her supervisor, told her, "That's a dumb idea; forget about it and go back to work." Because of this and other ham-handed actions by Jack, Mary began just to go through the motions. She completed assignments lethargically, her cynicism grew worse, and her enthusiasm and creativity all but disappeared. Consequently, she was labeled a malcontent by management.

Several years later, a new supervisor, Horace, was appointed. He asked all group members what he could do to make their jobs better, but Mary refused to participate in any discussions. Horace did not press the issue with Mary, but when the latter noticed the rapidly improving mood of her colleagues, she approached Horace and shared her previous bad experience. He replied, "Your idea seems worthwhile; are you still interested in pursuing it?" When Mary answered in the affirmative, he suggested she take charge of the project and start by setting up a meeting with the engineers and appropriate manufacturing employees. The first experimental device was soon purchased and installed, the project was a success, and under Horace's nurturing supervision Mary's "attitude problem" disappeared completely. The cost of the device? Fifty dollars!

Note that in this case is would have been unfair and unsuccessful to try to solve the problem by coming down hard on Mary and her "antagonistic" attitude. Likewise, it would have been terribly unfair to terminate her if she had failed to respond positively to harsh, corrective managerial pressure.

More Drastic Actions

Every attempt should be made to solve performance problems without taking drastic action such as transferring or terminating employees. However, when leaving employees in their present job is no longer a viable option, three successively severe steps need to be considered:*

1. Keep the employee in the same work group but assign different, perhaps reduced, duties.
2. Transfer the employee to a different department where the responsibilities will be better matched to his or her abilities and interests.
3. Terminate the employee from the organization, but help him or her locate another position, preferably before termination.

Let's take a look at each of these options.

Different Duties Within the Same Work Group

Finding other work for an employee is sometimes feasible, especially if the performance problem is not too severe and if the work group is sufficiently large and varied (see the case study of "Rocco" in Chapter 17 for such a situation). But this approach must not be abused; too many managers procrastinate by rotating a problem employee until retirement. This is usually undesirable for all concerned, especially the employee.

Transfer to a Different Department

Switching a problem employee to another department has proved to be a workable option in many cases, especially if as a manager, you are—

▲ *skilled* at hiring, because then the employee is probably above average compared to the company-wide labor pool—other departments usually are interested in such people;

---

*This discussion assumes problems unrelated to alcohol or other drugs. Handling those cases depends on corporate policies and is beyond the scope of this book; however, the R&D manager, employee, personnel department, and medical department should work together. If an employee is proved guilty of theft on the job, immediate termination is usually the only appropriate action.

▲ *competent*, because then the employee comes from a growth environment and most likely has positive attitudes toward work and management;

▲ *honest* with other managers about the individual's strengths and weaknesses so those problems aren't just transferred to someone else; and

▲ *perceived by* other managers as a leader whose judgment and word they can trust.

Such transfers usually work out, primarily because the employee is enthusiastic about a fresh start and is eager to succeed and feel good about him or herself. Internal transfers can also be a positive force in employee growth, especially for R&D scientists who are starting to burn out in their present position.

Case Study: Transfer to a More Suitable Position

George was a bench scientist with chronic performance problems. He had a reasonable understanding of technical matters and always started a project with great enthusiasm. However, his laboratory skills were limited, his attention span short, and he spent too much time socializing. Consequently, year after year he was relatively unproductive and, equally problematic, he distracted his colleagues from their work. Management procrastinated for years, shifting George from project to project in the vain hope that the problem would somehow go away.

Finally, a new supervisor tried unsuccessfully to relocate George in the purchasing department, where his technical knowledge, enthusiasm, and tendency toward loquacity would serve him and the organization well. An even better fit was finally found (with George's enthusiastic concurrence) in Chemical Sales. The problem disappeared—for both the organization and for George. The benefit to George is emphasized because, as is almost always the case, the employee was not happy in a job where he was doing poorly and where management was dissatisfied with his performance.

Termination

Termination is, of course, a profoundly serious action, and we cannot grasp the devastating effect it has on the recipient unless we have gone through it ourselves. Consequently, managers who have never been laid off or fired need to understand this process and its impact on the individual. They need to learn as much as possible so that, when confronted with the necessity of performing this disagreeable task, they can and do act responsibly—with wisdom, honor, competence, understanding, sensitivity, and compassion.

Before deciding to terminate an employee, it is especially important that you define the problem carefully and accurately. Only after you have ruled out all other, less severe options do you have the right to take such drastic action. Furthermore, you must be certain that the employee is primarily at fault, because the problem could be caused by poor management.

Let's now assume that as manager you are convinced an employee must be terminated because of irreparable performance or attitude problems. What procedure do you follow?

1. Consult the personnel and/or employee relations departments for official guidance; in fact, it's wise to work with them unofficially at a much earlier stage. Many organizations have a formal probationary process to ensure against unfair treatment by a supervisor and to protect the company's legal position. There may be rules that must be followed before making a final decision on termination.

2. After ensuring that your actions have been consistent with company policy (e.g., documentation of performance problems), bring the employee into your office for a private, uninterrupted conversation having essentially no time limit. It is unconscionable to try to have this initial discussion at a time when you or the employee has another commitment in thirty minutes or even an hour. The meeting may take less than an hour but it could take longer, and ending the conversation early because of another commitment further demeans the subordinate. During the meeting, offer probation as an option before termination.

3. If the employee opts for probation (that is obviously his or her right), bear in mind that experience shows probation is seldom successful. This is an extremely stressful period; the individual tries, under dire threats, to be someone he or she is not. Social science tells us that people under such menacing pressure almost always do worse than usual. Even if performance improves initially, the relationship between you and the subordinate is almost certain to be permanently scarred.

4. Assuming the employee eschews probation, then one highly success-ful approach is to suggest that this is a problem the two of you need to solve *jointly*. Then say that you don't expect him or her to leave tomorrow, but that you would have trouble if he or she were still on the job six months from now. Sometime between tomorrow and six months from now the employee has got to find employment elsewhere.

Case Study: Amiable Termination

Don Smith was an above-average laboratory scientist, but he needed detailed, day-to-day guidance to focus his activities. His present and near-future situation did not allow for close supervision and his management decided, reluctantly, that drastic action had to be taken. Working together, Don and his immediate supervisor, Betty, contacted managers in competi-tive companies. Because of Betty's reputation for honesty and candor, her reputation for hiring good people, and especially because of Don's assets, he was able to join another organization. Provided with close guidance in his new setting, Don performed well. (Note: The basic cause of the problem was Betty's recruiting error.)

Offer to help in any way you can and reassure the person that you'll make every effort to keep him or her on until the worker finds something else. But emphasize that finding another job is primarily the worker's responsibility. Then give the employee the opportunity to talk—all the time needed. Since R&D managers deal primarily with technically trained college graduates, positions elsewhere often are soon found; very few individuals dally under such circumstances.

Here are some hints to make termination proceedings smoother:

1. The success of any management action depends heavily on the quality of the existing work environment. The more trusting and caring the relationship between a manager and the employees, the less traumatic and more successful (for both parties) will be any termination episode. Realistically, however, in most cases the rejected employee will have residual resentments against the manager.

2. The need to be straightforward is especially important with termination actions. When the employee comes into your office to hear the terrible news, don't beat around the bush or make ominous preliminary statements. Start right off by saying, "Tom, we've got a serious problem and I think you're going to have to find another job." Then go into the details.

3. If an employee vents her wrath and frustration on you, don't take it unkindly and don't argue. As calmly as possible tell her you have a different view and give her short, straight answers when she asks questions. Considering the situation, she's entitled to be upset and may need to blow off steam. What she needs most from you is honesty, plus concern for her as a fellow human being in considerable personal difficulty.

4. When you see a performance problem developing, and especially if you become convinced it's terminal, don't procrastinate—deal with it. Otherwise you're asking for big trouble down the road—for everyone concerned. Terminating someone is never easy, but delay only makes it worse. Furthermore, management has a responsibility to the organization, but especially to the individual, to perform such "surgery" cleanly and quickly.

5. It's probably best to talk to the employee early in the day, early in the week. Then he has a number of options: (a) stay at work, (b) talk further with you that day or the next to help deal with the emotional aspects of rejection, or (c) go home immediately after the discussion. Too often a manager drops this bombshell a half hour before quitting time on Friday. This allows the manager to have a reasonably good weekend (the difficult task of breaking the news being completed) but gives the subordinate the problem of dealing with the shock at home over the weekend. A manager must consider the employee's emotional needs first in this traumatic situation.

As emphasized earlier, whenever we perceive a performance problem, the first question should be, "What, if anything, am *I* as a manager doing wrong, or is there a deficiency in his work situation?" Related to the above, any termination episode should cause us to review where management went awry, perhaps in the hiring process.

6. When dealing with terminations, managers tend to rush through the process; they want to get the unpleasantness behind them as quickly as possible. However, keep in mind that an employee in such dire difficulty needs as much of your time, respect, patience, and understanding as possible. If any situation demands your best, it's this one.

There are times when termination, even though justified by the "facts," is not a defensible option. If a thirty-year employee has been mishandled by previous management, or if his performance problems have been ignored for twenty-nine years, management may have to do the best it can until his retirement, treating him with as much dignity as possible. Certainly the individual should not be made to pay the full price for thirty years of inadequate, procrastinating management. (Fortunately, federal laws on age discrimination protect many, but not all, such individuals.)

In the same vein, managers bear considerable responsibility for how well their subordinates perform, from both a hiring and an everyday managing standpoint. If a manager has a history of problem employees, his lack of management skills may be the biggest problem of all. On the other hand, the manager who acts honorably and in a caring manner while performing this "toughest task in management" will earn the respect of other members of the organization.

In summary, transferring or terminating substandard researchers is part of an R&D manager's basic obligation to his or her three "clients":

1. *The Corporation.* Management's obligation is to optimize productivity and increase the overall quality of the work group; terminating poor performers is one of the best ways to do that.

2. *The Work Group.* Each member of the group has a personal stake in its overall performance; if someone is not pulling his or her weight, other group members have to take up the slack or see group productivity decline.

3. *The Transferred or Terminated Employee.* One must exercise caution here; it's tempting to salve a troubled conscience by saying an employee was fired for his or her own good. However, assuming the process was carried out competently, fairly, and in a genuinely caring manner, the affected individual is usually well served (at least ultimately), in spite of the temporary trauma. If people are in a work situation where they are unable to do well, no one has more trouble than they (self-esteem suffers, as does their peace of mind). A fresh start in a better-matched position usually helps the individuals more than anyone else.

It's appropriate to conclude this serious subject with a quotation from the writer Lloyd Shearer:

> Resolve to be tender with the young, compassionate with the aged, sympathetic with the striving and tolerant of the weak and the wrong. Sometime in life you will have been all of these.

Reference

Gaylin, Willard. *Rediscovering Love*. New York: Viking Press, 1986.

Chapter 20

Promoting Laboratory Workers Into R&D Management

The grounds for [natural leadership among men] are virtue and talent.

Thomas Jefferson

[I speak of] industries...which have been drastically changed by persons who trust their own power, do not feel a need to have 'power over,' and who are willing to foster and facilitate the latent strength in the other person.

Carl Rogers, *Carl Rogers on Personal Power*

Selecting new R&D supervisors and promoting technical management people to positions of greater authority have important, far-reaching consequences: for society as a whole, for the organization, for those who will be supervised by that person, and for the promoted individual.

Why are decisions on managerial promotions so crucial? Because people's impact on the organization increases in direct proportion to their level of responsibility. For example, if a well-performing bench scientist increased her productivity by 50 percent, we would regard that as a great accomplishment. But a group leader supervising ten laboratory people can, with moderately good management practices, increase the group's productivity by *at least* 20 percent. Ten times 20 percent equals two FTEs (full-time equivalents). Therefore the group leader, with only modest effort, can have a fourfold greater impact on the group's output than can the most productive bench scientist. It follows, then, that management should be at least four times more careful in choosing new supervisors. (To put the importance of productivity into proper perspective, Robert Samuelson, in an article in *Newsweek* ["The Peace Dividend," June 26, 1989], estimated that a 1.5 percent increase in America's national productivity would increase the gross national product, after a decade of such growth, by $800 billion.)

In a democratic society, most adults grow accustomed to the freedom they have outside the workplace. We decide where to work, where to live, what to eat, what to buy, how to spend our leisure time, and who shall have power over us in the government. In industrial organizations, much of that freedom tends to disappear. At work, a chosen few hold the power. A good boss can make our workdays challenging, fulfilling, and enjoyable; a terrible boss can make our lives (on and off the job) miserable. Consequently, deciding whom to promote into management is not a decision to be taken lightly; it affects the organization and the lives of many people for decades.

Like everyone else, management people will (and must) behave within their individual limitations, so if an inappropriate person is promoted into supervision, no amount of training or counseling will remedy the problem. Equally important, consistent experience says poor managers are seldom removed from their positions until long after they have damaged their subordinates, their bosses, and the organization.

This chapter discusses the problems and challenges of promotion, with a view toward the widespread consequences of both good and bad promotion decisions. Let's begin by looking at why certain people shouldn't be promoted.

Promoting the Wrong People

The three most common mistakes made when choosing people for R&D management positions are—

1. Assuming the best laboratory worker will make the best supervisor;
2. Choosing people with traditional "boss" characteristics; and
3. Going outside of the company instead of promoting from within.

Promoting the Best Laboratory Worker

A scientist's natural inclinations and training—where objective reasoning is paramount—are both in direct conflict with the world of management and interpersonal relations, where personal bias is a fact of life. This can lead to all sorts of problems, especially an inability to see and accept different ways of perceiving reality.

When there is a need for a new R&D supervisor, the person most likely to be selected is the technical employee who has demonstrated the greatest proficiency at the hands-on laboratory work of the organization. Although this may turn out well, if the selection process is based solely on technical skills, the organization is in danger of suffering twice: (1) It gains a poor supervisor and (2) it loses a productive worker.

In their book, *Organizational Psychology*, David Kolb, Irwin Rubin, and James McIntyre have shown that different learning, problem-solving, and decision-making skills are needed for management than for laboratory science or engineering. This does not mean that technical people cannot become good managers; it simply means that the scientist-turned-manager must learn new skills.

According to Kolb, Rubin, and McIntyre, scientists and engineers are inclined to take one of two approaches to learning, problem solving, and decision making: (1) "an analytical, conceptual approach . . . that relies heavily on logical thinking and rational evaluation. . . . [They] tend to be oriented more toward things and symbols and less toward other people" or (2) "an active, 'doing' orientation . . . that relies heavily on experimentation."

Good managers, on the other hand, usually possess strengths opposite to those of technical laboratory people. For one thing, they are inclined to have "a receptive, experience-based approach that relies heavily on feeling-based judgments"; for another, they are "interested in people and tend to be imaginative and emotional."

Thus, when management decides which laboratory workers to promote, it should make sure that the chosen individual has the necessary problem-solving and decision-making skills to do well in the Looking-Glass World of R&D management—or at least the flexibility, desire, and capability of developing these skills.

Look back to the case study "Noncommunication" in Chapter 12 to see a typical situation. William was promoted into management because of his technical competence. But his interpersonal skills were minimal, and he was finally removed from his position. Surely you know of many similar cases; how many of these people are still managers?

Promoting People with "Boss" Characteristics

Peter Drucker, in *Management: Tasks, Responsibilities, Practices* has said that a manager "cannot expect to succeed by continuing the practices of the last two hundred years. He will have to develop new approaches, new principles, and new methods—and fast." Unfortunately, over the years, too many organizations have developed a management culture based on the traditional but archaic image of "the boss"—a forceful, intimidating, hard-driving he-man, barking crisp orders to passive, often cringing, subordinates. This role flowered during the industrial revolution and has been propagated, even nurtured, ever since. As business columnist Robert Samuelson has quipped, "The truth is that most top executives believe in a divine right of management."

The vast majority of management people are still male, and "good" management behavior is often associated with traditional male qualities (see Alice Sargent, *The Androgynous Manager*). For example, successful female executives are depicted on television advertising—that mirror of contemporary social values—as brisk, no-nonsense, dominating individuals barking orders in the true subculture fashion.

Typical "boss" culture values tell us being strong (dominating, cold, and businesslike) is good; being weak (deferring to subordinates, admitting one's limitations, being warm, friendly, and caring) is bad. Likewise, being objective (sticking to the "facts") is good; being subjective (allowing feelings to enter discussions and decisions) is bad. For example, a management advertising brochure states, "Leaders who let personal feelings and emotions color their thinking aren't doing the job they're paid to do." In short, managers know more—about all things—than workers, vice-presidents know more than managers, and the president is wisest of all.

Social scientists consistently debunk these values (see References at end of chapter). They point out that:

▲ In the "boss" culture of management, *strong* equates with "results oriented" and *weak* equates with "people oriented"; while both orientations are important, experiments have consistently shown that increased emphasis on people improves productivity while primary concern for results is self-defeating.

▲ Managers are no more "rational" than anyone else; every human being's view of reality is clouded by personal bias. Douglas McGregor (*The Human Side of Enterprise*) says, "The emotional and the rational aspects of man are inextricably interwoven; it is an illusion to believe they can be separated." More simply, we see things, not as they are, but as we are. At the same time, Abraham Maslow (*Motivation and Personality*) points out that some people's judgment is influenced more by emotions than that of others, but that it is also true that people who appear unemotional are often just concealing strong feelings from others *and from themselves*.

In fact, psychiatrist Willard Gaylin (*Rediscovering Love*) emphasizes that emotions are a necessary part of decision making:

> One of the most mischievous false perceptions is the casting of emotion as the enemy of reason. Feelings are a necessary adjunct to—not the antagonist of—our freedom from . . . [instinct] and intelligence. Because we have so many options for actio..s that are not dictated by automatic responses, we depend on these emotional signals to indicate the best immediate response, and if it turns out our judgment was incorrect, the emotions will guide us to alternative behavior to modify the unproductive response after the fact.

When position and power are blindly and unequivocally equated with wisdom, everyone suffers. Managers are deprived of employee input and therefore tend to make sterile, lower-quality decisions, workers feel demeaned, and the organization becomes less healthy.

The "boss" image is so pervasive and the behavior flowing from it seems so normal and right that many managers accept the culture without thinking. Then, quite logically, when vacancies occur at the first level of R&D supervision, individuals with perceived "boss" characteristics are promoted, thus perpetuating the species. In addition, the new supervisors hone their "boss" skills because, looking around them, they assume it is the appropriate way for a manager to behave. This is not to say that all "boss" characteristics are bad; rather, blind fealty to those qualities can lead to big trouble.

Tom Peters criticizes the archaic "boss" culture in an article in the *Arizona Daily Star* (April 4, 1989). First he lists survival requirements for the future, including:

▲ Hierarchy replaced with boundaryless, ambiguous networks of organizations

▲ Empowerment, ownership, information, and power-sharing

▲ Team-centered organizations, without cop-supervisors

Quoting Beverly Forbes, Peters goes on to state that to do well in management men will have to abandon their "macho" approach. To survive in the 1990s, managers must, for example, (1) subjugate individual ego concerns to cooperation, (2) "consider commitments in the context of life and moral relationships [rather than] in terms of their careers," (3) minimize domination and control, and (4) learn to "value egalitarian relationships rather than hierarchy."

Peter Drucker also decries the "boss" culture:

[It] assumes that the manager is healthy while everybody else is sick. It assumes that the manager is strong while everybody else is weak. It assumes that the manager knows while everybody else is ignorant. It assumes that the manager is right, whereas everybody else is stupid. These are the assumptions of foolish arrogance.

Bringing In People From the Outside

When management brings in people from the outside to fill managerial positions rather than promoting from within, it lowers employees' morale and speaks volumes about management's deficiencies in hiring quality entry-level people and developing leaders from within the organization.

Because of the complexity and long-range nature of R&D, it is difficult for corporate management to evaluate the performance of R&D management. However, if the latter consistently goes outside the company to fill middle-management positions, top management should take a careful look at what is going on inside the R&D group, because something is seriously wrong. If R&D management is not developing its people for supervisory careers, it may be suppressing their creativity and development in technical areas, too. Equally bad, R&D management may have a well-qualified insider to promote, but they migrate toward an outsider because they see only his or her good points, while being familiar with the insider's bad points. The Bible says it best: "A prophet is without honor in his own country."

Promoting the Right People

A key element in promoting the right people into R&D management is having the right people to promote. Thus recruiting and hiring the best candidates, and then creating a growth-fostering environment, are crucial. It's also critical to learn to recognize the personal qualities needed to make a good manager.

Avoid promoting people with little talent for or interest in supervision. Unless management does its job well, few technical workers will reject the chance to move into supervision, even if they have questionable interest in it, because (1) that's where the power, status, and money are; (2) in organizations lacking an effective scientific ladder, that's the only path for substantial growth, especially in responsibility; (3) they don't want to appear unambitious to their boss; and (4) few workers are exposed to the management side of supervision—for example, required skills and subtle responsibilities—so they don't know what they are getting into.

On the next page are some tips to help you spot managerial potential.

Case Study: "No, Thanks" to Management

Celia was a Ph.D. scientist in an R&D department. She supervised one laboratory technician, but was interested in becoming a formal group leader so that she could investigate other areas of research. Celia was an excellent scientist who loved laboratory work, but she was quiet and introspective. She got along well with colleagues but preferred the relative solitude of the lab to the busy discussions with employees from other R&D disciplines.

Bob, the department manager, became aware of Celia's interest in management. After several detailed discussions with her, he learned that her primary motivation was to assemble the human resources to do more personal research. He said, "Celia, if you become the supervisor of several Ph.D.s, they should not be regarded as your laboratory assistants; rather, you will be obliged to help them become premier scientists in their own right, and they should have as much independence as possible. Some of your focus will change from laboratory work to interpersonal matters. How do you feel about that?"

Celia replied that she hadn't realized all the ramifications of being a group leader, and quickly admitted that she preferred laboratory work. She and Bob then agreed to work toward Celia's having an additional technician on a trial basis to see if that might be the best solution.

It should be noted that this experience brought Bob and Celia closer together and made Celia feel valued and respected, since Bob spent considerable one-on-one time with her discussing her career.

---

1. *Hold group discussions*. As part of the teaching or coaching function, managers can hold individual and group discussions wherein laboratory workers learn about interpersonal and management matters, and also where managers can get a better feel for subordinates' talents and true interest in this area. It's best to have a brown-bag group session once a week during lunch hour; participation should be voluntary and open to all employees.

2. *Use mutual evaluations*. As part of the evaluating activity, managers will get to know their subordinates very well. And during this process, employees will learn more about the subtle facets of management responsibilities. These evaluations will help managers pick the right people for supervision as well as help laboratory workers decide if they would like—and would do well in—management.

3. *Urge self-evaluation*. Because self-evaluation is a major component of a fertile work environment, employees can decide for themselves what their

---

Case Study: Self-Evaluation

Mark, Marie, and Paul, veteran engineers, all applied for the position of section head when their incumbent boss retired. Martha, their manager, got each of them to evaluate themselves and their compatibility with management responsibilities. The results were as follows:

- ▲ Mark came to the realization that he would not do well as a section head, primarily because he preferred working with others on engineering projects as opposed to supervising people and giving up most of his technical responsibilities.
- ▲ Marie wrote Martha a three-page memo listing her qualifications and the reasons she was interested in moving into management. Martha perceived that Marie had good interpersonal skills and was creative, dedicated, and group oriented. After extensive discussions with the manager, Marie was promoted to section head and performed well.
- ▲ Paul was never able to see or admit to his shortcomings. He lacked self-discipline in conducting research projects and seldom completed them on time. He also lacked insight and judgment in interpersonal areas, and failed to keep his technician busy and challenged.

Martha told Paul that, right or wrong, it was her judgment that Marie would make the best section head, and that Paul should think seriously about concentrating on his technical career. Over the years, Paul has been reasonably productive as a bench engineer and his interest in management has appeared to subside. Mark has remained happy with his decision and gets along well with Marie as his boss.

personal level of talent and interest is. There are social science instruments that can assist people in self-evaluation (see David Kolb et al., *Organizational Psychology*).

4. *Offer practice management.* In most R&D organizations, there are numerous opportunities for employees to practice their management skills on a temporary, experimental basis. These include short-range projects and informal group effort.

5. *Promote other career pathways.* In a fertile work environment, in which management is concerned about growth opportunities for all, people not interested in management will see other career pathways. Make sure this is possible through a technical career path. The scientific ladder is discussed later in this chapter.

Case Study: Climbing the Scientific Ladder

Brian was an excellent scientist but a poor supervisor of technicians. After four or five years of productive laboratory effort, he began to suffer burn-out and approached his boss for a possible change into management. After much discussion, Brian became convinced that the most appropriate career path for him was the scientific ladder. Soon afterwards a challenging and different laboratory position became available in another R&D department. Brian transferred and attacked his new responsibilities with fresh enthusiasm; two years later he was still doing well.

It is preferable for unqualified subordinates to take themselves out of the running for first-time supervisory positions rather than feel passed over when someone else is chosen. This does not mean there will be no problems, but the difficulties can be minimized with wise management. In addition, scientists keep their lab careers on the right track. When R&D laboratory scientists are promoted into supervision, some fledglings do well while others fail. Alerting your management candidates to these potential problems can minimize subsequent failures. Here are the primary hazards they should guard against.

Eight Potholes in the Road to Managerial Excellence

1. *Unfamiliarity With Human Nature.* Management candidates need to understand the fundamentals of social science, especially regarding motivation and behavior. Trying to manage people without understanding these basics is like trying to balance the books without knowing how to add or subtract.

2. *Career Ladder Distraction.* Focusing on one's next promotion rather than concentrating on the job at hand is a dangerous situation. Managing an R&D group and becoming skilled at that job is difficult enough, demanding constant

attention. Focusing on the promotion in the distance shortchanges the group and the company. Furthermore, experience tells us that the best path to promotion and personal growth is excellence in one's current position.

3. *Stealing the Show.* When a new R&D group leader runs a theatrical, autocratic show as "the star," he or she is not building the necessary strong group cohesiveness and high performance. Laurence Peter, author of the well-known *The Peter Principle*, says, "Fame is a case of hero today, gone tomorrow." Leaders who hog the spotlight at the expense of their subordinates may have some fleeting success, but they are more dependent on the group than the group is on them. Such managers will struggle throughout their career because they are fighting human nature—their subordinates' need for recognition—and in that battle the employees are on the opposite side.

4. *Personal Flaws.* Psychological and behavioral limitations, including immaturity, fear, uncertainty, and an unwillingness to share power with subordinates can cause extensive problems. Most "givers" are realistically self-confident and do well in management. "Takers" are often insecure and fearful, and struggle throughout their managerial careers.

5. *Increased Pressure.* Personal limitations are magnified under management stress. We all have psychological and behavioral limitations, but moving from the laboratory into supervision may exacerbate a problem. For example:

▲ Power over and responsibility for other adults is a new, euphoric, and intimidating experience for most people. Since many new supervisors are thrust into their positions with little or no management training and very little advance notice, their initial tendency is to rely on parental behavior. But subordinates are not children, and treating them as such will meet with resistance, thus creating confusion and frustration.

▲ As mentioned earlier, management requires skills very different from— or at least in addition to—those necessary for hands-on laboratory work. When a good lab performer becomes a barely adequate supervisor, feelings of inadequacy on the job can lead to anxiety and frustration.

▲ Increased responsibility almost always translates into more psychological pressure because of new expectations. The organization expects more from new leaders and new leaders expect more of themselves. Furthermore, as new supervisors gain more power, prestige, influence, and salary, additional pressure is generated because the individuals have more to lose if things go wrong.

▲ Managers must depend on others to do the hands-on work, and being at least once removed from basic tasks requires a large measure of trust. This can mean anxiety and frustration, especially when trouble arises.

Increased psychological pressure, confusion, anxiety, and frustration all tend to intensify a person's behavioral limitations, causing normal, healthy supervisors to regress psychologically at the very time they need full use of their talents and energy.

6. *Misconceptions.* There's a tendency to assume that most growth in managerial competence takes place at seminars and by reading the social science and management literature. These are important, especially for learning basic principles and for broadening one's horizons, but most progress toward managerial excellence takes place on the job.

Effective supervision is difficult, complex work that must be tailored to particular individuals and actual situations. Even more important, seminars and literature provide primarily cognitive learning, whereas experiential learning provides the real growth in managerial competence. What cognitive learning of basic social science principles does is to guide experiential learning into positive, realistic directions, with minimal distortion from personal bias.

Unfortunately, after laboratory people are promoted into management, many spend most of their day "minding the store" and, even more unfortunately, that is precisely what their bosses want them to do. As a result, except for an occasional three-day seminar and a few evenings with a book, most management careers are spent running an organization and meeting R&D deadlines. There simply isn't any time to worry about something as ethereal as personal growth. As mentioned earlier, the inherent pressures of management tend to cause regression, not growth, unless the steps emphasized throughout this book are taken to reverse that trend.

7. *Remaining Ignorant About Oneself.* People can learn from and utilize advances in knowledge about the physical world, but growth in managerial skills is primarily limited by what they learn—or don't learn—about themselves. This is because understanding ourselves is a prerequisite for understanding others—people in general and coworkers specifically. Self-knowledge involves primarily experiential learning and, as any parent knows, such understanding cannot be hammered into one generation by the experiences of its predecessors. A new supervisor can inherit a limited amount of interpersonal wisdom from a mentor, but the rest must come from within through hard work, diligence, and patience.

This already difficult situation is exacerbated by the following, creating a vicious circle:

▲ Fledgling supervisors often lack self-understanding, thanks to the selection criteria (those having "boss" characteristics and those showing interest and competence in technical areas, often at the expense of "people" skills). For example, a self-centered person with burning personal ambition for power is often viewed positively by management as a hard driver who gets things done. In many instances, this self-orientation creates a sterile environment for subordinates, but few self-centered individuals would view themselves in that light.

▲ The "boss" culture of management exerts great pressure on individual managers to conform, which can impede movement toward self-understanding. Likewise, many mentors teach traditional management values, thus the blind lead the blind.

8. *All Sweat and No Result.* The last pothole on the road to managerial excellence can best be described by telling a true story (see the case study on the next page).

Most likely, you are acquainted with one or more managerial Freds. Well-dressed and impressive, they look like executives. They know all the buzz words, and when to speak and when to keep silent. They follow the rules, move smoothly along the corridors of power, blend into the background, and never make waves. They are polite to everyone, although not always to their subordinates, and they are well thought of by their bosses and by casual observers (though perhaps not by their subordinates and peers).

But when you step back and take stock of what they accomplish over a month, a year, or a career, the screen is blank—no significant accomplishments, no observable growth or improvement. In fact, these types have very little impact on the organization. Upon closer investigation, however, you find a negative impact on their subordinates: frustration, malaise, and discouragement as a result of working in a sterile environment for years with no one in management noticing or caring. Also, their peers are often frustrated because these "Freds" do not carry their share of the managerial or organizational load.

Case Study: Fred "The Flash"

Years ago I joined an intramural basketball league. One of the players was a young man named Fred, and if anyone ever looked like a basketball player, it was he. He was 6'2", well-proportioned, well-coordinated, and in excellent physical condition. During a game, Fred would guard his man with vigor. He dribbled well, passed crisply, and was a "holler guy." He took very few shots, scored very few points, and had even fewer "assists," but he always played hard and worked up a good sweat.

One evening while observing Fred play, I suddenly realized that, as good as Fred looked out there on the court, *he never really accomplished anything!* He never made any difference in the game; he just went through the motions of being a basketball player.

The point of the story is not to ridicule the Freds of the world. Fred the basketball player was probably doing the best he could. But everyone must acknowledge their "Fred" tendencies and work to avoid this last—and perhaps most dangerous—pothole.

Despite these formidable obstacles, there is cause for optimism, at least for the new R&D leader. Not everyone can be the best, but everyone can grow and improve. Although many seminars and books, like the Sirens and Sophists of yore, promise quick and easy paths to better performance, the wise, experienced manager knows better. Supervising people is difficult, complex work and genuine, lasting progress comes slowly. With patience and perseverance, it can be done.

An Alternative to Management: The Scientific Ladder

For maximum growth and productivity, laboratory employees must see within their organization opportunities for promotion and formal recognition. As in nontechnical companies, the number of available R&D management positions is severely limited, especially in a flat organization. The best solution to this problem is a scientific ladder with grade levels equivalent to those for management.

Basically, a scientific ladder recognizes and rewards laboratory scientists for technical accomplishment, expertise, innovation, experience, and good judgment. When operating well, such a system is beneficial to employees and the organization.

1. Scientists at all educational levels who excel in laboratory work are rewarded for concentrating on what they do best.
2. Technical employees with no interest in or talent for management are provided with an alternative.
3. Scientists who are interested in moving into management find a less crowded field of candidates.
4. A dual-ladder system provides more opportunities for employee freedom, recognition, responsibility, and involvement.
5. Two career paths make it easier to identify scientists with whom top management can formally interact.

The net results of a dual-ladder system are: (1) an increase in the quality of R&D management, and (2) lower employee turnover, especially among veteran scientists. Also, a meaningful scientific ladder will attract high-quality job candidates (many interviewees ask about this).

Note the caveat "when operating well" mentioned above. A good scientific ladder can be of considerable benefit, but if poorly designed or improperly maintained, it can be a costly demotivator. For example, if the scientific career path is viewed as a consolation prize for demoted R&D managers, or for average laboratory scientists who are rejected for openings in management, its prestige value is considerably reduced.

Characteristics of a Good Scientific Ladder

A scientific ladder that operates on the following principles will succeed as a career pathway parallel to the management hierarchy for the following reasons:

1. Promotions are based on scientific accomplishment, expertise, creativity, and judgment.
2. The first two to four levels are available to all scientists who have a record of solid accomplishments. Selection is made by department management with approval of the department manager's boss.

3. The upper rungs (e.g., senior scientists) are reserved for those demonstrating excellence in science, as evidenced by internal accomplishment (especially being on the cutting edge of their field), creativity, external publications* (including patents), and peer recognition, both internal and external.

4. The nomination or election procedure for senior scientists is rigorous but simple and efficient, and involves both R&D management and laboratory scientists. For example:

   ▲ Within each R&D department, a nomination advisory committee composed of laboratory scientists (senior scientists plus representatives from various worker levels) assists department management in deciding which nominations to forward.

   ▲ Top R&D management and select senior scientists together make the final decision. For example, a selection committee, composed primarily of incumbent senior scientists, "elects" new members; their decisions are, with rare exception, confirmed by top R&D management.

5. Scientists outside the company are involved in the nomination or selection process, either as candidate references or, if appropriate, as members of department nominating or R&D selecting committees.

6. Great care is taken to preserve the scientific integrity of the program. Demoted managers and rejected managerial candidates who do not meet the requirements are not given a position as a consolation prize.

7. No numerical quotas are imposed. If a person deserves to be a senior scientist, he or she is elected, no matter how many candidates there are. On the other hand, if none of the nominees is worthy, none is selected.

Senior scientists—those at the top of the ladder—should be recognized in as many ways as possible: For example, they should get the same salary and perks (e.g., stock options and company automobile) as equivalent management grades. In addition, they should be respected within the corporation as much as their managerial equivalents.

Likewise, new senior scientists should be honored at a formal dinner that includes incumbents, R&D management, and corporate management; the groups should intermingle as much as possible. Plaques, rings, wall photos, articles in company and local newspapers, special laboratory coats, and laboratory wall nameplates are examples of such recognition.

As important as recognition and scientific freedom are, however, a scientific ladder is much more effective if its occupants also acquire more organizational responsibility and involvement. For example, when appropriate, senior scientists representing relevant scientific disciplines should attend board of directors

---

*In some situations, the individual may be working in a "proprietary" area in which external publications are restricted. However, this should not be used as a convenient excuse for not publishing externally, and in such situations internal publications and patents may be substituted.

meetings, give lay-level technical presentations to stockholders, and accompany management during inlicensing or outlicensing negotiations with competitors.

Ideally, the highest-level scientists should serve as technical advisors to R&D management and corporate management, while senior scientists should serve as mentors to other laboratory workers as long as those relationships arise spontaneously. Good scientific ladders are difficult to build and maintain, but they are a cornerstone of a successful R&D division.

References

Argyris, Chris. *Personality and Organization*. New York: Harper & Brothers, 1957.

Drucker, Peter F. *Management: Tasks, Responsibilities, Practices*. New York: Harper & Row, 1974.

Gaylin, Willard. *Rediscovering Love*. New York: Viking, 1986.

Hall, Jay. *Ponderables: Essays on Managerial Choice–Past and Future*. Woodlands, Tex.: Teleometrics International, 1982.

Kolb, David A., Irwin M. Rubin, and James M. McIntyre. *Organizational Psychology: An Experiential Approach*, 3rd ed. Englewood Cliffs, N.J.: Prentice-Hall, 1979.

Likert, Rensis. *The Human Organization: Its Management And Value*. New York: McGraw-Hill, 1967.

———.*New Patterns of Management*. New York: McGraw-Hill, 1961.

McGregor, Douglas. *The Human Side of Enterprise*. New York: McGraw-Hill, 1960.

Maslow, Abraham H. *Motivation and Personality*, 2nd ed., ed. Wayne G. Holtzman and Gardner Murphy. New York: Harper & Row, 1970.

Peters, Tom. "Control Paradox: Less Yields More," *Arizona Daily Star*, April 11, 1989.

———. "Firms May Be Dancing Last Macho Tango," *Arizona Daily Star*, April 4, 1989.

Rogers, Carl R. *Carl Rogers on Personal Power*. New York: Delacorte, 1977.

Rogers, Carl R., and Barry Stevens. *Person to Person: The Problem of Being Human*. Lafayette, Calif.: Real People Press, 1967.

Sampson, Robert C. *Managing the Managers*. New York: McGraw-Hill, 1965.

Samuelson, Robert, J. "The Peace Dividend." *Newsweek*, June 26, 1989.

Sargent, Alice G. *The Androgynous Manager*. New York: AMACOM, 1981.

PART IV
The R&D Function

Parts II and III concentrated on R&D management's responsibilities pertaining to the supervision of technical people. Part IV deals with other management matters concerning the R&D division and its various functions, although some discussion of interpersonal relations cannot be avoided.

The emphasis here is on the crucial subtleties in each area—the secrets of success that largely determine how well a manager does in the R&D division, no matter what the hierarchical level. You should, of course, discover the additional subtleties in your own situation.

Chapters 21 and 22 cover the factors that come into play when R&D management interacts with peers and supervisors, or in committees and multidisciplinary project teams. Chapter 23 provides some tips for handling R&D budgets, while Chapter 24 describes some applications of computers for R&D that heighten productivity. In Chapter 25, the subject of outlicensing and inlicensing is discussed, along with government contracts and other regulations. Chapter 26 concludes this part of the book with a view of the role academia plays in industry, particularly R&D.

But before dipping into these matters, let's review the basic role that R&D plays in the organization, and how the productivity of this vital division of the corporation can most accurately be measured.

R&D's Primary Goal

As a manager, you should recognize that the primary goal of R&D is to develop useful, profitable new products (or processes) of consistently high quality. The more exclusive those products are (e.g., patentable), the better. In addition, the manufacturing process for these products should be consistently trouble free.

R&D is also charged with bringing products to the marketplace as quickly as possible. As a manager, you can minimize the elapsed time between idea and market in three ways:

1. Hire the most competent, highly motivated laboratory workers.

2. Hire or promote the most competent, highly motivated, person-centered group leaders, who will:
   ▲ Create a fertile work environment wherein productivity is maximized.
   ▲ Manage people in an enlightened way so as to maximize employee loyalty, enthusiasm, and cooperativeness, with a sense of urgency; and so that energy is focused primarily on creative, productive work.
3. With the help of your subordinates, organize your R&D group and assign your resources to maximize efficiency and optimize progress.

The R&D manager needs to back up the department's or group's developments. This is especially true if the product is a radical departure from present technology, because many decision makers tend to be conservative and might be inclined to "jump ship" at the first sign of serious trouble.

Likewise, if the product is highly technical, even though conventional, it needs support. The more complex the product, the longer the time frame and the greater the number of bugs during development. Without a champion to supply both patience and persistence, such a project may die of attrition or neglect.

Some products are first viewed as failures because they don't meet present criteria for success. For example, 3M's highly successful Post-it notes weren't marketed for eleven years after development, reportedly because, until its champion sold the idea of removable notes, the product's key quality—moderate adhesiveness—was considered inadequate by 3M's high standards.

R&D Productivity

Measuring the productivity of your R&D division is like trying to catch butterflies while wearing boxing gloves. Ultimately, R&D productivity is reflected in the success or failure of new products and processes. But a fair and accurate measure of R&D productivity is extremely difficult because so many factors enter into the equation:

▲ Long lead times—for example, it was ten to fifteen years from idea to profitability for 3M's traffic-control materials
▲ Luck, including the vagaries of science, introduction of competing products, and other variables in the marketplace
▲ Effectiveness of the manufacturing and production planning divisions in doing their jobs
▲ Government regulations and red tape
▲ Competence and priorities of the company's sales and marketing divisions in promoting a new product
▲ Degree and consistency of support from corporate management

In spite of—or better, because of—these difficulties, R&D managers must take care not to make one of these factors an alibi for mediocre R&D performance. For example, in the pharmaceutical industry, it's tempting to blame the

Food and Drug Administration for delayed approval or rejection of new drug applications, rather than questioning the quality of the submissions.

The following illustrate several reasonable methods of estimating R&D productivity. However, caution should be exercised because none is a complete and accurate measure.

1. The percentage of yearly sales coming from products introduced within the last, say, five years.
2. The percentage of total R&D projects resulting in marketable products.
3. The number of new products marketed each year.
4. A comparison of the R&D division's performance against that of competitors.
5. The return-on-investment (but while R&D expenditures are measurable, the sales-profit figures for new products depend heavily on the performance of marketing and sales departments, how efficiently and consistently the manufacturing division produces high-quality material, and the effectiveness of the production planning department—for example, do sales suffer from poor inventory control, with many customers on back order?).
6. Customer feedback; is the company viewed as marketing good, innovative products over a long period of time?

The Hughes Aircraft Company (*R&D Productivity: An Investigation*) studied R&D productivity; as an idea of the complexity of the subject, their report lists over 700 references. For additional help on measuring productivity, see the References that follow.

References

Drucker, Peter F. *Technology, Management and Society.* New York: Harper & Row, 1970.

Hazen, Robert M. *The Breakthrough: The Race for the Superconductor.* New York: Summit Books, 1988.

"Research and Development: Key Issues for Management." Conference report from The Conference Board, edited by James K. Brown and Lita M. Elvers. New York: The Conference Board, 1983.

Steele, Lowell W. *Managing Technology: The Strategic View.* New York: McGraw-Hill 1989.

Suggested Readings

Chakrin, L. W., and D. A. Byron. "Labs Labor Lost? R&D in an Era of Change." *Pharmaceutical Executive*, July 1987.

Collier, Donald W., John Monz, and James Conlin. "How Effective is Technological Innovation?" *Research Management* 27, no. 5 (September–October 1984).

Davy, M. F. "Economic Evaluation of Research Projects—A Procedure." *AACE Transactions* (1983).

Evans, James R., and Samuel J. Mantel, Jr. "A New Approach to the Evaluation of Process Innovations." *Technovation* 3, no. 4 (October 1985).

Foster, Richard N. "Boosting the Payoff from R&D." *Research Management* 25, no. 1 (January 1982).

Gilman, John J. "Factors that Affect Development Investment Values." *Research Management* 29, no. 6 (November 1978).

———. "Market Penetration Rates and their Effect on Value." *Research Management* 25, no. 2 (March 1982).

Griliches, Zvi. "Issues in Assessing the Contribution of Research and Development to Productivity Growth." *Bell Journal of Economics* 10, no. 1 (Spring 1979).

Hambrick, Donald C., and Ian C. Macmillan. "Efficiency of Product R&D in Business Units: The Role of Strategic Context." *Academy of Management Journal* 28, no. 3 (September 1985).

Jaffe, Adam B. "Characterizing the 'Technological Position' of Firms, with Application to Quantifying Technological Opportunity and Research Spillovers." *Research Policy* 18, no. 2 (April 1989).

Kravitz, H. "R&D and Diminishing Returns." *Chemtech* 16, no. 11 (November 1986).

Krogh, Lester C. "Measuring and Improving Laboratory Productivity/Quality." *Research Management* 30, no. 6 (November–December 1987).

Krogh, Lester C., Julianne H. Prager, David P. Sorensen, and John D. Tomlinson. "How 3M Evaluates Its R&D Programs." *Research-Technology Management* 31, no. 6 (November–December 1988).

Kudla, Ronald J., and Thomas H. McInish. "A New Tool for R&D Project Evaluation." *Industrial Management* 22, no. 6 (November–December 1980).

Levin, Richard C., Alvin K. Klevorick, Richard R. Nelson, Sidney G. Winter, Richard Gilbert, and Zvi Griliches. "Appropriating the Returns from Industrial Research and Development; Comments and Discussion." *Brookings Papers on Economic Activity* 3 (1987).

Manners, George E., Jr., and Joseph G. Louderback. "Sales Potential Guidelines for Research Investment." *Research Management* 23, no. 2 (March 1980).

Mechlin, George F., and Daniel Berg. "Evaluating Research—ROI Is not Enough." *Harvard Business Review* 58, no. 5 (September–October 1980).

Mittermeir, Roland, and Karin D. Knorr. "Scientific Productivity and Accumulative Advantage: A Thesis Reassessed in the Light of International Data." *R&D Management* 9, Special Issue (1979).

O'Brien, C., and B. Chiplin. "Proposed Research into a Method for Assessing and Modeling Design Productivity in the Electronics Industries." *Engineering Costs and Production Economics* 12, no. 1-4 (July 1987).

Pake, George E. "Business Payoff from Basic Science at Xerox." *Research Management* 29 no. 6 (November–December 1986).

Ramsey, Jackson E. "Selecting R&D Projects for Development." *Long Range Planning* 14, no. 1 (February 1981).

R&D Productivity: An Investigation of Ways to Evaluate and Improve Productivity in Research and Development. Los Angeles: Hughes Aircraft Company, 1974.

Sarnat, Marshall. "On the Use of Risk Analysis for the Evaluation of Industrial R&D Expenditures." *Managerial and Decision Economics* 8, no. 3 (September 1987).

Scherer, F. M. "R&D and Declining Productivity Growth." *American Economic Review* 73, no. 2 (May 1983).

Teitelman, R., and A. Baldo. "Grading R&D: Which Companies in the Drug Business Get Their Money's Worth out of Research Spending?" *Financial World* 158, no. 2 (January 24, 1989).

"Using R&D as a Guide to Corporate Profits." *Business Week,* May 29, 1978.

Zaidman, Beno, and Guido Cevidalli. "Project Evaluation: Externalities Must Not Be Disregarded." *R&D Management* 17, no. 4. (October 1987).

Chapter 21

Interacting With R&D Peers and Superiors

In addition to managing subordinates, there are two additional constituencies with which the successful R&D manager must be concerned: peers and superiors. Much of so-called organizational politics is based on how well a leader relates to these groups. Many otherwise promising careers have been stymied because of a lack of understanding, tact, and diplomacy in these areas.

Interacting With R&D Peers

People who are effective as managers of subordinates but ineffectual in relating to their peers tend to isolate their staff and diminish their department's impact on the overall R&D effort. R&D projects are complex ventures, often requiring cooperation among many different department and scientific disciplines. As Tom Clancy (*Cardinal of the Kremlin*) writes:

> Progress depended on the free transfer of information and ideas. They were people who got excited about new things, and talked about them among themselves, unconsciously seeking the synergism that makes ideas sprout like weeds in the disordered garden of the laboratory.

To effectively relate to peers, an R&D manager must understand thoroughly the "big picture"—that is, how the overall R&D process works in the company. The manager must also treat peers with the same respect, understanding, and deference he or she shows all others, including subordinates and superiors.

The Big Picture

The ultimate goal for R&D is useful, high-quality, and profitable products. Wise R&D managers become well acquainted with how such products become reality in their company. The best way to do this is to talk with appropriate department managers (e.g., all those in R&D plus Marketing, Sales, Manufacturing, Engineering, and Quality Control). You want to learn—

▲ the project or product flow from idea to manufacture;
▲ the responsibilities of each department;
▲ how each group fits into the overall operation; and
▲ the interactions among various R&D departments.

It's worthwhile to construct a flow sheet briefly describing this process.

Respect, Understanding, and Deference

Many managerial tasks involve peers as well as subordinates. These tasks are best accomplished with understanding and empathy, respect for others, deference to more-informed people, communication, and trust.

1. *Understanding and Empathy.* The process starts with understanding (and, as much as possible, empathizing with) other managers and their groups' role in the overall operation. It is only after you have this understanding, only after you can see things from *their* point of view, that you can relate to them and do well in peer-interaction tasks.

2. *Respect for Others.* When you have respect for managerial peers and show that respect, everything else falls into place. You need to respect them as individuals with their own managerial style, which requires getting to know them as individuals, and you need to respect their departments for the important role they play in R&D and product development. This requires that you understand their department's function.

3. *Deference to More Informed People.* You need to defer to your peers and their departments when appropriate, in order to minimize turf problems and to ensure the best decisions.

4. *Cooperation.* Because of its complex nature, R&D *is* cooperation. You need to willingly offer your services to sister departments when help is needed. Many times, others don't realize what you can do for them, so you need to communicate. For example, in the pharmaceutical industry, scientists in product development are trained to determine the physical (e.g., pH-solubility profile) and chemical (e.g., pH-stability profile) properties of potential new drugs. This information can help synthetic chemists choose the most appropriate salt of a compound and can help pharmacologists and toxicologists select the most bioavailable presentation of a compound to ensure the most meaningful data. It is a cooperative effort.

5. *Communication.* The complexities of science necessitate good communication, in both the technical and nontechnical sense. Interdepartmental communication devoid of a strong interpersonal component tends to be sterile, incomplete, and susceptible to misinterpretation. Equally important, good interpersonal communication among various R&D groups fosters creativity and

innovation. Scientists often build on the ideas of colleagues from other disciplines (two heads *are* better than one), and management must encourage such cross-fertilization.

Although it cannot be accomplished by administrative fiat, interaction can be initiated by management's suggestion; it is then up to individual laboratory workers to nourish and perpetuate the relationships. Leaders should set a friendly, cooperative intergroup example; if department managers are at each other's throats, respective group members will be hesitant to antagonize their leaders by cooperating with the "enemy's" employees.

6. *Trust*. It's important that scientists and technical managers trust each other—that they trust one another's judgment, honesty, candor, and dedication. In addition, they need to have confidence that everyone is, in general, placing company welfare over the R&D division's, R&D's welfare over the group's, and group welfare over personal interests.

In summary, the interests of all concerned are best served by knowledgeable cooperation among peers. The catalyst for this is the R&D manager.

Interacting With R&D Superiors

Building good relationships with one's immediate superiors* is a crucial managerial task. To be effective as an R&D manager, you must have the support of your boss and top R&D management. Without this backing, your effectiveness as a manager will be severely diminished; with that support, you can focus your efforts on optimizing the growth, creativity, and productivity of your employees, and the impact of your department on the overall R&D division.

Your Relationship With Your Boss

How can R&D managers optimize their relationship with their boss? Here are some tips.

Get to Know the Individual. Become familiar with your supervisor as a unique individual. You will want to deal with your boss (within your limits as a person) in a manner that is most compatible with his or her way of doing business.

You'll notice that you are advised to adjust to the personal characteristics of others, whether they be subordinates, superiors, or peers. If you ask, "Why does it always have to be me who does the adjusting?", here are five reasons:

▲ What is your definition of a leader, and don't you want to be a leader in everything you do?

*The discussion here deals only with R&D management. Interaction between R&D management and corporate management is discussed in Chapter 29.

▲ You have control only over your own efforts and accomplishments, so wouldn't you prefer to take the initiative here also?
▲ Adjusting to others is the essence of deferring.
▲ Accepting others means valuing people and dealing with them as they are rather than trying to change them to what you would like them to be.
▲ Adjusting is contagious; when others observe you working hard to accommodate their idiosyncrasies, they will be more forgiving of your imperfections as well.

It's important to insert a note of caution. Adjusting to your supervisor does *not* mean compromising your principles and "cozying up" to the boss. Good managers stand up to their boss when appropriate and necessary. They are honest, open, and candid with them whenever possible. They also present the same face to subordinates, peers, and superiors.

This takes courage and, at times, may cause difficulty. But it must be done if you want to be a strong, principled leader. It's possible to be flexible, diplomatic, politically successful, and principled, but you have to strike your own balance.

Case Study: Don't Rush Marvin

Marvin was a conservative, cautious, deliberate, but flexible veteran R&D manager. Barbara was a new first-line supervisor in Marvin's department. She frequently became frustrated because Marvin resisted her attempts to instill new ideas and a new spirit in the department. Soon Barbara realized that her brash, frenetic style made Marvin nervous, and she knew she had to alter her approach. From then on, when she presented an idea to Marvin she added that there was r.o hurry; he should think about the idea for a week or so. Their relationship improved greatly and Marvin became much more receptive to Barbara's proposals.

Learn About Your Boss's Responsibilities and Pressures. It will also be helpful if you learn more about the totality of your boss's job. What are the pressures? What are the individual's overall goals for the organization and his or her career? What are his or her priorities? If your boss doesn't approve something you want to do, is it because that would conflict with some other plans? If your boss does something that appears to be unwise, perhaps it's because he or she is responding to *his* or *her* boss.

Help Your Boss Learn More About You. If you want your boss to supervise you wisely, it's your responsibility to help him or her to learn as much about you as possible. Tell your boss what's important to you and what isn't. If you need your boss's help in a particular area of management, ask. If you have special problems with several employees and this affects your department's perfor- mance, request your boss's patience and forbearance (but commit yourself to a target date for solving those problems). Encourage your boss to tell you any time he or she is unhappy with how you're managing.

Your boss deserves the same ethical, well-mannered treatment you give your subordinates and peers, but here are some additional suggestions:

1. A supervisor-subordinate relationship demands an extra measure of deference and respect from you.
2. Let your boss know you are committed to the goals of the organization and to making him or her look good.
3. Help your employees understand the pressures your supervisor is under so that they give the individual the benefit of the doubt if any actions cause them concern.
4. Encourage your boss to interact directly with your subordinates, espe- cially when there are questions. This will reduce distance and promote understanding. If you have the right relationship with your employees and boss, both will keep you informed about these interactions.
5. Be honest and straightforward with your boss whenever possible. Tell the truth, not what you think he or she wants to hear.
6. Encourage your boss to adopt your ideas and suggestions, but be patient; give the individual time to adjust and adapt.
7. Find out the extent to which your supervisor wants to be kept informed about your operation. Most important, if trouble develops in your department, make sure your boss hears about it from *you* first.
8. Solve as many of your problems as you can without your boss's help. Offer *solutions*, not problems. Be as relaxed, friendly, cheerful, courte- ous, and helpful as you can. Like your subordinates, your boss should feel better, not worse, after interacting with you.
9. Trust your boss. Most supervisors will respond honorably and posi- tively to such an assumption on your part.
10. More than anything else, your loyalty and enthusiasm will ensure a good relationship with your boss.

One last word of caution: Because of the "boss" culture of management, you cannot expect all leaders to respond as you would like to your attempts to build a good relationship. But in every case, you can make progress and be content knowing you've done your best.

Your Relationship With Top R&D Management

How can R&D managers optimize their relationships with those in higher R&D positions? Here are a few rules to live by.

1. Help your immediate boss look good to top management.
2. Don't bypass your boss to communicate with top management unless asked to do so.

3. Without making a pest of yourself, take every appropriate opportunity to interact with top R&D management on the job or at social functions.
4. In all interactions, be respectful but friendly. Also be yourself and don't pontificate. Most important, listen and learn.
5. When making presentations to top R&D management, be prepared. Be appropriately brief. Don't upstage your boss; help your boss look good. And, if you don't know the answer to a question, say so.

Reference

Clancy, Tom. *The Cardinal of the Kremlin*. New York: G. P. Putnam's Sons, 1988.

Chapter 22

Working With Committees and Project Teams

Committee—a group of men who keep minutes and waste hours.

Milton Berle

Any effective group has three core activities: (1) accomplishing its goals, (2) maintaining itself internally, and (3) developing and changing in ways that improve its effectiveness.

David W. and Frank P. Johnson, *Joining Together: Group Theory and Group Skills*

Although your primary work will be in conjunction with your subordinates, there will be times when you, as R&D management, will be involved in committees and project teams. This chapter looks at both, with an eye toward initiating a cooperative effort that reaps success.

The Two Worthwhile R&D Committees

While one may agree with often-expressed derogatory comments about committees, two groups can have inestimable value in R&D if constructed well and used wisely. These are the R&D Managers Committee and the R&D Advisory Committee.

The R&D Managers Committee

The R&D Managers Committee, as the title suggests, is composed of the managers from each R&D department, with a leader elected for a term of one year from within the group. The committee's primary function is *communication* among its members. Its purpose is *not* to duplicate the efforts of project teams; rather, it discusses and works to solve organizational, managerial, and philosophical issues.

Case Study: More Technician Grades

A major pharmaceutical company had a single job category for all its technicians. A number of R&D managers felt this policy limited promotional opportunities, growth, and performance incentives for their laboratory assistants. Several individuals discussed the problem with their personnel representative, but were unable to make any progress. Then they brought the matter before their R&D Managers Committee, and, with their vice-president's support, drafted a position paper for Walter, the vice-president of Personnel. Within six months the policy was changed, and two job categories for technicians were approved.

Case Study: R&D Project Accounting

R&D projects in a large electronics firm were tightly controlled by an oppressive, progress-dampening accounting system. The R&D Managers Committee invited Miriam, the manager of Accounting, to a series of meetings to discuss the situation. Within a year many of the more vexing regulations were rescinded, the entire operation grew more efficient, and both Miriam and the R&D managers gained a better understanding of the pressures and complications of one another's job. Equally important, the R&D vice-president and corporate management continued to receive the information they needed and retained the control they desired. Thus the committee turned a serious problem into a classic win-win solution.

Case Study: Project Management

Some problems arose in the area of project management in a major computer company. The R&D Managers Committee (which included Toby, the manager of the project management department) addressed the issues, and the discussion drifted toward trying to solve each of the problems in detail. Toby reminded his colleagues that the committee's role was to delineate the difficulties and reiterate R&D goals; he was responsible for specific solutions. He also assured them that he would ask his project managers to come up with recommendations before the next monthly meeting. The project managers did and the problems were resolved by them and Toby within three months.

The R&D Advisory Committee

The R&D Advisory Committee is usually composed of carefully selected academicians, private citizens, and—occasionally—scientists from noncompetitor companies, all with appropriate scientific expertise and experience. Its functions should include—

▲ evaluating and advising on the general direction of the company's R&D effort;

▲ examining and commenting on individual R&D projects;

▲ recommending which projects to continue and which to terminate;

▲ providing outside technical information and fresh views; and

▲ advising corporate management on the overall quality of the R&D group and its performance.

To help ensure a competent, effective advisory group, committee members should be nominated by laboratory scientists, R&D management, and corporate management, with final appointments made jointly by the vice-president of R&D and selected members of corporate management. Members should be chosen on the basis of their expertise, experience, broad vision, and relevance to the company's business, not solely on their reputations, which may be political and misleading.

The three most important character traits for these advisers are integrity, independence, and candor. It is vital that the committee does not become a rubber stamp for the R&D vice-president. Very few, if any, members should be friends of the R&D vice-president. Intentional or not, friends are inclined to stick together (groupthink), which decreases the board's ability to disagree with the vice-president when necessary. At the same time, members should not be close friends of corporate management; this may foster spying and cronyism.

The size of the Advisory Board will vary depending on the size of the company and the complexity of its technology. If the committee is too small, expertise and diversity will suffer; if too large, it will become cumbersome and ineffective.

Committee members should be paid an appropriate salary so that they take their duties seriously. All concerned must work to create an atmosphere wherein the committee is viewed as a source of help and useful counsel, not as auditors and critics.

The Advisory Committee should have direct access to and contact with department managers and laboratory scientists. The group should meet at least two or three times a year, more often when circumstances (complexity and criticality of projects) dictate. On each visit to the company, the board will typically first meet with R&D personnel, then together as a group, and finally with top R&D and corporate management.

R&D Project Teams

A key element in many R&D divisions is the project team; the more complex and multidisciplinary the project, the more critical the need for an effective group to bring it to fruition in the shortest possible time. R&D managers may not be directly involved in project teams, but at the very least, they need to ensure that the groups—

▲ are properly constituted;

▲ are effectively led;

▲ function effectively; and
▲ have sufficient resources to reach their goals within the allotted time.

Project teams may be formal or informal, and their success depends upon two factors:

1. The group's technical skills and performance
2. The interpersonal skills of team members, especially the team leader

Because the first is usually a given while the second is ignored, R&D managers should encourage all laboratory scientists and project leaders to become familiar with the general principles of group dynamics. (See David W. and Frank P. Johnson, David A. Kolb et al., and George H. Labovitz.)

The members of such a group will primarily be R&D laboratory workers, but marketing, manufacturing, engineering, and other relevant personnel should also be represented. The latter may not need to attend every team meeting, but the general rule should be more, not less attendance. At the very least, they should participate in planning and then again as the project moves from the feasibility stage into development.

Project teams may be organized and led differently depending on the technology, the company, and the philosophy of R&D management. Furthermore, depending on the specific project, an R&D group might have different teams organized and led in more than one way. Basically, teams are formal or informal, intradepartmental or interdepartmental.

Formal Project Teams

The leader of a formal project team has managerial authority over members of the group and thus functions as an R&D supervisor. Parts I, II, and III of this book address this situation, so only a few additional comments will suffice.

For instance, leading such a team can be an invaluable aid in assessing the managerial potential of laboratory scientists who express an interest in supervision. The scenario might proceed as follows:

1. The laboratory worker judged to be the most promising candidate for R&D management is selected as project leader.
2. The manager and the project leader work together to develop the basic guidelines (group and personal goals, estimated length of project, size and composition of the team, available resources including total budget, and performance evaluation criteria). It's important to involve the project leader in the planning and decision-making process rather than placing the individual in charge of a predetermined group or situation.
3. The project leader is given an appropriate amount of freedom to lead as seen fit.

4. The manager strongly encourages the project leader to practice participative management; for example, that person should involve team members in decisions related to organizing and operating the team.
5. The manager assists the project leader when appropriate, but preferably waits to give help when asked.
6. At the completion of the project, the manager and project leader evaluate the new leader's performance, with self-evaluation by the employee predominating.

All relevant R&D departments and other functions should be represented on the team (within reason; this is another case where "more is better"). Also, R&D management must work to minimize unhealthy competition among various project groups.

Informal Project Teams

In the informal project team the leader functions only as a coordinator and has no line authority over group members. There are three general types of such teams: (1) intradepartmental; (2) interdepartmental with one of the members serving as leader (internal coordinator); and (3) interdepartmental with a staff project manager as leader (external coordinator).

Intradepartmental. The projects of these teams are usually less complex, narrower in scope, and of shorter duration. They provide the coordinator with new challenges even though he or she may not be interested in management as a career, and they help group members focus on a common goal; this facilitates progress and promotes personal growth.

Interdepartmental With Internal Coordinator. As the name implies, these ventures are multidisciplinary, more complex, broader in scope, and include members of two or more functional departments. Participants are appointed by their department manager, and their primary loyalty is to the manager and their formal work group.

Work on the project is centered in the various R&D departments, with team meetings primarily interdepartmental (including non-R&D departments if appropriate) coordination, communication, and schedule setting. The project coordinator is often designated by management, but social scientists (Johnson and Johnson) aver that it's best if the group chooses its own leader. Elected leadership often changes as the project enters various stages.

Interdepartmental With External Coordinator. The coordinator is a staff project manager who belongs to a project management department. Such departments have one or more of the following functions:

▲ "Managing" (more accurately, coordinating work on) projects;
▲ Developing project plans and schedules;
▲ Calculating and then monitoring project budgets;
▲ Monitoring project progress for top R&D management; and
▲ Determining (with the help of line R&D managers) priorities among projects—not in the commercial sense, but in assigning key service resources among projects. For example, in discovering and developing new pharmaceutical products, a single Safety Evaluation (toxicology and pathology) department usually services all projects. As project needs and schedules change, limited Safety Evaluation resources must be reallocated.

When staff project managers serve as project leaders or coordinators, three factors come into play:

1. The head of the project management group usually reports directly to the vice-president of R&D. Often both individuals (and therefore all staff project managers) see project management's primary function as monitoring the progress and budgets of R&D ventures and alerting the R&D vice-president when problems arise.
2. Project team members and their functional managers inevitably view project managers in that same way and therefore consider them outsiders.
3. The staff project manager, while usually technically trained, is seldom an accomplished laboratory scientist. In addition, he or she may be relatively unfamiliar with the inner workings of the various R&D departments.

Case Study: Project Management—Correcting the Wrong Way

Bruce, an R&D vice-president, presided over a bimonthly consolidated project team meeting in which he attempted to ensure that nothing had been left undone in the fifteen to twenty informal project teams in his area of responsibility. The meetings were held in a large conference room with about fifty people attending; individuals came and went as their segment of the agenda came up for discussion. Not surprisingly, the meeting was time-consuming (two to three hours), clamorous, and somewhat confusing and disconnected. A number of items needed attention because the individual project team leaders did not feel that they were "in charge."

Eventually Bruce retired and Suzanne, his replacement, discontinued the consolidated meeting. Instead, she made it clear to the project team leaders that it was their responsibility to see that *all* project matters were taken care of. The team leaders embraced their new responsibilities. Not only did the problems disappear, but projects progressed more rapidly because of employees' enthusiasm and sense of involvement. (No one mourned the "maxi-meeting" that cost the company up to 150 person hours—plus preparation time—every two months.)

Because of these factors, the external coordinator has difficulty becoming a full participant in the project and seldom can facilitate its progress. Ultimately, success depends upon the level of cooperation among the various departments, separate from any contribution by the externally appointed project manager.

This does not mean that the external project management concept is worthless, although, for these reasons it is probably inferior to the other options. What it *does* mean is that when staff project managers are team coordinators, functional R&D managers must find informal ways to ensure the success of the various technical ventures. This usually involves close cooperation among R&D managers and, even more important, among laboratory scientists who are intimately involved, both with the experimental work and the project team.

Because the success of most technical projects depends on the efforts of a team, the wise R&D manager and project team leader will acquire knowledge and experience in the field of group dynamics (see References at the end of this chapter). The following organizations conduct workshops, publish books, and provide interpersonal and group dynamics training materials:

American Management Association
135 West 50th Street
New York, New York 10020–1201

University Associates, Inc.
8517 Production Avenue
San Diego, Calif. 92121

NTL Institute
1240 North Pitt Street
Suite 100
Alexandria, Va. 22314

Information specific to R&D project management is also available (see References).

References

Johnson, David W., and Frank P. Johnson. *Joining Together: Group Theory and Group Skills*, 2nd ed. Englewood Cliffs, N.J.: Prentice-Hall, 1982.

Kolb, David A., Irwin M. Rubin, and James M. McIntyre. *Organizational Psychology: An Experiential Approach*, 3rd ed. Englewood Cliffs, N.J.: Prentice-Hall, 1979, especially Chapters 8, 12, 13.

Labovitz, George H. *Motivational Dynamics II: Managing Groups: The Key to Productivity*. Minneapolis: Control Data Corporation, 1980.

Suggested Reading

Group Dynamics

Brightman, Harvey J. *Group Problem Solving: An Improved Managerial Approach*. Atlanta: Business Publishing Division, College of Business Administration, Georgia State University, 1987.

Brown, Rupert. *Group Processes: Dynamics Within and Between Groups*. New York: B. Blackwell, 1988.

Cleland, David I. "The Cultural Ambience of Project Management: Another Look." *Project Management Journal* 19, no. 3 (June 1988).

Cooper, Cary L. *Improving Interpersonal Relations: A Guide to Social Skill Development for Managers and Group Leaders*. Englewood Cliffs, N.J.: Prentice-Hall, 1982.

Corey, Gerald. *Group Techniques*, rev. ed. Pacific Grove, Calif.: Brooks/Cole, 1988.

Kadunc, Nancy J., and Desmond L. Cook. "Psychological Attributes of Project Managers in Educational Research and Development." *Journal of the Society of Research Administrators* 18, no. 3 (Winter 1987).

Kernaghan, John A., and Robert A. Cooke. "The Contribution of the Group Process to Successful Project Planning in R&D Settings." *IEEE Transactions on Engineering Management*, EM-33, no. 3 (August 1986).

Luft, Joseph. *Group Processes: An Introduction to Group Dynamics*. Mountain View, Calif.: Mayfield Publishing, 1984.

Napier, Rodney W., and Matti K. Gershenfeld. *Groups, Theory and Experience*, 2nd ed. Boston: Houghton Mifflin, 1981.

———. *Making Groups Work: A Guide for Group Leaders*. Boston: Houghton Mifflin, 1983.

R&D Project Management

Allen, Thomas, Ralph Katz, J. J. Grady, and Neil Slavin. "Project Team Aging and Performance: The Roles of Project and Functional Managers." *R&D Management* 18, no. 4 (October 1988).

Aptman, Leonard H. "Project Management: A Process to Manage Change." *Management Solutions* 31 (August 1986).

———. "Project Management: Criteria for Good Planning." *Management Solutions*, vol. 31 (September 1986).

Barr, Gerald W., James P. Furaus, and Charles G. Shirley. "Showcase Project: Particle Accelerator Research and Development at Sandia National Laboratories." *Project Management Journal* 19, no. 1 (February 1988).

Blackburn, T., and J. Lane. "Project Management at the Mill Level." *Technical Association of the Pulp and Paper Industry Journal* 69, no. 3 (1986).

Fleetham, Charles. "Project Management Keeps Quality Job 1 at Ford." *Industrial Engineering* 21, no. 8 (August 1989).

Fleming, Mary M. K. "Keys to Successful Project Management." *CMA—The Management Accounting Magazine* 60 (November–December 1986).

Frumerman, Robert, Daniel Cicero, and Charles Baetens. "R&D Programs with Multiple Related Projects—I." *Research Management* 30, no. 5 (September–October 1987).

Funk, Fred P. "The Development of an Integrated Project Management System in the Medical Development Section of Lederle Laboratories." *Project Management Journal* 20, no. 3 (September 1989).

Gray, Clifford F. *Essentials of Project Management.* Princeton, N.J.: Petrocelli Books, 1981.

Gupta, Balarko. "Everybody Wins with Joint Project Management." *AACE Transactions* (1989).

Harrison, F. L. *Advanced Project Management.* New York: John Wiley and Sons, 1981.

Imam, Muhammad H., and Jasjit S. Dhillon. "Project Management in Telecommunications: A Case Study." *AACE Transactions* (1989).

Kezsbom, Deborah S. "Leadership and Influence: The Challenge of Project Management." *AACE Transactions* (1988).

Klimstra, Paul D., and Joseph Potts. "What We've Learned Managing R&D Projects." *Research-Technology Management* 31, no. 3 (May–June 1988).

Kopitowsky, Ronald. "Telecom Project Management Tips." *Computerworld* 22, no. 18A (May 4, 1988).

Krusko, Diana, and Robert R. Cangemi. "The Utilization of Project Management in the Pharmaceutical Industry." *Journal of the Society of Research Administrators* 19, no. 1 (Summer 1987).

Larson, Erik W., and David H. Gobeli. "Significance of Project Management Structure on Development Success." *IEEE Transactions on Engineering Management* 36, no. 2 (May 1989).

Liberatore, Matthew J., and George J. Titus. "Managing Industrial R&D Projects: Current Practice and Future Directions." *Journal of the Society of Research Administrators* 18, no. 1 (Summer 1986).

Manglik, P. C., and Arabinda Tripathy. "Uncertainty of a Research and Development Project." *Project Management Journal* 19, no. 5 (November 1988).

Medley, Larry G. "Systems Approach to Project Management." *AACE Transactions* (1989).

Murphy, Patrice L. "Pharmaceutical Project Management: Is It Different?" *Project Management Journal* 20, no. 3 (September 1989).

Oldham, Connisue B., Carl T. Ripberger, and Judith E. Cook. "Project Management in a Federal Research and Development Laboratory: An Application of the Elusive Budgeted Cost of Work Performed." *Project Management Journal* 17, no. 4 (September 1986).

Pinto, Jeffrey K., and Dennis P. Slevin. "Critical Success Factors in R&D Projects." *Research-Technology Management* 32, no. 1 (January–February 1989).

Rad, P. F. "Elements of an Effective Project Management System." *Clinical Research Practices and Drug Regulatory Affairs* 4, no. 6 (1986).

Randolph, W. Alan, and Barry Z. Posner. "What Every Manager Needs to Know about Project Management." *Sloan Management Review* 29 (Summer 1988).

Schlick, James D. "Developing Project Management Skills." *Training and Development Journal* 42, no. 5 (May 1988).

Syrett, Michel. "New Paths for Project Management." *Director* 41, no. 6 (January 1988).

Tucker, J. G. "Satisfying the Scientist and the Marketer Through Computers, Team-building, and Project Management." *Pharmaceutical Technology* 10, no. 8 (1986).

Chapter 23

R&D Budgets

An article in *Business Week* (June 16, 1989) reported that the National Science Foundation estimated 1989 R&D spending by American industry at $95 billion (current dollars) or $75 billion (constant 1982 dollars). The American Association for the Advancement of Science (AAAS), a cooperative scientific group, in its comprehensive Report XIV (1989) on federal R&D spending, noted that the FY 1990 budget included approximately $45 billion (current dollars) for national defense R&D and $25 billion for nondefense R&D. Gene Koretz, in an article in *Business Week* (August 21, 1989), estimates that real R&D spending fell in 1989 compared to 1988.

Interesting information, but of what use is this to the R&D manager preparing a budget for the upcoming fiscal year? It's not at all helpful, nor is any other piece of general information. I make this point to emphasize that a lengthy discussion of R&D financing or budgeting would be a waste of time; it would also be out of my area of expertise. However, R&D managers cannot ignore financial matters completely; they must become familiar and deal effectively with their organization's unique budgeting system. In that spirit, here are ten budgeting rules to live by.

☐ **Rule 1:** *Take your budget seriously.* R&D has the reputation (too often well deserved) of being in an ivory tower, not appreciating the realities of the bottom line. R&D managers who take their budget seriously and monitor it carefully are being fiscally responsible. They are also 95 percent of the way toward having a good relationship with the accounting department and making their department's finances a nonissue with their superiors.

☐ **Rule 2:** *Involve subordinates in the budgeting process.* R&D managers who involve their employees (to the extent they prefer) in planning the department's budget will construct a better financial plan. They will also find their subordinates more committed to staying within those budgetary guidelines.

☐ **Rule 3:** *Don't overburden your employees.* Although input from subordinates is valuable in *planning* a budget, the manager should *monitor* it. Subordinates prefer to concentrate on science; when you need their assistance controlling spending, they will know it's a serious matter and will respond helpfully. Most times, a department head or vice-president will have a staff accountant to monitor the total R&D budget.

☐ **Rule 4:** *The budget is not etched in stone.* Several company controllers have emphasized that budgets are—up to a point—flexible guidelines, not etched-in-stone numbers. In general, and except for emergency austerity periods, if R&D managers stay within 1 to 3 percent of their budget (even though some line items may be higher or lower), the accountants will be happy. Everyone connected with budgets, while taking them seriously, should heed North Carolina University's basketball coach Dean Smith's words: "If you treat every situation as a life-and-death matter, you'll die a lot of times."

☐ **Rule 5:** *On-budget R&D managers live more freely.* If R&D managers do consistently well keeping to their budgets, they will experience more freedom within the corporation's financial corridors. When the boss and the company accountants view you as a pragmatic, reasonable, responsible individual concerning budgets, your financial constraints will be minimal, certainly tolerable. For example, if you occasionally need special budgetary relief because of unforeseen circumstances, most controllers will be understanding and helpful.

☐ **Rule 6:** *Find an in-house financial adviser.* To learn about your company's budgeting system, ask the help of someone in the accounting department. Find out, for example, the difference between capital dollars* and expense dollars, which expenses are fixed and which are variable, what each line item means, and what the capital depreciation schedule is. Ask for hints on how to live with "the system." If the accountant strikes you as a rigid, by-the-book person, look for another adviser until you find someone who is informed, has common sense, and is flexible (see the case study on page 217).

Then when "the system" says there's no solution to a budgetary problem, ask your adviser for help. More often than not, you'll be pleasantly surprised.

☐ **Rule 7:** *Don't let your budget become a fetish.* If R&D managers become infatuated with budgetary matters, they may neglect their subordinates and other important duties. The case study on page 219 proves that point.

☐ **Rule 8:** *Fixed expenses ain't . . . necessarily.* Even fixed expenses should be monitored for changes and anomalies. For example, departmental office and laboratory floor space are fixed expenses. When a department gains or loses floor space, the change should be reflected in the following year's fixed expenses. Also, errors can creep into budgets; managers should challenge any unexplained increase in both fixed and variable expenses. Naturally, accountants also appreciate being informed whenever a department is undercharged.

☐ **Rule 9:** *Employee salaries are the primary variable expense.* For most R&D departments, the major variable—and therefore controllable—expense is sala-

---

*As the reader probably knows, capital money is different from expense money in many ways, including tax treatment. Most important, in the annual report capital items appear in the asset, or plus, column until they are fully depreciated, while expense items appear in the liability, or minus, column. Your financial adviser can give you a more detailed view of how capital vs. expense money is handled in your company.

Case Study: Help! Or Challenging the System

Greg was an R&D manager who had underspent $38,000 earlier in the current year on a laboratory renovation project in the "over $100,000 capital" budget category. Unexpectedly, he needed $35,000 later in the year for a separate renovation project. Greg's boss, along with two managerial peers and three lower-level accountants, told him that the rules forbade spending leftover money from "over $100,000 capital" projects on "under $100,000 capital" items.

Unwilling to accept a rule that made little sense to him, Greg went to Myrtle, the division controller, and asked the same question, emphasizing that the second renovation project could be deferred until next year only with difficulty. Myrtle replied that she saw no problem with moving the funds from one account to another, since it was a semi-emergency and the funds were available within Greg's own budget. The latter informed his boss and the accountants, and the way was cleared. (Greg approached Myrtle because he once heard her give a talk in which she mentioned that the company's budgeting system was meant to be flexibly helpful, not rigidly onerous, to line managers.)

Table 1. R&D expenses.

Industry	Percentage Change From Previous Year	As Percentage of Sales
Overall composite	11%	3.4%
Aerospace	1	4.1
Automotive	12	3.2
Parts and equipment	12	2.1
Chemicals	10	3.6
Conglomerates	2	2.2
Consumer products	9	1.6
Containers and packaging	3	1.0
Electrical and electronics	13	5.3
Food	3	0.7
Fuel	6	0.7
Health care	19	8.2
Housing and construction	0	1.9
Leisure time industries	12	4.6
Manufacturing	8	2.6
Metals and mining	-2	1.2
Nonbank financial	27	0.8

(continued)

Table 1. R&D expenses. (*continued*).

Office equipment and		
computers	18	7.5
Paper and forest products	12	1.0
Service industries	4	1.2
Telecommunications	6	5.7

ries and other people-related expenses such as laboratory supplies. Thus, prudent management is especially careful about adding headcount. For instance, an additional $300,000 in a particular year's budget for new people can, with a relatively stable work force, mean a financial commitment for years to come.*

☐ **Rule 10:** *Expect limited budget growth.* For most functions in a corporation, yearly budget growth, after inflation, is usually limited to 5 percent or less. In general, R&D divisions need more money than that if the corporation is to stay competitive. R&D managers must use general R&D growth statistics to support their budgetary requests to top management and have defensible reasons for additional funding. Relevant statistics are widely available, as for example in Table 1.

Case Study: The Budget-Computer Hacker

Roy, an R&D manager, became infatuated with his computer and the company's newly installed project tracking system. He created extensive, complicated software and spent uncounted hours monitoring the financial progress (including the hours each employee spent on each item) of every project in his department. He became a laughing stock, and the work environment suffered until Juanita, a group leader, informally took over the management of the department.

---

*I have heard it said many times (e.g., during periodic layoffs to ensure short-term profits) that top management's primary obligation is to the shareholders. Perhaps, but we need to carefully weigh that obligation against a corporation's basic responsibility to its workers. After all, shareholders invest money, but employees invest much more, including their careers. In some high-risk industries, they invest their health and their lives. Also, workers will repay top management's ministrations with increased loyalty and productivity, which is the surest path to increased shareholder benefits. Finally, where should a company draw the line between its obligations to shareholders and its obligations to society (e.g., environmental pollution)? These issues are not easily resolved, but they need to be thoughtfully addressed.

In summary, wise R&D managers will strike a balance on budgeting matters by being—

▲ *resourceful* in finding ways to generate the money for their department to make optimum progress;
▲ *responsible* in balancing the needs of the corporation and those of their employees;
▲ *responsive* to the requirements of "the system," their boss, the accountants, and their subordinates; and
▲ *realistic* by recognizing that there are finite budgetary constraints to what they would like to do as R&D manager.

References

"AAAS Report 14: Research and Development FY 1990." Washington, D.C.: American Association for the Advancement of Science, Committee on Science, Engineering, and Public Policy, 1989.

"Innovation in America." *Business Week*, Special Bonus Issue (June 16, 1989).

Koretz, Gene. "Business Talks a Better R&D Game Than it Plays." *Business Week*, August 21, 1989.

Chapter 24

Computers and R&D

As every R&D manager and laboratory worker knows, computers have become an indispensable tool in research and development. Except, perhaps, in the computer industry, R&D managers need not, and should not, be experts in computer science, but it is important that they (1) understand the general capabilities and limitations of computers in R&D work, and (2) appreciate the need for computer expertise within or available to their department.

Computers have been around for years, but their proliferation in R&D, especially in the laboratory, began with the widespread availability of the moderately priced personal computer (PC) in the 1980s. Today computers are used for any of the following:

▲ Word processing, including spelling and grammar checks and thesaurus
▲ Electronic mail
▲ Automated data acquisition and data base construction; for example—
  —Periodic weight determination when studying vapor transmission through films
  —Control of analytical instruments such as HPLC
  —Physiological data acquisition (e.g., blood pressure) and subsequent digitalization
  —Data treatment, including statistical evaluation
▲ CAD-CAM (computer-aided design and manufacture)—for example, allowing designers to formulate concepts, replacing manual tools such as T-squares and French curves
▲ R&D and manufacturing process control and automation. For example—
  —Lyophilization, remotely monitoring and controlling temperature, pressure, and time
  —Compression of solids, controlling weight variation
▲ Process and scientific equation or theory simulation
▲ Spreadsheets for budget monitoring and number crunching
▲ Control of complicated administrative procedures such as project management

Perhaps the best way to illustrate the appropriate management of computers in R&D is through this case study.

I wish to acknowledge the contributions of my colleagues at Abbott Laboratories for most of the information in this chapter.

Case Study: A Department Meets Its Computer Needs

Wilhelm was the newly appointed manager of four interrelated R&D departments. Over the past few years some individuals had acquired PCs, but as the departments had no master plan for the general use of computers, intercomputer communication was limited.

Only about 25 percent of the employees operated the computers, but those who did used them extensively. The group included several self-taught computer experts, but in every case their computer activities were secondary and supplementary to their research responsibilities.

Recognizing that extensive, integrated use of computers was vital to the future of his operation, Wilhelm set up a task force whose purpose was to recommend a master plan for computer acquisition and use. The group proposed (1) a large increase in the number of PCs and (2) enlisting the help of a specialist who would develop and implement the plan. This would ensure that departmental computer acquisition and use were coordinated, with all units having the ability to "talk" to each other. Also, it would guarantee that the most appropriate hardware and software would be purchased, focusing especially on flexibility to upgrade and modernize. Lastly, employees would have ready access to a teacher or consultant who would facilitate and expedite their computer training.

The above objectives could be achieved by means of one of the following:

▲ "Rent" an expert from the company's MIS (Management Information Systems) department to get the group started.
▲ Hire a full-time specialist as part of the department's regular work force. This individual would be a scientist so that after the plan was implemented, he or she could shift focus to laboratory research while remaining readily available as an in-house computer consultant.

The latter course was chosen, primarily because an in-house employee would better understand the department's unique technical projects, and, as a bona fide member of the department, the person's commitment to the group would be ensured.

Wilhelm, committed to promoting from within, first posted the position in the four departments and in other R&D areas as well. Dexter, a laboratory technician with a flair for and interest in computers, was offered the position but decided to stay where he was.

Subsequently, Marcia, a newly graduated B.S. electrical engineer who had specialized in computer hardware, software, and programming, was hired. She proved to be a competent computer specialist and a dedicated employee with excellent interpersonal skills. Furthermore, she was enthusiastic about becoming a researcher in the group's engineering section as her computer responsibilities diminished. As a result, within twelve to eighteen months all four departments were functioning smoothly with the optimum type and number of interactive, compatible PCs.

Computers in the R&D setting

The computer enables scientists to broaden their experimental approach. Before PCs, scientists often gathered samples, sent them to another department for assay, to still another group for statistical treatment, and then evaluated the treated data when it was returned to them. PCs enable scientists to perform these satellite services themselves, making optimum use of their intimate knowledge of the project.

PCs also enable researchers to design better experiments; gather more precise, more complete data at lower cost; and prepare better graphs and charts for presentation.

However, the primary danger here is that scientists may remove themselves from the laboratory, spend all of their time at the computer, and force technicians to work in relative isolation. It should be remembered that the research process works best when scientists are readily available to: (1) make firsthand observations while an experiment is in progress and (2) interact with technicians while they work, to advise and help them and be available to answer questions.

Some researchers may become so infatuated with the magic of computers and programming that they forget that the PC is only a tool for their *real* job, which is conducting laboratory research and developing new products. Thus, they become more proficient in computer use and less effective in research.

If computer use is managed wisely, however, these problems can be avoided. The computer has multiple uses in R&D.

Applications for Technical Work

1. Before PCs, scientists had to spend considerable time with a calculator to get their experimental data into manageable form. Now they can use a computer to do that work, giving them more time for analyzing, thinking, and planning.

2. Using a PC to model physical processes has many advantages, especially when the process is complex and dynamic: (1) It allows scientists to have more insight into the process under study, and (2) with computer modeling, according to James Gleick (*Chaos: Making a New Science*), scientists are less likely to understate or overstate the effects of a particular variable.

However, actual laboratory experimentation is as important as ever: (1) The validity of any model, no matter how realistic, needs to be tested experimentally, and (2) laboratory experimentation forces scientists to be quantitative about their assumptions.

3. Computers can interface with fax machines so that the scientist can send and receive fax communications without leaving the laboratory.

4. Computers can be used with videos for on-screen presentation of data, replacing overheads and slides.

5. Literature searches can be conducted with a PC and modem when the

scientist's needs are too selective for the normal company library services or when the company is too small to have a full-service library. Copies of the reference or patent are then immediately available.

6. With remote access to computers in the laboratory, intercontinental connections can be made. Likewise, remote access allows scientists to work extra hours at home if they so choose.

7. Computers are especially helpful in the field of project management—for example, to construct critical paths, coordinate activities, and monitor progress of complicated research projects (see References at the end of this chapter for more examples). One enterprising project manager used impressive computer spreadsheets to convince management of the need to hire more people for his project!

Potential Problems

Computers are invaluable, but unless their limitations are recognized, there can be complications and setbacks. Here are some examples:

1. While electronic mail has obvious advantages, it can get out of hand. If coworkers communicate only by E-mail and never interact face to face, their relationships are sure to deteriorate.
2. Some scientists send formal communications via computer without going through the department secretary. While this can be appropriate and efficient in some cases, there are disadvantages:
   ▲ It reduces scientists' time for research.
   ▲ Formal letters and memos do not have the benefit of the secretary's expert editing and formatting.
   ▲ The secretary may not know of letters and memos that should be placed in departmental files.
   ▲ The secretary is out of the information loop and may feel uninvolved and discontent.
   ▲ The secretary may be unaware of scheduling conflicts when confirming dates for meetings.

Managing With Computers

Managers often think the primary use of computers is to help scientists work *faster*, but equally important, computers should enable the scientist to work *more wisely*. To ensure that, managers need to understand the group's computer needs and applications. For example, the R&D manager should become familiar with the many valuable services offered by the corporate computer department, including expert advice and mainframe capacity. However, the disadvantages of always bringing in computer experts from a corporate department or an outside firm can best be illustrated with the following case study.

Case Study: The Experts Were Gone

An R&D department wanted to install a computer system to monitor product stability. Departmental scientists investigated programs offered by outside firms, but decided against this approach because future upgrading would be difficult, since the consulting firm would need to be educated as to the details of the stability system, a difficult task. Also, the consulting firm would need to protect its trade secrets, forcing departmental scientists to work blindly in many instances. Lastly, specialized modifications to the system could be prohibitively expensive. Instead, the group enlisted the help of the internal corporate computer services department.

At first the installed system satisfied the department's requirements, but subsequent changes in technology and governmental regulations necessitated major revisions. Unfortunately, this could be done only with great difficulty and expense because the individuals who designed the system were no longer with the company, so someone new had to be oriented to the special needs of the department. Rita, the R&D department's computer specialist (hired after the program had been in place for several years) was unable to get into the system to make the necessary modifications.

Rita and several departmental scientists developed another system themselves, one that could be modified in the future if necessary. Because the department had a history of low employee turnover, and because several individuals were knowledgeable concerning the new system, the danger of history repeating itself was minimized.

Equipment Considerations

Too often, R&D managers wring their hands over decisions (need vs. cost) about computer use in their departments. As with any other situation, management should let employees decide what tools they need, and then work up a feasible budgetary schedule to provide those tools.

Always remember, of course, that frequent, continuous improvements in hardware and software necessitate buying units that are capable of being upgraded. In R&D, supercomputers can be justified only when treating mega databases, as in molecular biology and weather modeling. Mainframe units are most appropriate for intermediate tasks, while PCs serve the day-to-day needs of laboratory scientists.

Automated control of complex, sophisticated physical processes such as lyophilization require both scientific (including engineering) and computer expertise. But the major problems are process, not computer, related. Therefore, it's best to have the engineers learn to handle computerization rather than try to teach computer specialists about the process.

Scientists must make sure software companies are aware of their technical needs—for example, many of the currently available spreadsheets are business, not laboratory, oriented. Also, scientific software may not facilitate intuitive data manipulation as well as business software does. But business software may not include error bars, and it often has limited statistical capability; this restricts its adaptation by scientists.

Staff Considerations

Although most current, educated scientists cannot function without a computer, some veterans who lack computer skills may not be inclined to learn. The wise R&D manager will accommodate both types of employees, as long as they are productive. However, it is important to emphasize to reluctant veterans that learning to use a computer is a growth opportunity, but you should not force the issue past their Plimsoll line. Most certainly, all new scientists and technicians should be encouraged to develop computer skills if they don't already possess them.

An appropriately computerized R&D department, with each scientist having a PC, becomes a recruiting tool; it demonstrates to job candidates two things:

1. The company generously supports R&D.
2. Potential co-workers are keeping themselves current in computer usage.

When recruiting a computer specialist for your department, look for more than just technical skills. Among other things, the individual must—

▲ work harmoniously with colleagues, be a patient teacher, and be well organized.

▲ remember that scientific software is sophisticated, complicated, and difficult for a neophyte to use (although the computer industry is working hard to make it more user-friendly).

▲ step back and look at problems from the user's viewpoint.

Representative references on computer use in R&D appear below. Some of them (especially those concerning software) may be obsolete, but they serve to identify journals where relevant information can be found.

References

Aptman, Leonard H. "Project Management: Successful Use of PC Software." *Management Solutions* 31 (December 1986).

Brackett, Stephen W., and Anne Marie Isbell. "PMIS—An Integrated Approach for the Management and Distribution of Project Information." *Project Management Journal* 20, no. 3 (September 1989).

Brousseau, John. "Project Management: Look Before You Leap." *Computing Canada* 14, no. 9 (April 28, 1988).

Cottrell, S. C. "Novel Applications of Project Management Software to Support the Clinical Development Process in the Pharmaceutical Industry." *Clinical Research Practices and Drug Regulatory Affairs* 6, no. 3 (1988).

Gleick, James. *Chaos: Making a New Science.* New York: Viking Press, 1987.

Hlinak, Anthony J. "Freeze Dryer Automation with Programmable Controllers." *Pharmaceutical Engineering* 7, no. 6 (November–December 1987).

Hlinak, Anthony J., and Edward A. Ingold. "A Computer Control System for Freeze Drying." *Pharmaceutical Engineering* 4, no. 5 (September–October 1984).

O'Neal, Kim Rogers. "Second Annual Buyer's Guide Lists Latest Project Management Microcomputer Software." *Industrial Engineering* 19 (January 1987).

Page, William G. "Using Project Management Software in Planning." *Journal of the American Planning Association* 55 (Autumn 1989).

Phan, Dien, Douglas Vogel, and Jay Nunamaker. "The Search for Perfect Project Management." *Computerworld* 22, no. 39 (September 26, 1988).

Rad, P. F. "Considerations in Computerizing a Project Management System." *Clinical Research Practices and Drug Regulatory Affairs* 5, no. 1 (1987).

"UPECS Speeds Up Design and Project Management." *Dairy Industries International* 52, no. 8 (August 1987).

Suggested Readings

Alak, Safa M., and Talib Obiad. "Spreadsheet Solution of Time-dependent Heat Transfer Problems." *Journal of Engineering Computing and Applications* 2, no. 4 (Summer 1988).

Blakely, Ken. "Dynamic Analysis: Application and Modeling Considerations." *Journal of Engineering Computing and Applications,* 2, no. 1 (Fall 1987).

Blundell, James K. "Expert Systems for Material Selection." *Journal of Engineering Computing and Applications* 4, no. 1 (Summer 1989).

Braun, Ori. "Transient Three-dimensional Numerical Simulations." *Journal of Engineering Computing and Applications* 2, no. 4 (Summer 1988).

Currie, Andrew O. "Getting Started with Finite-Element Analysis for Product Design." *Journal of Engineering Computing and Applications* 2, no. 1 (Fall 1987).

Fraade, David J., ed. *The Aster Guide to Computer Applications in the Pharmaceutical Industry: An Overview of Manufacturers' Hardware and Software.* Eugene, Ore.: Aster, 1984.

———. *Automation of Pharmaceutical Operations.* Eugene, Ore.: Aster, 1983.

———. *Automation of Pharmaceutical Operations—Supplement.* Eugene, Ore.: Aster, 1984.

Harris, James R. *The Aster Introduction to Microcomputers In Pharmaceutical Operations.* Eugene, Ore.: Aster, 1984.

Hohne, Bruce A., and Thomas H. Pierce, eds. *Expert System Applications in Chemistry.* Washington, D.C.: American Chemical Society, 1989.

Jensen, Klaus F., and Donald G. Truhlar, eds. *Supercomputer Research in Chemistry and Chemical Engineering.* Washington, D.C.: American Chemical Society, 1989.

Light, Bob. "Using Spreadsheets for Data Analysis." *Journal of Engineering Computing and Applications* 2, no. 1 (Fall 1987).

Meyer, Daniel E., Wendy A. Warr, and Richard A. Love, eds. *Chemical Structure Software for Personal Computers*. Washington, D.C.: American Chemical Society, 1988.

Nwosu, Harold U. "Evaluating Product Design Alternatives." *Journal of Engineering Computing and Applications*, 3, no. 3 (Spring 1989).

Onwubiko, Chinyere, and Heeyong Park. "Constrained Optimization Using a Modified Pattern Search Method." *Journal of Engineering Computing and Applications* 3, no. 3 (Spring 1989).

Ouchi, Glenn I. *Personal Computers for Scientists: A Byte at a Time*. Washington, D.C.: American Chemical Society, 1986.

Provder, Theodore, ed. *Computer Applications in Applied Polymer Science II: Automation, Modeling, and Simulation*. Washington, D.C.: American Chemical Society, 1989.

Putnam, Frederick A. "Data Acquisition and Control: Technology Trends and Applications." *Journal of Engineering Computing and Applications* 2, no. 2 (Winter 1988).

Schwartz, Thomas J. "Expert Systems Come of Age." *Journal of Engineering Computing and Applications* 1, no. 1 (Fall 1986).

"Software: It's a New Game." *Business Week*, June 4, 1990.

Tou, S. K. U., C. Y. Lin, and H. Chu. "A Microcomputer-based Data Acquisition Monitoring System." *Journal of Engineering Computing and Applications* 3, no. 3 (Spring 1989).

Warr, Wendy A., ed. *Chemical Structure Information Systems: Interfaces, Communications, and Standards*. Washington, D.C.: American Chemical Society, 1989.

———. *Graphics for Chemical Structures: Integration with Text and Data*. Washington D.C.: American Chemical Society, 1987.

Watson, Henry, and Asok Ray. "An Overview of Robotics Implementation." *Journal of Engineering Computing and Applications* 3, no. 1 (Fall 1988).

Chapter 25

Outlicensing and Inlicensing Concerns/ Government Contracts and Regulations

Research-oriented corporations prefer to get new products from internal efforts, with enough prospects left over to license to competitors, but in reality most organizations engage in both out- and inlicensing. Most commonly, a small department reporting to top management is responsible for identifying, evaluating, and processing opportunities for licensing.

It is important that R&D be closely involved with this function, especially in the evaluation stage of inlicensing, because it has the scientific expertise to help top management make wise, informed decisions. In addition, it is especially important to involve laboratory scientists in technical evaluation and decision making. Too often R&D managers, confident of their own judgment and eager to impress, give scientifically obsolete, naïve, or incorrect snap opinions to top management.

An in-depth discussion of this topic is beyond the scope of this book, but R&D managers should be aware of several general points and subtleties.

Financial Arrangements

In most licensing agreements, one of three options, which may or may not include up-front money, is commonly negotiated:

1. A lump-sum payment
2. A percentage of sales in the ± percent range, with percentages varying with volume
3. Some combination of the two

Outlicensing

A wise, active outlicensing program is beneficial to the corporation and to R&D morale and productivity because scientists see more of their efforts reach the marketplace.

R&D's Interaction With the Marketing Department

While top management makes the final decision about whether to outlicense a particular product, R&D and marketing people should cooperate before making recommendations because technical and commercial factors are closely interwoven. Both groups must avoid the "dog-in-the-manger" syndrome, fighting outlicensing and then letting the product die internally.

The following key questions will help R&D and Marketing reach a consensus:

1. Should the product be outlicensed or developed and sold internally? R&D needs to accurately convey to the marketing department the item's technical advantages and disadvantages. Marketing people must express to R&D their degree of enthusiasm for the product. The process requires trust, candor, and courage while eschewing game playing, protectionism, and finger pointing.
2. Should R&D complete development and offer the finished product or sell the rights and let the outlicensee do most of the development work? This depends on technical factors and priorities:
   ▲ Must R&D be involved to ensure technical success because of its unique expertise and capabilities? Do not let hubris and scientific chauvinism distort the perception.
   ▲ How does this project fit into the company's financial, time, and resource priorities?
3. Which competitor is likely to be best, and how can they be sold on the idea?
4. Is joint marketing advantageous?
5. Will licensure endanger the success of the company's other products?
6. Will too many technical secrets be given away, especially if a fully developed product or process is outlicensed?
7. What effect will outlicensing have on R&D morale? Will workers feel the fruits of their labors were given second-class status? In a supportive work environment, *and if the reasons behind any particular outlicensing decision are explained to them*, R&D workers will understand, appreciate, and usually endorse management's decisions.

R&D's Interaction With the Licensing Department

The keys to a good relationship are understanding, empathy, communication, respect, candor, trust, deference, and cooperation. Wise R&D managers will recognize that the licensing department's performance and personal satisfaction depend almost entirely on *culminating* outlicensing and inlicensing contracts. Therefore, if R&D consistently vetoes each project, the licensing department may become frustrated and alienated. To avoid this, R&D must—

▲ keep an open mind regarding all proposals;
▲ recommend approval when that makes sense technically; and
▲ explain at length to the licensing department the reasons behind rejection of a project and be willing to listen to counterarguments.

If the licensing department views R&D as competent, reasonable, flexible, and enthusiastic about the outlicensing function, the relationship will be positive and productive.

Inlicensing

R&D must exercise special care in the area of inlicensing because, compared to the situation in outlicensing, R&D will be less familiar with the details of the technology. Also, the potential licensor's data are usually sparse and almost always incomplete. In particular, R&D must temper Licensing's and top management's enthusiasm for proposals that sound tempting but are short on experimental proof.

At the same time, R&D must avoid the NIH (not invented here) syndrome, in which company scientists undervalue someone else's accomplishments because the scientists may look bad by comparison. (Why didn't *we* think of that?) This is less likely to occur if R&D has a history of success and if scientists feel valued and appreciated by management. Secure, confident people are much more apt to look at outside technical proposals objectively and realistically. The need for broad-visioned, well-read scientists in R&D is especially important here, both in the sense of having a feel for the offered technology and in being aware of who might make a good consultant.

Many of the comments and questions for outlicensing also apply here. Other key questions include:

1. Is the product or process technically sound and feasible? If R&D is relatively unfamiliar with the technology behind an offered product, independent consultants can be valuable.
2. What are the chances of technical success? Seldom are they 100 percent. Does the marketing potential justify proceeding if R&D estimates 50 percent probability?
3. What needs to be accomplished internally to ready the item for the marketplace? For products involving complex technology, the temptation is to ask the offering company to do all the development work. This may be appropropriate, especially if the licensor is also going to be the manufacturer. But if the licensee wants to manufacture a technically complex product developed wholly by the licensor, then when trouble arises in Manufacturing, internal R&D cannot be of much help because

they have not done the development work. This can lead to serious problems for Manufacturing. Therefore, negotiations should include a service contract whereby the licensor agrees to provide technical support. A provision must ensure responsiveness so that Manufacturing is not shut down for extended periods of time.

4. If the licensor is responsible for all R&D work, does the estimated timetable ensure, to the extent possible, that the product won't be outdated by the time it reaches the marketplace?

5. What provisions are made in the contract so that near-future advances in the technology by the licensor will be made available to the licensee?

6. How reliable, technically and businesswise, is the offering company?

Case Study: You Can't Rely on Schmidt

Felice, an R&D scientist for Hyteck, was invited by Klaus, the manager of Product Licensing, to hear a presentation by a visitor, Dr. Schmidt, who was trying to convince the company to license a unique technology he had developed. When Felice shook Schmidt's hand, she thought she recognized his name. During the presentation, Felice remembered that Schmidt had consulted for Louteck, her previous employer. Although she had had no personal knowledge of the visitor's competence or integrity, Felice knew three present Louteck employees (whose judgment and candor she trusted) who had worked closely with Schmidt.

The next day Felice called her three friends, and they all related the same story: Five years ago Schmidt had taken a $200,000 fee from Louteck to do some work in his laboratory; unfortunately, his experimental technique was of such low quality that the data were worthless. Felice called the R&D vice-president and Klaus to share this information; both were appreciative. Schmidt was politely told, "No, thank-you."

In some cases, a promising new technology may arise and become popular, but for various good reasons R&D elects not to establish a major research effort in that area. Nevertheless, it often pays to have a modest program in the field so company scientists can quickly test inlicensing proposals in the laboratory and, equally important, detect scientific Sophists before the company makes an up-front payment.

Any company with an active inlicensing program should establish a standing evaluation committee composed of laboratory scientists from all relevant disciplines. Not only will the committee assess the worth or potential of any one proposal, but it will also be able to compare a current suggestion with similar ones made over the past two or three years. In addition, it may be able to recommend and institute quick, definitive laboratory evaluation.

Most technical companies have highly successful inlicensed products in their history. R&D can provide a valuable service to the corporation by paying close, careful, and consistent attention to all such proposals. Who knows? The next billion-dollar product may be on tomorrow's agenda for consideration!

Patenting Technical Achievements

The rewards of innovative industrial science can be greatly magnified if laboratory workers work closely with the patent department to ensure maximum protection of new products and technological discoveries.

The R&D manager should help ensure careful day-to-day documentation of ideas and data in laboratory notebooks and the witnessing thereof by a colleague. In patent disputes with competitors, millions of dollars can be and have been gained or lost by a few days' difference in the first written record.

The manager should also ensure that scientists understand the legal importance of "diligence"; that is, if an idea is recorded but no laboratory work is done, the patent position will be weak. Scientists should interact frequently with the patent department's R&D liaison personnel to ensure: (1) protection for any and all potentially useful and profitable ideas or laboratory results, and (2) that all patents are as broad as possible.

R&D personnel should understand the need for confidentiality (from outsiders) in their work. This includes:

1. Proper filing and disposal of written material.
2. Prudence in conversation, especially at scientific meetings and conventions.
3. Delaying publication in journals until patents can be filed. This is not usually a problem because in most companies the patent department must approve all proposed publications.

Lastly, be careful that overzealous patent attorneys don't produce weak patents that reveal proprietary information but do not, in fact, give the company legal protection.

Securing Government Contracts for Research and Products

Depending on the company and the technology, business with the federal government may be a significant or insignificant part of a corporation's business. If the former, many companies have a person or staff of individuals (e.g., a government sales or contracts department) located in the Washington, D.C., area.

Even companies with normally small government business may find it advantageous at times to engage in R&D contracts for the federal government.

For example, when corporate financial conditions threaten a temporary (one to three year) cut in R&D personnel, the government can, at times, provide the necessary funding continuity. The activity may lead to new products (e.g., in cancer chemotherapy). And in some situations, a company's unique R&D expertise can provide a public service at a fair profit.

Many technical companies supplement their product sales with contracts with state and federal governments. At times R&D can provide technical service to Manufacturing so that products can meet goverment specifications, or products can be manufactured more efficiently to allow lower bids.

R&D managers are in a unique position here to combine technical knowledge, business sense, and a broad view of the corporation to suggest opportunities to the R&D vice-president and corporate management.

Governmental Regulatory Affairs

Some technical industries (e.g., computers, electronics) have minimal goverment oversight,* while others (e.g., pharmaceuticals, tobacco) are highly regulated and still others (e.g., food, oil, automobiles, diagnostics) fall somewhere in between. The regulatory affairs department in affected industries is important; the more government regulation, the more crucial this function becomes. For instance, in a highly regulated industry, disregard for government regulations can, at best, cost money; at worst, it can put a company out of business. R&D managers in regulated industries need to learn the subtleties of their companies' interactions with the government.

The pharmaceutical industry provides a good example. Pharmaceutical companies in the United States deal primarily with the Food and Drug Administration (FDA). If a company wants to market a new drug, it must first prove its safety, efficacy, and stability, and submit a New Drug Application (NDA) to the FDA national office. (Research and development, preparation of the NDA, and the FDA approval process can take as long as fifteen years and cost the company hundreds of millions of dollars.) In addition, inspectors from the FDA's regional offices periodically audit a company's facilities and records to monitor compliance with regulations, especially good manufacturing practices (GMP).

The functions of the regulatory affairs department in major pharmaceutical companies center on interactions with the FDA, with special emphasis on the preparation of NDAs. Sections within the NDA (e.g., clinical, drug safety, manufacturing and controls) are prepared by the appropriate R&D departments, but the regulatory affairs group is responsible for the overall organization, thrust, assembly, and submission of the application and subsequent interactions with the FDA.

R&D managers should realize that a company's main interest is to get a

---

*All industries are regulated in the sense that they must conform to federal (EPA) and state safety and anti-pollution laws. Regulation is used here in the sense that a company (1) needs federal approval to market some or all of its products and/or (2) experiences periodic auditing by government inspectors to ensure compliance with regulations.

high-quality product on the market, but a government agency is interested primarily in protecting the public—and itself (self-interest and self-protection are normal for us all.) Within these boundaries, the agency will try to accommodate the company.

For instance, a former general counsel for the FDA pointed out to me that processing NDAs is about fifth or sixth on the agency's priority list—the first being testifying before Congress, the source of the agency's funding. He also emphasized that within government bureaucracies (using the word in a descriptive, not derogatory, sense) "the system" does not reward quick approval of data, but it does punish mistakes such as approving new drugs that subsequently cause deaths or harmful side effects in some patients.

Therefore, regulated companies should expect and understand the deliberate, nonhasty pace and extraordinary caution (which is often laudable) on the part of NDA reviewers. R&D managers who accept these realities will spend less energy ranting against the "goddam FDA" and more energy ensuring that their company does the best possible job on submissions.

For the R&D manager, the following personnel considerations are crucial:

▲ The regulatory affairs department is the narrow pipeline through which hundred-million-dollar data flow to FDA (and upon which hundred-million-dollar sales and profits depend), so competence—and incompetence—in this group are magnified accordingly. Thus, for a highly regulated industry, the manager of Regulatory Affairs *must* be one of the R&D division's very best people, and he or she must hire equally capable subordinates.

▲ Regulatory Affairs personnel need good interpersonal skills to deal with both government employees and company colleagues. Equally important, they should have a good overall understanding of the company's technology.

▲ A highly regulated company needs good attorneys to deal with regulatory legal problems, but in most cases they should be part of the legal department. Regulatory Affairs specialists should be technically trained people, preferably with some laboratory experience within the company.

An adversarial relationship between government regulators and regulated companies is inevitable and proper, but it should be minimized because hard feelings, mutual disrepect, poor communication, and misunderstandings can only hurt the company. After all, the government holds the high cards.

A company that develops a good reputation with a regulatory agency will reap immeasurable benefits. The twelve requirements of such a reputation are:

1. Corporate and personal integrity, including concern for the public good
2. Products of consistently high quality
3. Good, modern science
4. High-quality submissions involving good, sufficient, well-organized scientific data that are presented clearly and objectively

5. Company representatives with whom the regulatory agency's personnel can work in reasonable harmony
6. Reasonableness, including a willingness to admit mistakes and the ability to appreciate the possible validity of an opposing point of view
7. Honesty and forthrightness
8. Courtesy toward and respect for government employees—their abilities, dedication, good intentions, and desire to do a proper, responsible, competent job
9. The ability to disagree without being disagreeable
10. Responsiveness to appropriate government requests
11. The ability and inclination to cooperate
12. A good sense of when to contest an agency decision and when to accept it

Chapter 26
Industry and Academia

Maintaining a close relationship between industrial R&D organizations and academia is advantageous for both parties as well as for society. But before we discuss these interactions, the R&D manager should appreciate certain realities about academia.

The primary responsibility of a university and its faculty is to provide a good education for their students. In science, this includes a number of interrelated factors:

▲ *The Fundamentals*. During the course of study a student learns the basic tenets of general science and of a specific field, primarily through basic course work, seminars, and the literature.

▲ *The Research Process*. Especially in graduate school, the student learns how to solve a research problem, primarily by working on a basic laboratory project. Here, the specific technical knowledge gained is secondary to understanding the process of research.

▲ *Lifelong Learning*. A good education teaches the student to be a continuous and lifelong learner. This includes more than just the technical field but is especially important in the ever-changing world of science.

▲ *Flexibility*. All else being equal, an education usually helps a person to be more flexible; the individual will be more comfortable with change, and will welcome—even seek—new challenges in his or her jobs.

▲ *Curiosity*. Young children are curious about everything; a good education helps a person retain that sense of wonder and investigation. This trait is, obviously, particularly important for a researcher.

▲ *Humility*. The student should learn that knowledge is similar to an inverted cone. The farther one gets from the apex—that is, the more knowledge one acquires—the better appreciation one should have for the infinite size of the unknown still there. Thus, the more a person learns, the more humble the individual will become about what he or she doesn't know.

While discharging these responsibilities to the students, the university, and society, faculty members want and need to grow personally and professionally. Interaction with business is one way they do this.

Academic salaries may be significantly lower than those in industry, and most faculty members welcome any appropriate opportunity to supplement their income, such as consultantships—another basis for interaction.

Financial support for academic research for the university and governmental agencies is severely limited; industry can and should help fill the gap.

Mutual Benefits

The wise, ethical industrial R&D manager will want to interact with academia in ways that are advantageous to all concerned. First, let's discuss the benefits of such interaction.

ADVANTAGES FOR ACADEMIA

Educational Benefits

1. Encourages the cross-fertilization of ideas.
2. Offers temporary, education-focused work in industry for faculty, undergraduates, and graduate students (also a financial benefit).
3. Develops joint projects for increased knowledge.

Financial and Other Benefits

1. Support for research.
2. Possible employment opportunities for students after graduation.
3. Consultantships for faculty.
4. Rapid commercialization of academic research (often benefiting society as well).

ADVANTAGES FOR INDUSTRY

1. An increased knowledge base for—
   ▲ cross-fertilization of ideas
   ▲ more options for new and better products
   ▲ more flexibility in R&D spending (e.g., academic support can be enlisted for an urgent but speculative project without making the long-term internal commitment of adding laboratory employees)
2. Greater professional development of employees, through—
   ▲ teaching and lecturing opportunities in academia
   ▲ research sabbaticals
   ▲ internal short courses given by academic consultants
3. Easier recruiting of new personnel, owing to—
   ▲ more thorough evaluation of potential job candidates via summer employment of students
   ▲ improved corporate image among students and faculty

As in any cooperative venture, it's important that the relationship be founded on mutual respect, interest, support, and long-term benefit rather than on selfish expediency. R&D managers who think only of how they can benefit from their academic colleagues while giving little in return will soon be ostracized, hurting both their subordinates and the company.

Examples of Industrial-Academic Interactions

There are numerous opportunities for interactions between R&D personnel and academicians. Here are some examples, with case studies when appropriate.

1. *Joint Projects.* These can be structured so that academics and industrial scientists both contribute. For example, the structure and behavior of solid materials, especially in the area of crystallinity, amorphism, and polymorphism are vital concerns for many technical industries, including communications, computers, fuels, chemicals, and pharmaceuticals. For a particular project, academic experts can determine fundamental properties while industrial scientists concentrate on the relevance of those properties to their particular systems.

2. *Consultation.* Academic consultants can supply "expertise on demand" when new opportunities arise for a company. Academicians can also serve on corporate R&D advisory boards.

Case Study: Finding Other Applications

Footkare, Inc., a pharmaceutical company, was presented with a unique opportunity for marketing theophylline products based on a serendipitous internal R&D discovery. Because this was an entirely new area for Footkare, it enlisted the help of Professor Bronchia, a world-class medical expert in treating asthma (theophylline's primary indication for use). Dr. Bronchia guided the company's medical investigations and interacted with Footkare's nonmedical R&D scientists so they could make the best decisions in the physical, chemical, and biological areas of research—for example, which physical form of theophylline was most likely to result in optimal efficacy and minimal toxicity.

---

3. *Academic sabbaticals.* These breaks can be renewing and refreshing for industrial scientists.

4. *Advanced Degrees.* B.S. and M.S. scientists can return to academia (part or full time) and obtain aditional degrees, often with company support.

5. *Faculty Work Experience.* Faculty members can spend a summer (or longer, if a sabbatical can be arranged) in industry, benefiting both parties. This can be especially valuable to academicians with nine-month appointments.

Case Study: Dr. Byrnout Goes Back to School

Dr. Byrnout was a bench organic chemist in Hardcharge Chemical Corporation's R&D division. He had performed well for over twenty years, but he recently began to suffer from ennui and advancing obsolescence. Over the years, Byrnout and his manager, Molly Wysdom, had developed a close relationship with Professor Elyment of the state university's department of chemistry.

The three of them, with corporate and academic approval, arranged for Byrnout to spend a year with Elyment, learning new techniques in radiolabeling organic molecules. Hardcharge Corporation was responsible for the R&D scientist's salary and gave the university a grant for the specialized equipment he would need. The university treated their "guest" as a valuable postdoctoral student, but he also lectured to students and faculty on his industrial research experiences. Twelve months later Byrnout returned to the company fully recharged, and became a key contributor to a new project related to his recent academic training. As a bonus, he and Professor Elyment published three acclaimed papers on their work during his sabbatical.

---

6. *Summer Employment.* Undergraduate and graduate students can arrange to work for a summer in industry. National programs may be available to arrange for placement, as in engineering and pharmacy, or individual companies can develop their own program.

7. *Mini-courses.* Academicians can be contracted to give one- or two-day short courses to R&D personnel on specific subjects.

8. *Adjunct faculty and guest lecturers.* Industrial scientists can teach courses or give lectures at the university.

Case Study: Telly Gets His Degree

Telly Smith, a B.S. electrical engineer, was a highly regarded manager of an R&D department in Eyebem, a rapidly growing computer company. As time went on, it became obvious to Telly and the R&D vice-president, Kelly, that both the company and Telly would benefit from his obtaining more technical education. A leave of absence was arranged, and Telly entered a master's program in the field of computer science. It was agreed that his education would be financed by his employer; his obligation was to return and work for Eyebem for at least three years. The experiment worked well, and Telly contributed significantly to the company for many years.

Case Study: The SVP Program

Forsyte, a large technical company, developed a Summer Visiting Professor program in R&D, whereby outstanding young academicians (two per year from various scientific disciplines) would spend their summer months at the company. Characteristics of the program ensured optimum benefit for all concerned:

1. Projects were discussed and agreed upon beforehand. Some managers took advantage of the academicians' expertise while others allowed them to investigate new areas. In either case, company scientists working with the visitors advanced their own knowledge.
2. Each visitor was sponsored by a company scientist. This facilitated rapid assimilation into the work group and fostered a close relationship between the two that often lasted a lifetime. (In one case, the academician was just beginning a new, important scientific area of investigation; his enthusiasm and competence inspired the company scientist to eventually become a world-class expert in the field.)
3. The visiting professors offered lectures to R&D laboratory personnel.
4. Mini-tours to other R&D departments, Marketing, and Manufacturing presented the academicians with a broad view of the company.

Additional benefits of the program were joint scientific publications, a better appreciation by academicians of work in industry that enabled them to better advise job-seeking students, and other close relationships that developed between the visitors and many company scientists and managers.

Case Study: NPC Summer Program

The National Pharmaceutical Council (NPC) acts as a clearinghouse by accepting summer job applications from undergraduate pharmacy students and referring those requests to various pharmaceutical companies. The companies then contact the students directly for summer employment. Their time is spent touring various areas of the company and also working on short R&D projects with laboratory scientists. The students become acquainted with pharmaceutical company operations, thus broadening their professional understanding of the drug products they will dispense to patients. In addition, they can determine if they would prefer industrial work after graduation. The company provides a service to the students, the institution, and the profession while building incalculable goodwill and developing a core of future job candidates.

Case Study: Summer Visiting Graduate Students

Some companies hire graduate students for the summer, often as part of a formal program. Contacts are made either with individual students and advisers or with graduate school departments. Their summer research projects are, appropriately, more challenging than those for undergraduates, with correspondingly less time spent on tours. Students experience industrial work, which helps them make a more informed industry vs. academia vs. government vocational choice after graduation. The company benefits in at least three ways:

1. It gains a chance to evaluate a potential job candidate in detail.
2. Assuming it has been a good summer experience, the student is more inclined to accept the company's job offer after graduation.
3. The student will spread the word about that experience to fellow graduate students and the faculty, enhancing the company's reputation.

Case Study: "Professor" Joplin

Dr. Jonas Joplin, a talented, veteran industrial scientist in the field of solid materials, crystallography, and solid-solid interactions, taught a biannual graduate course in his area of expertise at a nearby university. Besides the obvious benefits for all concerned, the corporation profited because students—future job candidates—were impressed with the company's high level of science and its flexibility concerning laboratory work schedules.

---

9. *Consortia.* Academic departments can set up a consortium whereby basic research, utilized for graduate student training, is jointly sponsored by a number of corporations interested in the same field. The companies share equally and openly in the information generated.

Conflict of Interest

Some individuals have simultaneous (e.g., half-time) salaried appointments in both academia and industry. While a few talented individuals may be able to handle this double duty, there are pitfalls.

For example, can the person retain academic scientific "purity" and objectivity? As a part-time adviser, is he or she shortchanging the graduate students? If the individual is interested in recruiting students for his or her industrial employer, can he or she objectively counsel them on other job opportunities?

Some academicians become entrepreneurs, commercializing their research findings by interacting directly with various industrial corporations. Here, too, distractions and commercial conflicts may endanger the individual's academic performance and integrity, although this is not inevitable, as David Connell explains in an article in *Industrial Management and Data* (Jan.-Feb. 1987).

For many years, the Wisconsin Alumni Research Foundation (WARF) has been an example of academic-industrial-societal synergy. It rewards professors for research findings of commercial value, but the state university remains the primary financial beneficiary. As of 1989, WARF's three most successful projects have been: (1) Irradiation to fortify milk with vitamin D (Professor Harry Steenbach); (2) use of vitamin K antagonists as rat poison and for treating cardiovascular diseases (Professor Karl Paul Link); and (3) fluidized bed granulating, coating, and drying (Professor Dale Wurster).

There is a story—a good one and very likely true—concerning Professor Link's discovery. As he was leaving UW's Agricultural Research building one afternoon, he met a farmer walking up the steps carrying a bucket of blood. Naturally intrigued, he turned and followed the fellow. The pail contained the blood of one of the farmer's cattle who had died of spontaneous hemorrhaging after eating (they discovered later) spoiled clover. This led to the isolation, identification, and commercial use of vitamin K antagonists.

Other examples of academic-industrial-societal synergy include Louis Pasteur (pasteurization of milk), Joseph Lister (antisepsis), Paul Ehrlich (antimicrobial therapy), and current research at Massachusetts Institute of Technology to develop a method to inhibit cataract formation in eyes.

To give an idea of the extent of industry-academia interaction in 1989, *Business Week* (1989 Bonus Issue) listed ten elite academic institutions in decreasing order of financial support, with Massachusetts Institute of Technology at the top with $35 million in funding from industry, then Georgia Institute of Technology, Pennsylvania State University, University of Washington, Cornell University, Carnegie Mellon University, University of Michigan, University of California at Los Angeles, Texas A&M University, Washington University of St. Louis, North Carolina State University, and University of Arizona.

In summary, wise R&D managers will optimize the interaction and synergy between their organization and the academic world, thereby benefiting both.

Suggested Reading

"An Exploration of the Nature and Quality of Undergraduate Education in Science, Mathematics, and Engineering," Report of the National Advisory Group of Sigma Xi (New Haven Conn.: Scientific Research Society, 1989.) Copies are available from Sigma Xi, 345 Whitney Avenue, New Haven, Conn., 06511.

Connell, David. "Bridging the Gap between Academic Researchers and Industrial Corporations," *Industrial Management and Data Systems* (January-February 1987).

Greenleaf, Robert K. "The Leadership Crisis: A Message for College and University Faculty." *Humanitas* 14, no. 3 (November 1978).

"Innovation in America," *Business Week*, Special Bonus Issue (June 16, 1989).

PART V

R&D and the Corporation

Up to this point, we have been concerned primarily with the R&D division and its employees. Now it is time to consider R&D in terms of the corporation. Even managers on the lower levels of R&D management will benefit from the overview this section of the book provides. This is the larger picture—how R&D fits in. Here also are tips on getting on with senior management, as well as ways to effectively manage in the international corporate world—subjects especially relevant for vice-presidents.

Chapter 27

Interactions With Other Divisions

Most scientific fields and technical businesses require a high degree of interaction and cooperation among the various disciplines, *each of which is convinced of its own preeminence..*

David Kolb, Irwin Rubin, James McIntyre, *Organizational Psychology: An Experimental Approach*

The position and arrangement of R&D in a corporation depend on several factors:

▲ *The company, its organization and history.* Some companies will have R&D in one centralized business unit, others will have divisional R&D, and still others will have both.
▲ *The marketplace.* Computer companies may have a mainframe industrial computer division and a PC division, each with its own R&D, while pharmaceutical organizations often have a centralized R&D subdivided into therapeutic areas (e.g., cardiovascular and anti-infective) requiring specialized pharmacological or medical techniques.
▲ *The relevant technology.* 3M has business groups called sectors, with most components of a particular sector using the same or similar technology (e.g., adhesives or reflective materials). Each business within a sector has its own R&D, but 3M also has a corporate central research organization.
▲ *R&D's management and its philosophy.* Personal and group biases and preferences often dictate how R&D is situated and organized; there is often little ordered reasoning behind such a situation.
▲ *The degree of governmental regulation.* The pharmaceutical industry is highly regulated by the federal government, consequently most R&D departments and practices are structured with an eye on getting FDA approval of products prior to marketing. In contrast, the computer industry is far less constrained.

Despite these differences, certain helpful generalizations can be made about R&D's relationship to other parts of the corporate puzzle.

Elements of the R&D Process

The primary components of R&D work are the idea; the feasibility study; and product development, scale-up, and transfer to manufacturing.

The Idea

New product ideas arise from many sources: laboratory workers (either as a creative idea or from experimental results), other employees, management (R&D or other), Sales and Marketing, new product committees, customers, competitors, and inlicensing contacts. This is discussed in greater detail in the introduction to Part III, but the key is to assume *all* product ideas are good ones unless and until careful consideration shows otherwise. Often good ideas are rejected out of hand because they are too new and different. People and organizations, even R&D, are conditioned to think in terms of here and now. Too many leaders give lip service to the "consider everything" dictum; they "consider" each idea carefully, but in reality, their minds are made up before they begin considering. Nothing is more stifling to the process of creating new products than closed minds, especially when they claim to be open.

Feasibility Study

When a new product idea is accepted in principle, the next step is to reduce the idea to practice. One of the major benefits of this phase is that it allows the researcher to give the marketing people a prototype they can "hold in their hands."

Depending upon the technology involved, the industry, the product idea, and the degree of governmental regulation, the time frame for determining feasibility may be short (several weeks to one year), medium (one to three years), or long (three to ten or more years).

Product Development, Scale-up, and Transfer to Manufacturing

In various industries and companies this phase may be regarded as one (all-inclusive development), two (development and transfer to manufacturing), or three (development, pilot/scale-up group, and transfer to manufacturing) steps.

The R&D group, particularly the product development unit, should be thought of as a bridge between the theoretical area of the company (basic research, often part of R&D but defined differently by different companies and technologies) and the practical side, primarily the marketing, sales, manufacturing, and engineering divisions. To ensure linkage, there must be good communication, plus mutual commitment, trust, and respect.

Interaction With Marketing

In most companies, the marketing division's function is strategic, working in the background to determine who the customer is and how best to meet his or her needs. Marketing combines products into product lines, establishes priorities among products and product lines, and then presents those product lines to the customer. It also supports the product lines for optimum sales and profits—for example, through its marketing strategy, including advertising.

Crossover Activities

▲ *Selecting New Products.* R&D must involve Marketing in evaluating ideas and selecting new projects for development. In fact, marketing people need to be brought into the R&D planning process as early as possible. This encourages their valuable input and ensures Marketing's support for the general direction that R&D wants to pursue. The success of any product is heavily dependent upon Marketing's enthusiasm, and, as with any group of people, enthusiasm is always in direct proportion to involvement. In addition, any new item must dovetail with Marketing's overall strategy, both short and long term. (On occasion, a product champion must "wear down" marketing people on strategy because, like the rest of us, they may be resistant to change.) Also, Marketing is a key player in the R&D budgeting process. The R&D manager who seeks top management's financial support without first getting Marketing "on board" is trying to win a rowing race with one oar.

▲ *Determining Desirable Product Characteristics.* Marketing has a much better idea of what sells than does R&D, so the former is a valuable resource in determining desirable characteristics, assuming they are technically feasible. On the other hand, R&D can educate marketing personnel on those areas of research that are new, promising, and exciting; this will encourage Marketing to develop new product ideas.

▲ *Fine-tuning Existing Products.* One of the keys to any company's success is flexibility and dynamism. As the marketplace changes (preferably *before* it changes), the company's product lines and mixes must change with it. This requires constant interaction between Marketing and R&D.

In return, R&D can offer marketing people technical help on advertising. Competitors' advertising challenges need to be answered quickly and forcefully. With technical products, this requires active involvement of R&D.

Responsible R&D managers monitor their company's advertising to ensure that it is justifiable, technically and ethically. It's best if company policy requires R&D sign-off on all advertising copy.

Cooperation Brings Success

A good relationship with marketing personnel requires *understanding*, *empathy*, and *communication*. Since marketing and R&D personnel come from and operate in different worlds, it is especially important that R&D managers work hard to understand marketing people both as individuals and as a group of professionals. It is equally important that managers work hard to communicate to Marketing the realities of R&D, especially its potential and its limitations. The two groups need to clearly, freely, and openly communicate all relevant information to each other.

As mentioned before, *respect* is another key to a good relationship. Some R&D managers make the mistake of treating nontechnical people as inferior, while the latter may criticize R&D for being in an ivory tower. But as Will Rogers reminded us, "Everybody is ignorant, only on different subjects." Wise R&D managers treat everyone with respect and learn to appreciate the talent, expertise, wisdom, and experience of marketing personnel. In most cases, this respect will engender similar treatment from others.

From understanding and respect come deference and *trust*. It's important that R&D people trust Marketing's judgment in its area of expertise or responsibility and vice versa. Unfortunately, diferences between the worlds of R&D and Marketing can create difficulties with trust. For example, the further removed we are from another group (functionally, geographically, educationally, or philosophically), the more mysterious they are to us and we to them. Both parties must work hard to understand, communicate with, and respect one another.

Marketing people also have different learning and problem-solving styles. For example, marketing employees tend to be intuitive while laboratory workers are quantitative and reflective. The R&D manager who understands these differences will have better relationships with marketing personnel.

Even though Marketing tends to be intuitive, in many ways its world is far more concrete and predictable than the realm of R&D, and this may create problems. For example, if R&D estimates the probability of success for a particular product or project as 75 percent (an optimistic estimate for scientists), Marketing will tend to make plans on the assumption that the product *will* reach the marketplace. Then if the project turns out to be technically unfeasible, there may be antagonism and finger pointing unless the two groups enjoy mutual trust and respect.

Therefore, wise R&D managers develop a good relationship with marketing personnel, but also encourage their subordinates to interact extensively with Marketing. The R&D manager who doesn't insist on being the main contact with Marketing will expand the group's impact on the organization, increase the flow of new product ideas, improve the efficiency and success of R&D in developing new products, and encourage the growth of subordinates.

Contact With Sales

R&D has much less interaction with sales personnel than with marketing, but some interaction does occur. First, to put things in proper perspective, all employees, but especially management, should recognize that a company really needs only two kinds of workers: someone to make products (manufacturing) and someone to sell them (sales). Everyone else, in the strictest sense, is overhead. Salespeople are on the firing line, selling the company's products, and therefore are in constant contact with customers.

At least once a year, key R&D managers and laboratory workers should accompany salespersons as they call on their customers. This gives the R&D person a feel for the marketplace and how well current products fit in. It also allows the salesperson to question the R&D person about various technical aspects of the products he's selling. And in the end, the process should generate new product ideas from both individuals.

R&D representatives should also occasionally attend sales meetings to instill among salespersons a knowledge of and enthusiasm for the company's products— especially new ones— and to encourage feedback to R&D about products.

Case Study: Sowing Seeds in Minneapolis

Two R&D managers, Molly and Wilfred, attended a scientific convention in Minneapolis. Before going, they arranged with Constance, the regional sales manager in that city, to visit her facility. Fortunately, there was a regional sales meeting in progress the day of their visit, so Constance asked Molly and Wilfred to address the group. Molly expressed her appreciation for the good job of selling the Minneapolis group was doing (she checked sales performance before she left and discovered that Minneapolis was tops).

Then Wilfred, who had served in the Swiss Army as a young man, told the group about a sophisticated automatic rifle that the generals at the Swiss "Pentagon" were enthusiastic about; unfortunately, under dusty field conditions the weapon jammed and was quite useless. Poor communication between the field soldiers and the generals kept the problem hidden for several years.

Wilfred used that story to emphasize that R&D needed feedback from the sales force as to the merits or deficiencies of the company's products. At the end of the session, Constance congratulated Molly and Wilfred for the effective, though entirely unplanned, strategy of first complimenting the sales group and then emphasizing its responsibility for giving field reports to R&D.

Constance was eventually promoted to president of the company, and the Minneapolis incident, along with continued interaction and communication, ensured a realistic, receptive top management ear to R&D's budget requests.

On the other hand, R&D management should encourage sales management to bring salespeople back to the company periodically—and include a tour of R&D, with talks by R&D managers and bench scientists.

Since most marketing people first serve the corporation as salespeople, many previous comments apply here. Perhaps the biggest difference is that it's much harder to keep in contact with salespeople who spend most of their time in the field. R&D managers can optimize communication with the sales department by meeting occasionally with top sales management and by nurturing friendships first formed on joint field trips with salespeople. They should urge their sales contacts to give them continual feedback on how products perform for customers.

Case Study: R&D Contributes to Sales

Pharmacee, a brand-name, research-oriented pharmaceutical company, periodically brought its salespeople into the home office and included a tour of R&D. Igor, an R&D scientist, was asked to address, with no preparation, one group concerning the technical aspects of generic competition. He did the best he could extemporaneously, and was pleased when he later received a phone call from the vice-president for Sales:

Igor, what did you tell those people? They all said that was the best talk they'd ever heard about the pros and cons of generic competition, and they are sure it will help them sell our products over generics when technical circumstances allow. If it's OK with you, let's make that a regular talk for all visiting sales groups.

Links With Manufacturing

R&D has much more in common with manufacturing people than with Marketing and Sales, simply because the manufacturing division mass produces what R&D has made on a small scale. However, in addition to the obvious differences between R&D and manufacturing, R&D managers should remember that the essence of R&D is *change* while Manufacturing correctly reveres *sameness*. R&D's *raison d'être* is to discover and develop the new and the different. Manufacturing's is to produce products with lot-to-lot consistency and predictability. This does not mean Manufacturing is not interested in improving products or processes; rather, it emphasizes that *experiments leading to improvements are the province of R&D, with Manufacturing's help*. R&D managers who understand, remember, and appreciate this essential difference are well on their way to having a good relationship with Manufacturing.

Certain organizational options involving the R&D, product development, and manufacturing divisions need clarification before we discuss the role of Manufacturing in the R&D process and R&D-Manufacturing interaction.

Product Development

Product development people usually are part of R&D, but in some companies they report to Manufacturing or Marketing, or stand alone. For example, Figure 8 shows three possible arrangements.

A case can be made for each option: for example, if R&D and Manufacturing are geographically separated (often the case, at least in the pharmaceutical industry), it may be wise to have Product Development report to the function from which it is physically separated. Thus a balance is struck: organizational

Figure 8. Three options for organization of product development.

Option A

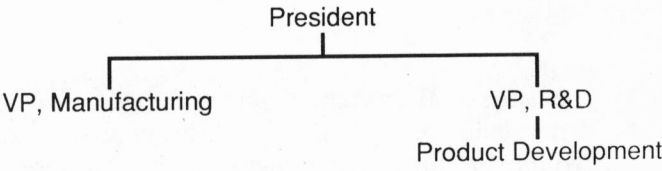

Option B

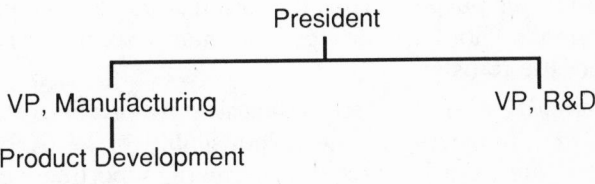

Option C

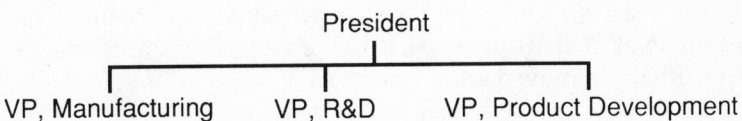

ties to one and geographical proximity to the other. In an article in the *Arizona Daily Star* (January 9, 1990) Tom Peters agrees: "And physical [proximity], not pecking order or even prior experience, is the premier variable that alters communication patterns."

In my judgment, option A is preferable (Product Development as part of R&D) because both groups share a common goal: new products. When Product Development reports to Manufacturing (option B), some of its innovative spirit may be lost because of Manufacturing's focus on uniformity. Product Development then tends to spend a major portion of its time reacting to Manufacturing's current problems. With Product Development standing alone (option C), organizational distance and rivalry between Product Development and R&D are likely to complicate and decrease the flow of new products.

Pilot Plant Group

A technical group (often designated Pilot Plant or Scale-up, expecially when separate from Product Development) needs to facilitate the transfer of new products from R&D to Manufacturing. Assuming that Product Development is part of R&D, four organizational options are available. For brevity, I designate those Product Development scientists who develop new products as "formulators."

Option A: *Formulators→Manufacturing.* Transfer of new products to Manufacturing is the responsibility of R&D's Product Development, and no separate group is set up within Product Development for this purpose. Formulators interact directly with Manufacturing personnel.

Option B: *Formulators→Pilot Plant→Manufacturing (within Product Development).* Transfers from R&D to Manufacturing are the responsibility of R&D's Product Development, but within Product Development there is a separate group designated for this purpose. Thus the formulators pass the product on to Product Development's Pilot Plant group, who then work with Manufacturing personnel to effect the transfer.

Option C: *Formulators→Pilot Plant→Manufacturing (within R&D but outside Product Development).* Transfers are the responsibility of R&D, but the Pilot Plant group is separate from Product Development, reporting directly to the vice-president of R&D. This is similar to option B but puts more organizational distance between the formulators and those who transfer products to Manufacturing.

Option D: *Formulators→Pilot Plant→Manufacturing (within Manufacturing).* Transfers into Manufacturing are the responsibility of Manufacturing, not R&D, and the Pilot Plant group reports to the vice-president of Manufacturing. This is a giant step removed from option C.

Depending upon the company, the technology, the product, and R&D–Manufacturing management, option B, C, or D may be preferable, but unless specific circumstances dictate otherwise, option A is generally best.

1. It enables manufacturing personnel to interact directly with those people most knowledgeable about the product (Pilot Plant workers cannot possibly know *everything* about the formulators' laboratory experiences).
2. The unavoidable disruptive competition between formulators and Pilot Plant workers (for example, who has final say concerning changes in the product or process?) is eliminated. This competition intensifies as one moves from option B to C to D.
3. Formulators will be more enthusiastic about their work because they will be involved with the harvest, not just with planting and fertilizing.
4. Formulators will do a better job of developing products because they will observe first hand the complexities of scale-up work.

Case Study: The Myopic Vice-President

A vice-president of R&D for a major pharmaceutical corporation, addressing a group of industrial scientists, described the R&D organization and process in his company. Product Development did not interact with Manufacturing; instead, a Pilot Plant group took new products or processes from Product Development and transferred them to production. During his talk, the vice-president made several sarcastic remarks about Product Development's narrow laboratory focus and lack of appreciation for the problems of large-scale manufacturing. After the presentation, a member of the audience pointed out that the organization (with Product Development isolated from Manufacturing by the Pilot Plant group) could be the primary cause of the problem. What the commentor didn't say was that there appeared to be more myopia in the vice-president than in Product Development.

---

5. When production problems arise after the transfer, Manufacturing will know where to turn and can draw on the already established good relationship with Product Development.
6. There is opportunity for job enlargement and enrichment for laboratory workers, a continuing concern for R&D management.
7. Product Development workers will become more familiar with the world of Manufacturing and vice versa, resulting in improved communication and cooperation between the two groups, a larger pool of well-qualified candidates for Manufacturing management positions, and increased promotional opportunities in Manufacturing for R&D personnel.

Case Study: A New Position

Pasqual was an effective mid-level R&D laboratory worker who had developed many new products over the course of his twenty-year career; he had often worked with Manufacturing personnel during the transfer of his products into that area. Muriel, his new supervisor, had a get-acquainted meeting with him and asked how he felt about his job. Pasqual confessed that, several years ago, laboratory work had lost its challenge and he was interested in a change. Muriel passed that information on to Manufacturing management, and within four months Pasqual accepted a first-line supervisor's job in Manufacturing. He felt refreshed and renewed, and proved to be an excellent leader.

---

8. Option A eliminates one management position (head of the Pilot Plant group) and, as we all are aware, minimizing management tends to optimize efficiency and productivity.

Successful Interaction

In addition to comments throughout this book on mutual respect and understanding, the very best service R&D can provide Manufacturing is to give it trouble-free products. In some companies, R&D is pressured to rush new products into production before they are fully debugged in order to get them on the market sooner. Then R&D and Manufacturing must wrestle with just about every batch to correct defects. Even worse, the company may lose credibility with customers because of inferior products. A good example is computer software found to be full of bugs.

Defenders of this practice say that R&D can finish its development work after the product is on the market, but priorities (including those on the next set of new projects) usually dictate otherwise. This philosophy brings to mind the classic saying, "If you don't have time to do it right, when will you find time to do it over?" The rationale has four basic defects:

1. Overall product quality is lower.
2. Scientists are pressured to do sloppy work. Not surprisingly, this encourages them to be sloppy scientists and is detrimental to their pride, morale, professional growth, and productivity.
3. A mediocre R&D organization will have difficulty hiring good scientists, perpetuating its mediocrity.
4. If careful cost-profit comparisons are made, companies will usually find the "quick and dirty" method inferior, especially if the product is one that will be on the market for a long time. Spending expensive R&D time on every Manufacturing batch devours the product's profitability and eats away at scientists' enthusiasm and morale.

Figure 9. Typical R&D–Manufacturing continuum.

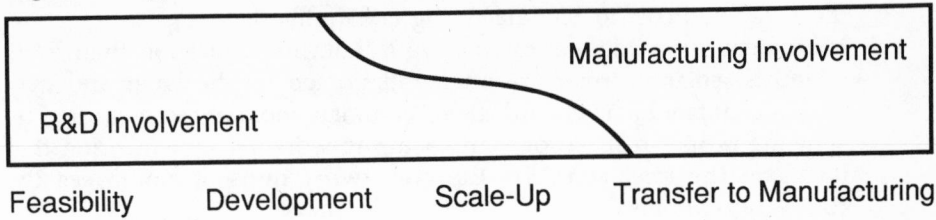

Feasibility   Development   Scale-Up   Transfer to Manufacturing

Only under rare and dire circumstances (e.g., to upstage a competitor who will be first and capture a lucrative market if the company doesn't move quickly), may such premature manufacturing and marketing be justified.

Here are some "secrets" for making the R&D-Manufacturing relationship smoother.

1. Listen carefully to Manufacturing personnel, especially when the latter have suggestions about improving a product or process. R&D people may be most familiar with the experimental details concerning their products, but they lack one key experience: producing the product day after day, year after year.
2. Bring Manufacturing into the R&D process well before transferring a product to that area. Usually the most appropriate time is during scale-up experiments. Figure 9 shows a typical R&D-Manufacturing continuum.
3. See that R&D's support of Manufacturing on established products is responsive and cooperative, via an informal system (e.g., a phone call initiating the request). Responses should be open-minded, in a spirit of cooperation.
4. Be sensitive to Manufacturing's cost concerns. For example, to a new R&D engineer in the auto industry, a $5 addition to unit cost may seem

---

Case Study: Never Our Mistake

In a computer hardware company, when a problem arose and manufacturing personnel came to Rockhead, the R&D scientist primarily responsible for manufacturing support, his stock answer was, "The product was designed correctly; if you can't make it, we'll get someone who can." When R&D management became aware of this situation, Rockhead was transferred to less interactive duties and replaced with Amy Able. R&D–Manufacturing relations improved considerably, as did product quality.

small for a $15,000 automobile; however, if a million vehicles are sold, the additional cost to Manufacturing is $5 million.

5. Manufacturing personnel often have less formal education than R&D scientists, so the former are often intimidated by the latter and may even feel antagonistic toward them. Eliminate most of these barriers by showing proper respect for manufacturing workers, remembering that they and the sales force are the only two groups of employees the company *really* needs.

6. To the extent feasible, assign to R&D technicians the responsibility for interacting with manufacturing personnel. This enlarges the technicians' jobs and minimizes educational differences.

7. Give R&D scientists a working tour of Manufacturing as soon as possible after they join the organization. This will bring them in contact with production employees, provide a firm foundation for future interactions, and give the scientists an appreciation of Manufacturing's world.

Case Study: One of the Gang

Connie, a new Ph.D. in R&D, was assigned to work in various manufacturing departments for the first month. She found it both educational and enjoyable, and she became familiar with many production employees. She spent the next-to-last day of her tour doing a physically hard, dusty, routine manufacturing job. At the end of the day, Walt, the foreman, came to her and said, "Connie, I know you're here to learn and I hate to ask, but the person who usually does this job called in sick. Would you mind doing the same thing tomorrow?"

Connie, an accommodating, hard worker, quickly and agreeably said she'd be glad to help out. From that time on, Connie was considered one of the gang, admired by Walt and all of Manufacturing; her later contacts with them were especially pleasant and productive.

Engineering Support

In most companies, engineering support is provided for both R&D and Manufacturing by an engineering department, especially when R&D's primary technical focus is not engineering. These engineers can be grouped in a separate department or dispersed throughout R&D and Manufacturing; each arrangement has its advantages and disadvantages.

Nonengineering R&D managers and scientists should foster good working relationships with engineers, because basic chemical, electrical, and mechanical engineering principles (e.g., mass and heat transfer, thermodynamics, field theory, solid and fluid mechanics, and material science) are critical to the development and manufacture of many products. When technical products are designed by engineers, such cross-fertilization is not as crucial, but the general principle still holds: laboratory scientists should seek help and opinions from technical colleagues in different disciplines and different functions.

Basic vs. Applied Research

A key question, somewhat related to industrial-academic interactions, is, Should industrial corporations conduct their own basic scientific research? In 1965, a large group of R&D managers from a variety of technical industries met for three weeks under the auspices of the Industrial Research Institute at the Harvard Graduate School of Business to discuss the challenges, problems, and opportunities in industrial R&D. Several times each day the discussion focused on the feasibility of conducting basic research in industry. Participants could cite only *one example* of a scientifically and commercially significant success in industrial basic research: the discovery and development of the transistor at AT&T's Bell Laboratories. Yet all participants were reluctant to say that no basic research should be attempted by industrial R&D groups.

The most realistic answer to that question seems to be yes, with certain qualifications.

1. For many reasons, private research contractors (e.g., Batelle Memorial Institute), certain federal agencies (e.g., National Institutes of Health), and academic institutions are the most appropriate settings for basic scientific research. The greatest share of industrial financial support in this area should go to academia. This financial assistance takes the form of unrestricted grants, with no strings attached; grants to university scientists as part of a consortium arrangement whereby all contributing companies have equal early access to experimental results; and restricted grants whereby the contributing company is solely privy to the generated information.

If a company puts excessive restrictions on the use of its donation— including the dissemination of information derived therefrom (usually in the form of publication in scientific journals)—it contradicts the whole idea of free-flowing basic academic research.

2. Some portion of a company's annual R&D budget should be devoted to some form of basic research, although the areas of investigation should be jointly selected by laboratory scientists and R&D management.* The amount of

---

*Some R&D managers fear that conducting basic research will cause scientists' interest and commitment to digress, even diverge, from those of the corporation. This has *not* been my experience, and such a concern is contradicted by social scientists who emphasize that, in a mutually supportive work atmosphere, employees are anxious to serve corporate goals.

money allocated will depend on the size of the company, the nature and complexity of its technology, the capabilities and interests of its scientists, and the philosophy of corporate and R&D management.

The primary benefits of having an R&D group conduct some basic research are:

▲ A major breakthrough is possible (e.g., the transistor).

▲ By demonstrating its commitment to science and scientific excellence, the company can recruit the best scientists.

▲ Laboratory workers' increased enthusiasm, growth, and productivity usually offset the cost of such research.

▲ If the corporation has a strong scientific image, it will attract inlicensing and outlicensing offers from other companies.

▲ Basic research often leads to improved applied technology and an influx of new product ideas.

▲ Having some laboratory workers at the "cutting edge" of a research area improves their relationship with academic scientists, facilitates consulting contacts when external expertise is needed, and helps R&D evaluate the new technology offered by other firms for inlicensing.

3. A company's commitment to basic research should be above a minimal, critical-mass level and reasonably long term. Turning the faucet on and off each year, depending on the current profit picture, is worse than no funding at all. A minimal level should be decided by corporate and R&D management, with annual fluctuations occurring above that figure.

Case Study: Corporate Grants

Abbott Laboratories has a worthwhile compromise policy: Each year corporate grants are available for high-risk research projects. The sponsoring division is then expected to provide funding starting the second year, although that requirement is not etched in stone.

Basic research is not for all R&D organizations, no matter what their size, technology, or products, but the decision should be a conscious, carefully deliberated one.

References

Bard, Jonathan F., Ramaiya Balachandra, and Pedro E. Kaufmann. "An Interactive Approach to R&D Project Selection and Termination." *IEEE Transactions on Engineering Management* 35, no. 3 (August 1988).

Danila, Nicolas. "Strategic Evaluation and Selection of R&D Projects." *R&D Management* 19, no. 1 (January 1989).

Hammonds, Keith H. "How a $4 Razor Ends Up Costing $300 Million," *Business Week*, January 29, 1990.

Kolb, David A., Irwin M. Rubin and James M. McIntyre. *Organizational Psychology: An Experimental Approach*, 3rd ed. Englewood Cliffs, N.J.: Prentice-Hall, 1979.

Liberatore, Matthew J. "A Decision Support System Linking Research and Development Project Selection with Business Strategy." *Project Management Journal*, 19, no. 5 (November 1988).

McGregor, Douglas. *The Human Side of Enterprise*. New York: McGraw-Hill, 1960.

Peters, Tom. "Firms Can't Ignore Space Management." *Arizona Daily Star*, January 9, 1990.

Rogers, Carl R. *On Becoming a Person: A Therapist's View of Psychotherapy*. Boston: Houghton Mifflin, 1961.

Chapter 28
Managing International R&D

In times past, most R&D managers were employed by a domestic corporation, but within the last decade or two, mergers and acquisitions have made that the exception rather than the rule. Now, and probably even more so in the future, most technical companies will be international in scope.

Domestic R&D managers face special challenges in a multinational corporation; in general, they need to do the following:

▲ Know the organizational specifics of their company's international operations.
▲ Learn as much as possible about the cultural, economic, technical, and governmental differences among the various countries.
▲ Establish close ties with their international R&D colleagues.

A multilingual R&D manager is especially valuable. Among other benefits, having one on staff shows respect for international colleagues.

Organizational Differences

Multinational companies differ in many organizational respects, and the wise R&D manager will become knowledgable in this area. For example, some firms have a separate international division while others do not. Even within the same company there may be anomalies. Abbott Laboratories, a major worldwide health-care firm, has an international division for most of its products, but the company's diagnostics division deals directly with its multinational markets.

International marketing may be separate from domestic operations, with R&D centralized in the home country. Often, a centralized R&D effort is coupled with small satellite development groups that deal with local market differences.

The history of a multinational company usually dictates its domestic-international characteristics. For example:

▲ If the company was founded outside the United States (Shell Oil, Ciba-Geigy, Unilever, Hoffmann-La Roche, and numerous chemical and automobile firms), the U.S. group may not have the final decision on marketing and R&D policy questions.

▲ When a large, well-established domestic company (e.g., Upjohn in pharmaceuticals) moves into other countries, those fledglings will often depend initially on the parent's products and will have little independence.

▲ When a small domestic firm (Riker Laboratories, now a pharmaceutical division of 3M) becomes internationalized through acquisition of already established companies (in Australia, England, France, and Germany), the latter, with their own product lines, tend to stay more independent. Thus an R&D manager at Riker would probably have a different relationship with his or her overseas peers than would an Upjohn R&D leader.

Cultural Differences

Cultural differences among various countries and international markets may have a significant impact on the development and marketing of products in those areas. For example:

▲ Automobiles in Europe and Asia are quite different in size and design from those in the United States.

▲ Oil companies and their automobile service stations operate differently in some countries.

▲ A popular form of medication in France is the "drinkable ampule," where a hermetically sealed 2 to 5 ml glass container with a thin neck is broken open and its liquid contents consumed orally. In contrast, the market in the United States for such dosage forms is nonexistent.

Equally important, social interactions with Japanese colleagues are quite different from those involving western Europeans. And Americans are different from the British, who are different from the French, who are different from the Germans.

Economic Differences

Economic differences among countries, often a result of internal legal requirements, dictate different strategies. For instance, in the United States, a pharmaceutical company with a unique oral presentation (e.g., controlled release) of an established generic drug can set a premium price, while in many European countries, governmental price regulations regard *all* oral dosage forms of that drug alike. Thus a U.S. R&D group would work to develop such a product while its overseas counterparts would probably not be interested. Based on these same economic factors, the international division of most major U.S. pharmaceutical companies is primarily interested in new, patentable chemical entities.

In Mexico, tariffs on imported "finished" products are several levels of magnitude higher than on raw materials or components intended for assembly in Mexico. At the same time, skilled labor in that country is limited, making it difficult to manufacture some complex technical products. Consequently, a U.S. R&D group will often design a product to be 80 to 90 per cent preassembled in the United States and then shipped (as components) to Mexico for final, perfunctory, assembly.

India restricts foreign ownership of corporations and limits profits that can be taken out of the country. Thus some multinational corporations have chosen to ignore Indian markets.

The U.S. tax code encourages U.S. companies to build manufacturing facilities in Puerto Rico; finished products are then shipped back to the continental United States. Since R&D usually remains in the continental United States, the development of new products and R&D-Manufacturing interactions become more complicated. In addition, significant tax savings on high-tech products depend on (perhaps learning from the situation in Mexico) the degree of assembly in Puerto Rico. If it is technically preferable to do some preassembly in the continental United States, R&D and company tax experts must assess the situation. Understandably, tax considerations dictate R&D's course of action unless the product cannot be successfully manufactured under those tax restrictions—and corporate management is never pleased with an R&D group that says "it can't be done."

Technical Differences

Highly technical companies seldom design the same products for sophisticated markets (U.S., Japanese, European) and Third World countries. For example, unless the underdeveloped country plans to import experts to operate large, complex computers, companies will offer only their more routine models to the Third World. Likewise, large, complex, expensive agricultural equipment would be inappropriate for a Third World country whose farms are of the mom-and-pop variety.

In a similar vein, hospital supply companies tend to sell only basic surgery and intravenous care accessories to hospitals in underdeveloped nations.

Governmental Differences

The R&D manager in regulated industry must be aware of governmental laws and practices.

For example, emission standards for automobiles and regulations concerning petroleum products differ from country to country.

In the United States, when a pharmaceutical company submits a New Drug Application to the Food and Drug Administration, its fate is primarily in the hands of FDA scientists and reviewers (although technical advisory groups are often used). In France, however, the government depends almost exclusively on independent experts, so the submitting company must understand the personal philosophy and idiosyncracies of that one person.

Establishing Closer Ties

As with any other facet of industrial operations, the R&D manager must become acquainted with his international colleagues and their projects. One way to do that is through international conferences.

Case Study: International R&D Conference

An enterprising multinational technical company held an annual international R&D conference. Attendees from each group were asked to make philosophical and scientific presentations. As a result new product ideas proliferated; technical expertise was shared; R&D managers and laboratory employees became more familiar with projects in each country and could make suggestions for improvements; and people became better acquainted personally with their international colleagues, improving trust, communication, and cooperation.

Technical interaction and communication among laboratories are usually among the most neglected aspects of international R&D. If five miles of separation between domestic R&D and Manufacturing can cause communication problems (as it often does), imagine what thousands of miles and different languages and cultures can do!

Intercontinental travel should be encouraged, but too often, it is limited to R&D management personnel. Whenever possible, laboratory scientists should also travel. It fosters technical interaction, improves communication, generates new product ideas, and broadens laboratory employees' horizons.

For laboratory personnel, occasional sabbaticals with overseas R&D groups can benefit everyone. For example, for many years, Ciba-Geigy has sent key new U.S. employees to its Swiss headquarters as part of their training program (see case study page 266).

R&D managers should recognize the educational differences that exist among people from different countries. For example, because of the school systems in some western European countries, high school graduates are more

---

Case Study: Millie Goes to Australia

Millie was a talented U.S. R&D scientist who specialized in improving complicated manufacturing processes. During an international R&D conference in the United States, Mortimer, the corporation's R&D leader in Australia, became aware of Millie's talents and interests. He suggested to Penelope, Millie's boss, that Millie be allowed to spend a month working in his group. With the scientist's enthusiastic concurrence, Mortimer and Penelope arranged the visit. The results were as follows:

1. Millie improved the quality and efficiency of four different manufacturing processes, saving the Austrailian subsidiary hundreds of thousands of dollars annually.
2. She picked up six new product ideas from discussions with local R&D scientists.
3. Communications between the two laboratories improved considerably; several persistent misunderstandings were cleared up.
4. Millie's subsequent approach to her R&D projects was broader and more imaginative.

---

advanced than those in the United States. At the same time, science Ph.D. candidates in England concentrate heavily on their research project and take relatively few formal graduate courses compared to their U.S. counterparts.

The references that follow offer more information on managing R&D in a multinational organization or an international setting.

Suggested Readings

Borrus, Amy. "Japan's Next Battleground: The Medicine Chest," *Business Week*, March 12, 1990.

Brooke, M. Z. *The Strategy of Multinational Enterprise*. New York: Elsevier, 1970.

Drucker, Peter F. *Management: Tasks, Responsibilities, Practices*. New York: Harper & Row, 1974, chapter 59.

Dunning, John J. *The Multinational Enterprise*. London: Longman, 1971.

Eells, Richard. *Global Corporations*. New York: Interbook, 1973.

Grabowski, Henry G. "An Analysis of U.S. International Competitiveness in Pharmaceuticals." *Managerial And Decision Economics*. Special Issue (Spring 1989).

Gross, Neil. "Japanese Biotech's Overnight Evolution." *Business Week*, March 12, 1990.

Hannay, N. B., and Lowell W. Steele. "Technology and Trade: A Study of U.S. Competitiveness in Seven Industries." *Research Management*, 29, no. 1 (January-February 1986).

Hiraoka, Leslie S. "Frontiers of Commercial Biotechnology: U.S. and Japanese Potential in a New Industry." *Futures* 19, no. 5 (October 1987).

Jouhar, A. J., et al., eds. *International Aspects of Drug Evaluation and Usage.* Edinburgh, Scotland: Churchill Livingstone, 1973.

Muroyama, J. H., et al., eds. *Globalization of Technology.* Washington, D.C.: National Academy Press, 1988.

Namai, Toshishige. "Japan's Drug Companies Venture Abroad," *Tokyo Business Today*, June 1989.

Rolfe, Sidney E., and Walter Damon, eds. *The Multinational Corporation in the World Economy.* New York: Praeger, 1970.

Samuelson, Robert J. "The Excuse Industry." *Newsweek*, December 11, 1989.

Spilker, B. *Multinational Drug Companies.* New York: Raven Press, 1989.

Taggart, J. H. "The Pharmaceutical Industry: Sending R&D Abroad." *Multinational Business* 1, Spring 1989.

Teeling-Smith, G., ed. *Science, Industry and the State.* Oxford, England: Pergamon Press, 1965.

Vernon, Raymond. *Sovereignty at Bay: The Multinational Spread of Private Enterprise.* New York: Basic Books, 1971.

Chapter 29

R&D Management
and Corporate Management

Without support from corporate management, R&D is out of business. Any questions?

For many reasons, the success of an R&D division depends greatly upon its corporate management. After all, corporate management hires the vice-president for R&D, the key position in a research organization. If that individual is capable and if corporate management supports R&D, the division will likely succeed; if not, things are almost certain to go poorly, no matter how much money the corporation pours into research.

Corporate management can provide a stable, supportive work environment for the R&D vice-president or a precarious, threatening, what-have-you-done-for-us-lately atmosphere. The former helps assure success, the latter usually pushes the vice-president into manipulating the information going to corporate management, leading to poor communication, confusion, and guaranteed failure. Top management must also provide flexible and dependable funding for R&D, assuring a relatively stable flow of "seed" money in spite of yearly fluctuations in sales and profits—except, of course, for dire, unusual circumstances.

Effective communication and mutual trust, respect, and confidence are important in every phase of organizational life, but these traits are especially crucial in R&D's interaction with corporate management, because the situation involves two quite different sets of people from very different worlds.

▲ The decision-making style of corporate management usually is intuitive while that of R&D management is more logical. This is because many

---

I wish to express my gratitude to the individuals in corporate management and R&D management at numerous organizations who generously shared their thoughts on this topic.

R&D judgments can be based on relatively "hard" laboratory data while the commercial world is far more conceptual and capricious.

▲ Financial people live in the highly competitive business world of stock prices, quarterly earnings, and shareholder concerns. The performance of laboratory scientists is usually not measured against their counterparts in other companies. R&D management, then, should serve as a bridge between these two disparate environments.

▲ Marketing personnel are good at dissecting history but not at soothsaying; their forecasts for the coming year are largely based on past performance. In contrast, R&D must look five to fifteen years into a radically different technical future.

▲ R&D managers usually have a deep understanding of fewer issues, while corporate management has a broader perspective—it is hoped that combining the two will lead to better decisions. Technically trained people tend to master the details of technical issues, but corporate management must take those R&D judgments and merge them with many other business and operational factors.

What can R&D management do to optimize communication and ensure success? The R&D leader must become well acquainted with the financial and commercial world of corporate management to better—

▲ understand and appreciate the views and concerns of the CEO, COO, and other non-R&D executives—in that same vein, the R&D leader should recognize that most corporate management people are bright, aggressive, and highly political, not necessarily in the bad sense;

▲ develop a broad vision for R&D that is harmonious with long-range corporate plans; and

▲ decide, with subordinates' help, what is in the best interests of the corporation.

Nevertheless, because of a scientific background and responsibilities, an R&D manager's perspective is usually different from that of colleagues in corporate management. Such diversity is desirable and necessary, but R&D managers should be mindful of these differences.

Likewise, corporate management must learn enough about the world of R&D to—

▲ appreciate R&D's point of view;

▲ understand the R&D process so that funding is steady, not sporadic; and

▲ recognize the danger signals (confusion, aimlessness, consistently poor decisions, laboratory worker malaise) of poor R&D management to distinguish them from bad-luck cycles inherent to all R&D.

Harmonizing R&D Objectives With Corporate Goals

One of the best examples of corporate and R&D management interaction is the melding of R&D and corporate goals. For an established company, the process proceeds as follows:

1. R&D, marketing personnel, and corporate management discuss the present and near-future state of the company's long-range goals, the company's finances, the marketplace, the company's present product line, and R&D's short-, medium-, and long-range research strategy.
2. Corporate management estimates how much funding will be available to R&D for the next year and over the next five years.
3. R&D management gives the status and prognosis for each project and recommends, on the basis of probable success and estimated time-to-market, which projects should continue and which should be dropped.
4. Marketing management estimates the present and near-future condition of the marketplace as well as the commercial performance and prognosis for present products and those near the end of the pipeline.
5. The group reaches a consensus on which projects should be discontinued and what portion of the available R&D funding should go toward continuing present projects (some may be accelerated, others decelerated), and what portion should go toward instituting specific new projects.

Marketing needs to do market research on the proposed new products. Then the entire group assesses the appropriateness of the mix of short-, medium-, and long-range and low-risk and high-risk projects. The process works best if Marketing and R&D management are on the same wave length before meeting with corporate management. For newly established companies, the deliberations will be different in ways that should be obvious, but the general process is the same.

Interviews with executives in corporate and R&D management in numerous, diverse corporations have led to the following ideas, thoughts, and recommendations for the mutual and harmonious attainment of corporate goals. First corporate management gives its advice to R&D management, then R&D has its say.

CORPORATE MANAGEMENT'S ADVICE TO R&D

General Matters

1. R&D should recognize that corporate and R&D management each have distinct, separate roles within the organization. Corporate management determines (after consultation with the R&D leader) the resources to be allocated to R&D, while R&D management decides (after consultation with appropriate members of R&D and with other groups, especially Marketing) how best to use those resources. R&D should see this consultation-decision

process as assistance, not interference. Furthermore, such discussion will broaden support for R&D's decisions, thereby taking some of the pressure off R&D management.

2. R&D management should try to prevent corporate management from making "micro" decisions on R&D projects.

3. R&D management should educate corporate management to be business leaders who look into the future, well beyond the next fiscal year.

4. The R&D vice-president is key in developing a vision of the future, but Marketing usually develops the corporate long-range strategic plan. Consequently, R&D must work closely with Marketing to ensure compatibility.

5. Salesmanship is a skill required for R&D management, not for an external customer, but to sell R&D's point of view to corporate management, including Marketing.

6. R&D management should educate its managers and laboratory people so they appreciate the financial conditions and priorities of the corporation.

7. R&D personnel need to get out of the laboratory and (usually accompanied by a salesperson) see the world from the customer's viewpoint, particularly how the company's products are used and if they perform consistently well.

8. The best R&D decisions combine scientific cogency with innovative "blue sky" thinking and lead to unique, profitable, trouble-free products. This approach involves higher risks but leads to greater payoffs.

9. Technical decisions should be made at the lowest possible level because, as issues move up the organizational ladder, risks tend to be filtered out and the decisions become less daring, less innovative. Also, the larger the decision-making group, the less daring will be the decisions. Therefore, although many opinions should be sought before coming to a conclusion, it's best if R&D decisions can be made by one person at the lowest possible level. Finally, the further back in the pipeline a project is, the less R&D management and corporate management need to be involved.

10. Corporate and R&D management must support laboratory risk-takers when they fail, because failure is inherent to research.

11. Corporate management needs R&D, not just for new products but to anticipate technological change. For example, if a particular technology is in a period of rapid change and a company must increase its manufacturing capacity, R&D management can advise corporate management to contract for outside production until more is known about imminent technological changes. Then a new manufacturing plant can be built that incorporates state-of-the-art equipment and processes.

12. R&D needs to build a strong technical base and do a proper job so that new products work well for customers. When a new item frequently malfunctions, customers not only get frustrated, they become apprehensive about the company's entire product line—and that loss of confidence can spread to Marketing and corporate management. The message: Do it right the first time.

13. There is more danger in overmanaging R&D than in undermanaging it.

14. The company does not need any particular R&D manager unless he or she contributes "value" to R&D, the research process, and the company's products. Said another way, R&D managers need to recognize that their jobs should be different from those above and below them; otherwise, their positions are redundant and therefore unnecessary.

15. R&D management must be aware that one of the problems with long-term projects is that key scientists and managers may not be around when success is finally reached; therefore sustaining excitement and a sense of commitment can be difficult.

16. R&D laboratory workers need to be closely tied to end results. This can be very difficult if the R&D process becomes too long, large and complex.

17. The less bureacracy in R&D the better, especially among staff people. When R&D vice-presidents have too many staff assistants, the latter tend to know the big picture while line managers may become isolated and compartmentalized.

18. R&D managment should assume its counterparts in other companies are intelligent and competent, so if competitors are well ahead in a particular field and unless the company has a unique idea, why waste R&D effort in that area?

19. The R&D vice-president must help R&D management and laboratory workers appreciate (1) the difference between scientifically interesting and commercially viable projects; and (2) the need for a mix of high- and low-risk and short-, medium-, and long-range projects.

20. It is usually best to leave the frontiers of basic science to academia, but industry should provide strong support for university research, financial and otherwise. Industrial R&D can then concentrate on developing technically sound new products based on academia's cutting-edge science.

Financial Matters

1. It is essential that R&D have sufficient ongoing resources so that, when a breakthrough occurs, R&D can concentrate sufficient energy and personnel forces to bring the product to market rapidly. This necessitates a balance between too few and too many laboratory workers, and it is R&D management's responsibility to determine that balance and then convince corporate management.

2. When the company's technology involves long-term projects, R&D management must remind corporate management that R&D must operate—within reason—by a set of budgetary rules different from most other corporate functions. For example, if R&D is constantly subject to annual budget cuts to preserve the corporation's bottom line for that particular year, R&D and the company will not succeed. At the same time, the R&D vice-president must understand that patience is difficult for a company president because the

individual's performance is often measured from month to month; in fact, he or she may not be there for the ultimate payoff of long-term projects.

3. Corporate management usually realizes that productive R&D is essential to a technical company's success; its primary concern is that the allocated funds be spent wisely.

4. When an individual project is terminated by management, R&D management should reassure its people that this does not signal a lack of corporate management support for research.

Organizational Culture

1. Corporate managment plays a major role in developing the overall culture of a company, and therefore bears some responsibility for R&D's culture. But R&D management is largely responsible for establishing the culture in its organization. R&D must encourage risk-taking and allow scientists to identify with the tasks and goals of both R&D and the corporation.

2. R&D management must place in charge of projects people who believe in those projects, who have confidence in the project's importance and its high probability of success.

3. Some R&D organizations are more successful than others because, in addition to laboratory and managerial competence, their people have a broad vision, common goals, confidence that their vision will come to pass, and a feeling that management trusts them and is not trying to overcontrol them. These qualities must originate with the R&D leader, with support from corporate management.

Case Study: A Higher Purpose

The progress in developing new U.S. aircraft in World War II was phenomenal; there were radical improvements every six to twelve months. Since then, even with adequate funding, progress has been relatively slow, primarily because there has been no national crisis, no higher purpose drawing people together.

---

4. R&D management must create an environment so that scientists can and will concentrate on developing new products while satisfying their personal scientific career goals. Scientists also should be encouraged to recommend ending a project if it's not in the company's best interest. It is they who are most familiar with project details and the chances of success at any given point in time. How much better for projects to be cancelled this way than by management making unilateral decisions, especially if the scientists don't agree.

5. A technical company should develop a culture where individual scientists are the stars, along with sales personnel. Other employees have support groups, but not lone scientists and salespersons—they need special recognition. In the case of scientists, R&D management must ensure this comes about.

Interpersonal Relations and Communications

1. For a productive working relationship, R&D management must establish credibility with corporate management.

2. A consensus is important among corporate and R&D management and laboratory scientists concerning the overall direction, purpose, and goals of a research program, but management should leave the day-to-day details to laboratory workers. Then individual scientists can operate more freely.

3. R&D should not bother corporate management with premature results; they should strike a balance between overpromising and complete silence. The best solution is to be candid, such as, "We're this far, but it's still a risk."

4. When laboratory workers become frustrated because of an unfavorable corporate decision, R&D managers should remind them that unresolved conflicts are part of life.

5. R&D managers should frequently get out of their offices and visit the laboratories.

6. In many situations, laboratory people hesitate to communicate positive results upward because then corporate and R&D management create premature pressure for a new product. In the right atmosphere, scientists push for a new product as soon as technical feasibility is demonstrated.

7. When R&D sees corporate management going off in the wrong direction on technical products (e.g., in advertising), even if there are no ethical transgressions, R&D management should raise questions—in a helpful spirit—with executives.

Case Study: No One Ever Told Me That

During a leisurely tour of R&D laboratories, a pharmaceutical executive asked a key scientist what he thought was the most important factor in his efforts to synthesize new antimicrobial drugs. The researcher replied, "lack of bacterial resistance." When the executive mentioned that Marketing considered lack of side effects to be, by far, the major advantage, the scientist said, "No one ever told me that." Concerned that a key researcher was working in the dark, without a clear mandate from the project team, his manager, or Marketing, the executive relayed his experience to the R&D vice-president. The latter discussed the problem with the scientist's manager and the Marketing personnel on the antimicrobial project team.

8. R&D management should be the communication link between corporate management and scientists (see the case study on page 274).

9. R&D management should avoid overexplaining technical issues to corporate management; the latter become uneasy and its confidence in R&D management may be shaken. One executive, formerly in R&D, emphasized, "Keep it simple. Corporate executives—even thought they are highly intelligent—are impressed by and most comfortable with technical simplicity."

R&D's ADVICE TO CORPORATE MANAGEMENT

General Matters

1. Too many members of corporate management shy away from evaluating the R&D vice-president's judgment and performance, but in a technical company that is an important part of their job.

2. Corporate management needs to be comfortable with the priorities set and decisions made by the R&D vice-president, but they must find ways to do this without interfering excessively.

3. Corporate management should guard against having R&D management that is technically sound but lacking in courage and self-confidence. Corporate management can bolster the R&D vice-president's feelings of security and self-confidence with overt support. However, if he or she is basically timid and insecure, it may be wise to replace the individual (or, better, not hire the person in the first place).

4. Mutual trust is an essential element of any good relationship. Trust comes from feeling secure, but the reverse is also true: Trust generates a sense of security.

5. Corporate management will receive less "managed" information from R&D if R&D vice-presidents feel secure and if they are given the final call in their area of responsibility.

6. At times corporate management will hire a star academician to be R&D vice-president. This can work out, but it is also fraught with danger. Corporate management must be aware of the hazards:

▲ Not promoting from within damages employee morale. It may mean the organization does not facilitate the growth of its employees, or that the issue of succession planning needs more attention.

▲ Severe problems can arise if the individual's goals and corporate goals aren't clearly and carefully aligned right from the beginning. This can be a real danger because long-range goals and priorities in academia are much different from those in industry.

▲ Managing 50 to 1,000 industrial scientists is vastly different from a scientific academic position, even if the individual chairs a large academic department. Corporate management should recognize this and emphasize the point to academic candidates for the position of R&D vice-president.

Because they lack managerial experience, academicians may eschew administrative duties, thereby avoiding overmanaging. But this should be a conscious decision and not the result of benign neglect. When crises arise, leaders who have abdicated their responsibilities tend to overreact and start to overmanage.

▲ If an outsider, especially from academia, is hired as R&D vice-president, it can take several years for the individual to "get up to speed" in a large, complex research organization, causing project delays of six to eighteen months and costing millions of dollars. Corporate management needs to ask, "Is this person worth it?"

▲ If an R&D group is in serious trouble, with low-quality people throughout the organization, depending upon a savior from academia usually results in disappointment—which, unfortunately, often leads to hiring another famous academician. In such a dire situation, the most likely path to success is to hire an experienced, inspirational industrial leader who is also a good organizer, a superior recruiter, and a patient person who recognizes that an R&D organization cannot be regenerated overnight.

7. Too often the people who rise to the top in R&D management are risk averse, have made the fewest mistakes, and are adept at "managing upwards." Before deciding on an R&D leader with such characteristics, corporate management should ask, "Is this the way to run the company?" Wise executives will promote a competent, judicious risk-taker and then help the individual feel secure by giving him or her strong support.

8. If R&D doesn't produce, corporate management should raise questions about the R&D vice-president's competence. In that same vein, if R&D management's estimates are faulty, corporate management should determine whether they are poor estimators (a tolerable deficiency) or poor leaders (intolerable).

9. Too often corporate management seems to have difficulty judging R&D management talent, allowing a poor research leader to remain in a position long after the problem is recognized by most R&D managers and scientists. Perhaps, as one executive suggests, it's because the R&D vice-president has but one talent—managing upwards.

10. Some corporate management people micromanage R&D as a substitute for making the required tough business and financial decisions. The result is poor decisions on R&D and procrastination in business and finance.

Financial Matters

1. There is great risk in trying to measure R&D productivity because mundane products tend to get better marks than they desrve. As one executive sees it, the real measure of R&D productivity is whether customers view the company as producing good, innovative, new products over a long time period.

Organizational Culture

1. Corporate management has a responsibility to help R&D management convince (honestly and genuinely) scientists that corporate management and R&D agree on common goals.

2. Corporate management must demonstrate to laboratory workers that high ethical standards are essential in both business and science.

Interpersonal Relations and Communications

1. Most technical companies have two hierarchies: R&D and financial or commercial. Many bridges, including social ones, are needed to maximize communication. For example, when new products are launched, the responsible R&D people should be invited to the initial sales conference and, when appropriate, be given a sample of the product along with associated sales accoutrements.

2. When corporate management brings R&D leaders in from the outside, it takes time to create effective, trusting relationships with both corporate management and R&D subordinates.

3. In an atmosphere of mutual mistrust, corporate management asks for more than it expects and R&D management promises less than it can deliver. Both should work to break the vicious circle by being candid and realistic.

4. Corporate management should try to make R&D managers comfortable in giving their opinions, assuming their views have been requested. The more comfortable they are, the more candid they will be.

5. Too often corporate management does too much talking and not enough asking and listening.

6. The assumption that intelligence is a function of rank is a poor one, especially in a highly technical organization.

7. Executives with high intelligence must temper that intelligence with wisdom—for example, they must refrain from making all the decisions themselves, or they will chase away top-notch subordinates.

8. At times corporate management may make a decision without explaining the reasoning to R&D. Because R&D assumptions are often different from those of executives, such decisions may frequently be hard to understand and accept.

9. Corporate management should spend quiet, philosophical time with R&D management. This helps both parties get acquainted, gives R&D managers a better feel for executive visions and the reasoning behind decisions, and helps integrate R&D goals with those of corporate management.

10. Corporate management can help the R&D vice-president by interacting with and reinforcing lower-level R&D workers. While doing this, executive confidence in R&D will grow—and vice versa.

Concluding Thoughts on Management

A few comments from management executives did not fit the above categories but are worthy of mention.

1. Scientific excellence is not the end product of R&D but the most efficient means of reaching the end product—dependable, profitable, high-quality products.

2. Because rewards in industrial science are often deferred, it's important that R&D managers share group accomplishments with laboratory workers; this fosters a sense of belonging, involvement, and group pride.

3. Corporations hire creative, ambitious R&D people, then (unrealistically) expect them to stay in the same job for years and years. Managers must attend to workers' developmental needs, either through job enlargement and enrichment or promotion up the scientific ladder or management.

4. A manager is the bridge between employees and the company, and should ensure that both parties are well served. Anyone ill suited for this role is not going to succeed in management.

5. Good R&D managers need the courage to hire people better than they are.

6. There should be synergism between R&D and Marketing: R&D encourages Marketing to look at the future while Marketing helps R&D keep one foot on solid ground.

7. Frequent changes in Marketing personnel can disrupt commitments to long-range R&D projects.

8. Bonuses for all employees should be structured so the individuals are encouraged to do the right thing for the long-term health of the corporation.

9. In management, the problem is not usually gaps in coverage but rather overlap. This can result in overhead that is 20 to 30 percent of total expenses—much too much.

10. When things go wrong, "the system" is usually trying to tell us something, but we seldom listen. Rather than asking why, we spend our time patching things up.

11. Success comes from helping people.

12. Good management begets good managers. Poor managers have usually been poorly managed early in their careers.

13. A good organization requires core values and beliefs while encouraging diverse viewpoints and multiple perspectives.

Index

AAAS, *see* American Association for the Advancement of Science
Abbott Laboratories, 262
academia
  basic research and, 259–260, 272
  financial support from industry, 242
  interaction with industry, 236–243
  R&D vice-president hired from 275–276
  see also recruiting
acceptance, 25, 89, 90, 127, 134–135
accounting department, 216
adjunct faculty, 239
advanced degrees, 238
advertising, 249
advisers, financial, 216
advocating, 74–77
  organizational, 76–77
  personal, 75–76
age discrimination, 177
agreeableness, 26
alcohol, 173n.
Alice's Adventures in Wonderland (Carroll), 48
All I Really Need to Know I Learned in Kindergarten (Fulghum), 122
American Association for the Advancement of Science (AAAS), 215
amiability, 26

Androgynous Manager, The (Sargent), 181
Annual Handbook for Group Facilitators, 1991, 97–99
anxiety, 4–5, 77, 187
applied research, 259
appreciation, 136–138
Argyris, Chris
  on growth, 125–126
  on performance appraisal, 159
arrogance, 27, 107
assistant scientists, characteristics of, 19, 57
associate scientists
  characteristics of, 19, 56–57
  role of, 20
  work group leadership and, 20
AT&T Bell Laboratories, 259
authoritarian control, 65–66, 71, 72–73
authority, delegation of, 68–71

basic research, 259–260, 272
Bennis, Warren S.
  on inspiring employees, 41
  on leadership ability, 31
  on self-confidence, 133
Berle, Milton, 205
Bernstein, Anne, on self-esteem, 119, 134
Blinder, Alan, 45
bonuses, 278

"boss" culture, 65–67, 71, 72–73,
   181–183, 188
brainstorming, 82
budgets, 215–219
  basic research in, 259–260
  national R&D spending, 215
  need for adequate R&D, 272–273
  rules for developing, 215–219
bulletin boards, 49
business of company
  developing familiarity with, 6
  potential employees and, 108–109

CAD-CAM, 220
Calder-Marshall, A., 94
candor, 26, 89, 201, 207
capital money, 216n.
Cardinal of the Kremlin (Clancy), 199
caring, 25, 88
Carl Rogers on Personal Power (Rogers), 11,
  179
Carroll, Lewis, 1, 4, 48
Carter, Hodding, 41
Catton, Bruce, 152
centralization, 60–61
Chalice and the Blade, The (Eisler), 92
Chaos: Making a New Science (Gleick), 222
Churchill, Winston, 130
civility, 25, 89, 113
Clancy, Tom, on progress, 199
cohesive group spirit, 27
Combs, Gary, on social influence, 97–99
commitment, 24, 88, 107
  reassurance and, 143
  to recruiting process, 104
committees, 205–207
  R&D Advisory Committee, 206–207
  R&D Managers Committee, 205–206
communication, 26, 89, 94–103, 106,
  200–201, 250
  between corporation and R&D
    division, 268–269, 274–275, 277
  in dealing with performance problems,
    170–172
  hearing vs. listening in, 95–97
  importance of, 49
  within the organization, 100–103
  persuasion vs. creating understanding
    in, 97–100
  R&D Managers Committee and,
    205–206

compatibility, 89
competence, 24, 29, 88, 89, 106, 234
competition, 3, 187, 272
  with self, 93
  within work groups, 90–93
computers, 220–227
  applications for, 220–223
  managing with, 223–225
  in the R&D division, 222–223
concern, 25
confidentiality, 232
conflict of interest, 241–242
conformity, ethics and, 37
Connell, David, 242
consortia, 241
consultants, 36, 237, 238
contracts, government, 232–233
controlling, 65–66, 98
cooperation, 26, 89, 90–93, 106, 200
coping behavior, 133
corporate culture
  "boss" culture and, 65–67, 71, 72–73,
    181–183, 188
  R&D managers and, 273–274, 277
corporate managers, advice to R&D
  managers, 270–275
counseling, performance appraisal and,
  162–164
creativity, 200–201
  growth and, 125
  manager role in, 81–82
  productivity and, 81–86
  tips for encouraging, 82–84
criticism, 139–142
  external, 139–141
  performance appraisals as, 158–160
  self-, 141–142, 167
curiosity, 236

decentralization, 60–61
decision making, 3
dedication, 88
deference, 27, 43, 89, 106, 200, 203
delegation, 68–71
  empathy in, 46–47
  employee involvement in, 68–69
  goals of, 69–70
  planned, 71
  reverse, 70
department secretary, 223
dependence, 161

DePree, Max, 122
Drucker, Peter, 73
  on "boss" culture, 183
  on communication, 100
  on control, 65
  on creativity, 83
  on education, 57
  on employee motivation, 17
  on growth, 122
  on management skills, 15
  on management style, 63
  on new approaches, 181
  on personal characteristics, 107n.
  on respect, 42
  on self-evaluation, 150
drugs, 173n.
dual-ladder system, 19–20, 190–192

Edison, Thomas, 57, 143
education
  of associate scientists, 56
  continuing professional, 129, 130, 188,
    236, 238
  importance of, 57, 58
  international R&D and, 265–266
  of manufacturing personnel, 258
  of R&D staff, 23
  of R&D vice-presidents, 34
  of scientists, 56, 57
  of technicians, 57
efficacy, 134
Ehrlich, Paul, 242
Einstein, Albert, 40, 125
Eisler, Riane, on competition vs.
  cooperation, 92
electronic mail, 223
empathy, 46–47, 64, 200, 250
encouragement, 138, 142
engineering department, 258–259
enthusiasm, 27, 88, 249
environment
  characteristics of effective, 22–28, 87–90
  for growth, 124–126
  role of R&D vice-president in, 36
ethics, 107
  in planning process, 52–53
  of R&D managers, 36–38
  see also values
Eupsychian Management (Maslow), 124,
  145
evaluation, 147–155, 185

developing skills in, 5–6
ethical considerations in, 52–53
formal performance reviews in,
  156–168
of manager by subordinates, 147,
  148–149
of potential employees, 109–110
of R&D vice-president, 35–36
self-, by manager, 147, 149–152
self-, by subordinates, 147, 152–154
of subordinates by manager, 147,
  154–155
expectations, growth and, 125
expense money, 216n.
expressive behavior, 133

faculty work experience, 238
faultfinding, *see* criticism
Fayol, Henri, 47, 63
FDA, *see* Food and Drug Administration
feasibility studies, 248
feedback, 158–161, 195
financial advisers, 216
firing employees, *see* terminating
  employees
fixed expenses, 216
flexibility, 4, 106, 216, 236
Food and Drug Administration (FDA),
  233–234, 265
Forbes. Beverly, 183
formal project teams, 208–209
freedom, 123
Freedom to Learn for the 80's (Rogers), 124
friendliness, 26, 89
frustration, 187
Fulgham, Robert, on growth, 122

Gaylin, Willard, 169
  on emotions in management, 182
  on growth, 123
genuineness, 27, 89, 106
Gilbert, Bil, on competition, 90–92
Gleick, James, on computer modeling,
  222
goal-focused activity, 24, 62, 88
goals
  of delegation process, 69–70
  harmonizing R&D with corporate,
    270–277
  of R&D division, 52–54, 193–194
  of work group, 89–90

government contracts, 232–233
government regulation, 233–235, 247
  in international R&D, 264–265
group discussions, 185
group dynamics, 211
group-think, 37, 207
growth, 106, 122–131, 186, 188
  applying understanding in, 124–126
  in budgets, 217
  manager as helper and, 126–130
  opportunities for, 108
  understanding learning process in,
    123–124
  understanding people in, 123
guest lecturers, 239

Hall, Jay, on effective management, 2,
    11, 39
hearing, listening vs., 95–97
hiring employees, *see* recruiting
honesty, 26, 89, 176, 201, 203
Hughes Aircraft Company, 195
Human Side of Enterprise, The
    (McGregor), 65, 66, 147, 156–165, 182
humility, 236

ideas, for new products, 248
independence, 27, 89, 107, 207
India, 264
individuality, 4, 25, 123, 125
Industrial Management and Data (Connell),
    242
informal project teams, 209–211
inlicensing, 230–232
innovation, 201
  manager role in, 81–82
  productivity and, 81–86
  tips for encouraging, 82–84
insecurity
  delegation and, 69
  of technical managers, 4–5
insistence, 160
inspiration, 41–42
integrity, 207
interdependence, 27, 89
internal transfers, 173–174
international R&D, 262–267
  cultural differences in, 263
  economic differences in, 263–264
  establishing closer ties in, 265–266
  governmental differences in, 264–265

organizational differences in, 262–263
  technical differences in, 264
interpersonal relations, 211
  between corporation and R&D
    division, 274–275, 277
  people skills and, 10–11
interviews, recruiting, 106–113
intradepartmental teams, 209–211
involvement, 24, 88
  in budgeting process, 215
  in delegation process, 68–69
  growth and, 125
  in planning process, 53–54
  in recruiting process, 105–106
  as role of R&D manager, 45
  scientific ladder and, 191–192

James, William, 135
Jefferson, Thomas, 179
Johnson, David W., 208
  on competition vs. cooperation, 91
  on effective groups, 205
  on experiential learning, 124
Johnson, Frank P., 208
  on competition vs. cooperation, 91
  on effective groups, 205
  on experiential learning, 124
*Joining Together: Group Theory and Group
    Skills* (Johnson & Johnson), 91, 124,
    205
joint projects, 238

Kanter, Rosabeth Moss, 89
Kettering, Charles, 57, 82
Kissinger, Henry, 115
Kolb, David A., 180–181, 186, 208
Koretz, Gene, 215
Kovach, Kenneth, on motivation, 17,
    116, 118, 135

labeling, 172–173
laboratory notebooks, 232
Labovitz, George H., 208
leadership
  ethics and, 36–38
  manager self-evaluation and, 147,
    149–152
  of R&D managers, 30–31
Leadership Is an Art (DePree), 122
learning
  performance appraisal and, 164–165

understanding process of, 123–124
Leavitt, Harold
   on changing employees, 120
   on individuality, 18, 25, 123
   on management skills, 15
   on motivation, 117
Lee, Harper, 46
Lemaire, Jacques, 127
licensing agreements, 228–232
   financial arrangements for, 228
   inlicensing, 230–232
   outlicensing, 229–230
licensing department, R&D interaction
   with, 229–230
Likert, Rensis
   on ethics, 37
   on growth, 125
   on people-oriented managers, 10
   on psychological health of managers,
      31
Link, Karl Paul, 242
listening, 170
   hearing vs., 95–97
   in supportive communication, 98–100
Lister, Joseph, 242
loyalty, 27, 76, 88, 203

Mabry, H., 42
Macaulay, Thomas, on delegation, 69
mainframe units, 224
major professors, technical managers as,
   4, 275–276
management skills, 15
   of successful R&D managers, 5–7
   technical managers and, 2–5
management style, 63, 200
   developing personal, 6–7
   encouraging growth with, 124–126
   establishing, 48–51
   people skills in, 10–11
   performance appraisal and, 157
   personal characteristics and, 9–11
*Management: Tasks, Responsibilities,
   Practices* (Drucker), 15, 42, 65, 100,
   107n. 122, 150, 181
Managerial Psychology (Leavitt), 15, 25,
   117, 120, 123
managers, *see* R&D managers
Managing the Managers (Sampson), 1, 2,
   25, 77, 89–90, 127, 156, 159

manufacturing department
   R&D division interaction with, 252–258
   transfer of new products to, 248–249
marketing department, 269, 278
   interaction of R&D division with, 147,
      249–250, 270
   in international R&D, 262–263
Marshall, Peter, 147
Maslow, Abraham
   on acceptance, 25
   on emotions in management, 182
   on growth, 124, 126
   on motivation, 117–120
   on performance appraisal, 161
   on psychological health of managers,
      31–32
   on reassurance, 145
   on secrecy, 101
Massachusetts Institute of Technology,
   242
matrix structure, 61, 62
McGregor, Douglas, 73
   on components of R&D groups, 22
   on control, 65, 66
   on emotions in management, 182
   on evaluation, 147
   on performance appraisal, 156–165
   on role of manager, 63
   on self-esteem, 16–17
McIntyre, James, 180–181
mediocrity, 3
Mexico, 264
mini-courses, 239
monitoring, 71–73
   effects of authoritative, 72–73
   impetus from below in, 72
   see also controlling; delegation
motivation, 107, 116–121
   performance appraisal and, 164
   personal needs in, 117–120
   self-actualization and, 93
   self-esteem and, 15–17
   supervisor vs. employee views of,
      116–117
Motivation and Personality (Maslow), 25,
   101, 117–120, 126, 161, 182
mutual support, 89

National Science Foundation, 215
NDA, *see* New Drug Application
needs, motivation and, 117–120

New Drug Application (NDA), 233–235, 265

New Patterns of Management (Likert), 10, 31

new products, 195
  desirable characteristics for, 249
  development of, 248, 253–256
  feasibility studies for, 248
  ideas for, 248
  scale-up and, 248
  selection of, 249
  transfer to manufacturing, 248–249

Newton, James, on reassurance, 143

NIH (not invented here) syndrome, 230

Ninomya, J. S., on inspiring employees, 41

Notes to Myself (Prather), 132

On Becoming a Person (Rogers), 22, 25, 99, 119, 139, 141, 152, 156, 158

openness, 26, 89, 106

Organizational Psychology (Kolb, Rubin & McIntyre), 180–181, 186

organizational structure, 61–62, 90

organizing of R&D work groups, 55–62

outlicensing, 229–230

Pasteur, Louis, 242

patent department, 232

performance reviews, 156–168
  argument against, 156–165
  communication and, 170–172
  positive kinds of, 165–167

Personality and Organization (Argyris), 125–126, 159

personnel department
  hiring process and, 114
  terminations and, 175

persuasion, 97–100

Peter, Laurence, on fame, 187

Peter Principle, The (Peter), 187

Peters, Tom, 73
  on "boss" culture, 183
  on communication, 254
  on control, 65
  on effective leadership, 29
  on ethics, 37
  on growth, 122
  on inspiring employees, 41

  on organizing function, 55
  on participation of employees, 45
  on supervising, 63

pilot plant group, 254–256

planned delegation, 71

planning, 48–54
  of budgets, 215–219
  delegation and, 71
  for R&D divisional goals, 52–54
  setting management style in, 48–51

politeness, 25, 89, 113

Ponderables: Essays on Managerial Choice— Past and Future (Hall), 2, 11, 39

power, 64, 180

praise, 5, 135–137

Prather, Hugh, on self-confidence, 132

predictability, 26

pressure, 4, 187, 202

pride, 27, 89

privacy, 75, 76

proactive management, 129

probation, 175

product development, 248, 253–256

productivity, 106
  authoritative monitoring and, 72
  "boss" culture and, 181–183
  of cohesive work groups, 87–93
  creativity and, 81–86
  delegation and, 68–71
  handling problems with, 169–178
  measuring R&D, 276
  nature of supervision and, 63–65
  promotions and, 179–180
  of R&D division, 194–195
  self-confidence and, 132–138

product line structure, 62

Professional Manager, The (McGregor), 22, 63

project management, 223

project teams, 207–211
  formal, 208–209
  informal, 209–211

promotions, 179–192
  from outside the company, 4, 275–276
  right people for, 184–189
  scientific ladder and, 19–20, 190–192
  wrong people for, 180–183

publications, external, 191

Puerto Rico, 264

purpose, sense of, 23, 88

R&D Advisory Committee, 206–207
R&D division
  basic vs. applied research and, 259–260
  centralized vs. decentralized, 60–61
  communication with corporation, 268–269, 274–275, 277
  computers in, 222–223
  elements of R&D process, 248–249
  engineering department and, 258–259
  goals of 52–54, 193–194
  interaction with academia, 236–243
  manufacturing department and, 252–258
  marketing department and, 147, 249–250, 270
  matrix vs. product line structure of, 61–62
  planning for goals of, 52–54
  productivity of, 194–195
  sales department and, 251–252
R&D managers
  advocating function of, 74–77
  characteristics of effective, 29–32, 39–40
  communication skills of, 100–103
  controlling function of, 65–66
  corporate managers and, 268–278
  creativity of work group and, 81–84
  delegation by, 68–71
  eliminating levels of, 55
  ethics of, 36–38
  evaluation process and, 147–155
  as good employees, 29–30
  as helpers, 126–130
  interacting with peers, 199–201
  interacting with R&D superiors, 201–203
  interacting with top management, 203–204
  in international R&D, 262–267
  key tasks of, 39, 41–47
  leadership ability of, 30–31
  organizing function of, 55–62
  planning function of, 48–54
  psychological health of, 31–32
  sheltering function of, 77–79
  supervising function of, 63–65
  tips for successful, 5–7
R&D Managers Committee, 205–206
R&D Productivity: An Investigation, 195

R&D staff
  characteristics of, 18–20, 23, 106–107
  diversity of, 23
  self-esteem and, 15–17
  typical job categories of, 18–20
  work groups and, 20
R&D vice-president, 207
  characteristics of effective, 33–35
  corporate managers and, 268
  educational background of, 34
  ethics of, 36–38
  evaluating performance of, 35–36
  hiring from academia, 275–276
  see also R&D managers
reassurance, 143–146, 167
  power of, 144–145
  tips for using, 144
reciprocal appreciation, 136–138
recognition, 26, 88, 136
  need for, 119
  praise and, 135–137
recruiting, 104–115
  best match in, 113
  candidate search in, 104–113
  computerization and, 225
  information sources for, 107–108
  long-term impact of, 114
  starting salaries in, 113–114
  summer employment and, 237, 239
  ties to academia and, 237
Rediscovering Love (Gaylin), 123, 169, 182
redundancy, 4
regulatory affairs department, 233–235
relegation, delegation vs., 68–70
respect, 5, 23, 42–43, 88, 119, 200, 203, 250
responsibility, 65
  of boss, 202
  delegation of, 68–71
  impact on organization and, 179
  pressure and, 187
  scientific ladder and, 19–20, 191–192
return-on-investment, 195
reverse delegation, 70
risk-taking behavior, 125, 271, 276
Roethlisberger, F. J., on communication, 95, 99
Rogers, Carl
  on acceptance, 25
  on communication, 95, 99

Rogers, Carl (*continued*)
  on criticism, 139, 141
  on evaluation, 152, 156
  on experiential learning, 124
  on nature of leadership, 87
  on people skills, 11
  on performance appraisal, 158, 162,
    167
  on power, 179
  on productive work groups, 22
  on self-esteem, 16, 17, 119
  on trust, 43
role models, 125
Rubin, Irwin, 180–181

sabbaticals, 238
salaries
  in budgets, 216–217
  for new employees, 113–114
  performance appraisal and, 168
  for R&D Advisory Committee, 207
sales department, 195, 251–252
Sampson, Robert C.
  on acceptance, 127
  on civility, 25
  on conditions for cohesive work
    group, 89–90
  on evaluation, 156
  on management skills, 1, 2
  on performance appraisal, 159
  on reassurance, 143
  on self-esteem, 15–16
  on sheltering, 77
Samuelson, Robert, 181
  on productivity increases, 179–180
Sargent, Alice, on manager
    characteristics, 181
scale-up, 248
Schulz, Charles, on competition, 92
scientific ladder system, 19–20, 190–192
scientists
  on scientific ladder, 19–20, 191–192
  see also assistant scientists; associate
    scientists
secrecy, 102
secretary, department, 223
security, 26, 127
self-actualization, 93
self-confidence, 107, 132–146

criticism and, 139–142
  encouragement and, 138, 142
  productivity and, 132–138
  reassurance and, 143–146
self-criticism, 141–142, 167
self-esteem
  criticism and, 159
  importance of, 15–17
  need for recognition and, 119
  trust and, 43–45
self-evaluation, 185–186
  by managers, 147, 149–152
  by subordinates, 147, 152–154
self-fulfillment needs, 119–120
selfishness, 107
self-knowledge, 188
senior scientists, *see* scientists
Shearer, Lloyd, 178
Shedd, W., 42
sheltering, 77–79
  nature of, 77–78
  qualities of effective, 79
  subtle, 78–79
social needs, 119
software, 224–225
stability, 26
staff, *see* R&D staff
Steenbach, Harry, 242
Steinbeck, John, 36, 81
suggestion systems, 83
summer employment, 237, 239
supercomputers, 224
supervision, 63–65
  control and, 66
  defined, 63
  developing skills in, 5
supportive communication, 98–100

Tannenbaum, Robert, on reassurance,
    143
tariffs, 264
taxes, 264
teachers, managers as, 129–130
technical managers, 2–5
  importance of science and, 4–5
  problems of, 3–4
  promotions and, 180–181
  technical vs. managerial focus of, 2–4
  tips for successful, 5–7

see also R&D managers
technicians
  characteristics of, 18–19, 57
  demonstrating respect for, 48–49
  role of, 20
technological change, 271
terminating employees, 174–178
  performance appraisal and, 168
  procedure for, 175–176
  tips for smoothing, 176–177
Third World countries, 264
thoughtfulness, 26, 89, 107
3M Company, 58, 147, 194, 247
Through the Looking Glass and What Alice Found There (Carroll), 1
To Kill a Mockingbird (Lee), 46
transferring employees, 173–174, 177
trust, 23, 26, 88, 201, 203, 250, 275
  authoritative monitoring and, 72
  in evaluation process, 148, 149
  guidelines for establishing, 48–51
  poor communication and, 102–103
  as role of R&D manager, 43–45
turnover, delegation and, 70

Uncommon Friends (Newton), 143
understanding, 200, 250

values
  performance appraisal and, 157
  scientific, 4
  see also ethics
vice-president, *see* R&D vice-president

Wisconsin Alumni Research Foundation (WARF), 242
Wooden, John, 9
work groups, 55–62
  arrangement of, 20
  building cohesive, 87–93
  as circular organizations, 90
  competition and, 90–93
  fertile environment for, 22–28
  providing information on, 109
Wurster, Dale, 242

Zaleznik, Abraham, on leadership ability, 30–31